Danielle Franz

MIKE LEWIS worked at Bain Capital before chasing his dream of playing professional squash. He is the founder and CEO of When to Jump™, a global community of people who have left one path to pursue a very different one. When to Jump™ has reached millions through media impressions, in-person events, and brand collaborations. *When to Jump*, a collection of case studies with clear guidance on how and when to jump, is Mike's first book. He received his BA from Dartmouth College and lives in San Francisco.

WHEN to **JUMP**

WHEN to **JUMP**

If the Job You Have Isn't
the Life You Want

MIKE LEWIS

PICADOR

HENRY HOLT AND COMPANY

NEW YORK

WHEN TO JUMP. Copyright © 2018 by Mike Lewis. All rights reserved. Printed in the United States of America. For information, address Picador, 175 Fifth Avenue, New York, N.Y. 10010.

picadorusa.com • instagram.com/picador
twitter.com/picadorusa • facebook.com/picadorusa

Picador® is a U.S. registered trademark and is used by Macmillan Publishing Group, LLC, under license from Pan Books Limited.

For book club information, please visit facebook.com/picadorbookclub or email marketing@picadorusa.com.

Designed by Kelly S. Too

The Library of Congress has cataloged the Henry Holt edition as follows:

Names: Lewis, Mike (Michael C.), author.
Title: When to jump: if the job you have isn't the job you want / Mike Lewis.
Description: First edition. | New York : Henry Holt and Company, [2018]
Identifiers: LCCN 2017035217 (print) | LCCN 2017036511 (ebook) |
    ISBN 9781250124210 (hardcover) | ISBN 9781250198143 (international) |
    ISBN 9781250124227 (ebook)
Subjects: LCSH: Career changes. | Occupational mobility.
Classification: LCC HF5384 (ebook) | LCC HF5384.L495 2018 (print) |
    DDC 650.1—dc23
LC record available at https://lccn.loc.gov/2017035217

Picador Paperback ISBN 978-1-250-29573-6

Our books may be purchased in bulk for promotional, educational, or business use. Please contact your local bookseller or the Macmillan Corporate and Premium Sales Department at 1-800-221-7945, extension 5442, or by email at MacmillanSpecialMarkets@macmillan.com.

First published by Henry Holt and Company, LLC

First Picador Edition: January 2019

10 9 8 7 6 5 4 3 2 1

For Corey Griffin,
a legend to us all

CONTENTS

Sheryl Sandberg

The most important jump of my life happened nearly a century before I was born.

My great-grandparents, Sadie and Gimpel, grew up not too far from each other, in different villages in what is now southern Ukraine. In the early 1900s, they and their families packed their bags and moved to a place on the other side of the world where Jews could live free from persecution—New York City. There, Sadie and Gimpel found the security and opportunity they hoped for. They also found each other. They met, married, and settled into a walk-up apartment in a tenement on the Lower East Side of Manhattan, sharing a bathroom with several other families on the floor.

They worked hard to build a good life for themselves. Gimpel was a street vendor, pushing a cart to sell his wares. Sadie gave birth to eight children: three girls, five boys. One of those boys was my grandfather Emanuel, whom everyone called Manny. In his twenties, Manny worked in the post office while going to City College at night. Later, he sold insurance. I used to ask him what life was like in that crowded apartment and how in the world they managed with just one bathroom. He'd say in his raspy voice, "You just waited your turn."

Eventually, I realized how ironic that answer was. I'm likely alive today because Sadie and Gimpel didn't wait their turn. Had they not left Europe, my family almost certainly would have died in the Holocaust. Instead, my great-grandparents found the courage to build a new life in a new land. They jumped.

Flash forward to the year 2005, when I met my second cousin Mike for the first time. He was in eleventh grade. I was recently married and working at Google. I loved Mike right away—he was funny and smart and way more thoughtful than I was as a teenager. In our first meeting, we sat down to figure out exactly how we are related. It turns out his grandmother Frieda was Emanuel's sister. They grew up together in that one-bedroom apartment—waiting their turn together. I wonder if they ever imagined that decades later, her grandson and his granddaughter would be sitting at a table in California, figuring out their family tree.

Since then, I've seen Mike graduate from high school and college and start his career. I've seen him take the audacious jump into becoming a professional squash player and saw how much joy that brought him. I've seen him study how and why people jump and the lessons we can all learn about courage, resilience, and leading fulfilling lives. And I've seen him take those lessons and put them into this book—one that I know will guide others as they face big decisions.

Like Mike, this book is smart, friendly, and ready to help people make a jump of their own. He explains the simple framework that many successful jumpers have followed and offers insights not just from his own experience but from people of many ages and backgrounds with dreams of all kinds. Some of their jumps led to small but meaningful changes in their lives. Others altered their futures in enormous ways. Not one of them regrets having jumped.

The question I've come back to again and again in my life is, "What would I do if I wasn't afraid?" That question gave me the push I needed to make big jumps: from government to the tech sector, from Google to a company called Facebook run by a twenty-three-year-old with a vision of connecting the world. Each time, some people I really trusted told me I was making a mistake. Each time, they might have been right. But my heart told me otherwise. I wanted to jump. And I've never looked back.

We all face moments in our lives when we have to decide: To jump or not to jump? That might mean leaving a familiar field to pursue a passion project or taking on a new responsibility at work. It might mean starting a new relationship or saying good-bye to one that's reached its end. It might be as small as embracing a new hobby or as big as moving to a new country. You never know exactly where those jumps will take you. They can be scary, and they don't always work out for the best. But they're how we pursue our dreams. They can make us stronger, more resilient, just plain more interesting, and help us have more impact in the world. They let us imagine things not as they are but how they should be—and then push us to do the hard work to make that change happen.

There are ways we can make those jumps more likely to lead somewhere great. This book tells you how.

Who knows? Maybe one day your great-grandchildren will talk about how that jump you made all those years ago changed everything for them—just like our great-grandparents changed everything for Mike and me.

WHEN to **JUMP**

Introduction: **Mike's Story**

SCOTT WAS MY cousin's friend before he was my friend. We had met during a party at my cousin's house and had grown close through coffee dates every so often, like the one just now ending on a neatly groomed sidewalk in downtown Palo Alto. It was a late February afternoon.

Midforties, tall, with a boyish smile and sharp blue eyes, Scott was soft spoken and a good listener, and he had a gift for making time spent with him feel important. With me, he played the thoughtful mentor, loyal older brother, and trusted confidant—a sounding board for the dreamer, the kid. As we parted that afternoon, I wasn't quite ready to let him vanish into the dusk. After taking a couple of steps in the direction of my car, I turned around.

"Is this crazy?" I asked. I was squeezing the stained coffee cup lid in my left palm. The culmination of several years of fantasizing and planning was a few hours away, and I was fishing for a final bit of reassurance.

Scott had started his hustle toward home, his lanky frame hunched over his phone, checking back in to his own work and life. Our time together had run a bit long, and for Scott, there were business calls to return and kids to pick up from school. But he slowed his step and gently returned his attention to me. The sun had disappeared behind us. New customers scurried into the coffee shop.

"What you have in mind is absolutely crazy," he said, quietly pushing his phone back into his jean pocket. "But there's a difference between crazy and stupid."

TWO years earlier, in an office toward the top of a pristine glass tower, above the bustling heart of Boston, I sat at my desk and stared at the wall. Taped to the top edge of my computer screen, printed in a size 50 font on leftover printer paper, was a quote from a commencement speech that Amazon's founder and CEO Jeff Bezos had made to graduating Princeton students in 2010: "When you are eighty years old, and in a quiet moment of reflection narrating for only yourself the most personal version of your life story, the telling that will be most compact and meaningful will be the series of choices you have made. In the end, we are our choices. Build yourself a great story."

What would I want my story to look like?

I knew my answer—I wanted to become a professional squash player—but I didn't know how to make that life happen.

Twenty-three years old, the youngest of six kids, born in New York City, raised in Nashville, Tennessee, and then in the beach town of Santa Barbara, California, I was the only child to live in Boston. A year out of college, I was ready to put down roots in Massachusetts. Or that was the plan, anyway.

I had moved to the city for what I viewed as my dream job, working in the shiny, wood-paneled offices of a venture capital firm. My job was the type of employment you get and don't give up, the type of work you ride into the sunset of your career if they'll let you. I had chased this job since the start of my senior year. I had been walking out the back steps of my fraternity house when I read the job description in a career services bulletin on my phone, and I'd immediately copied and pasted the text into an e-mail, sending it straight to my parents. I told them I'd seen an opening for the perfect job, working at Bain Capital Ventures, the venture capital investment arm of the international private equity firm Bain Capital. My parents agreed that the role seemed written for me: go out and meet entrepreneurs, listen to the stories behind their start-up companies, review their business plans and ideas, analyze and help decide if that start-up might be a good investment for the firm. Fast-forward to the wood-paneled office. I was only months into this plum job but performing well. I read everything I could, listened to everyone who would talk to me, and the effort was starting to pay off: one of the first entrepreneurs I came across was launching a company that, a couple of years later, would disrupt the health care industry and become one of the largest investments by our firm ever brought in by an analyst.

My coworkers were engaging, my bosses thoughtful leaders, my hours manageable: in by 8 a.m., out by 7 or 8 p.m. every day. I earned a couple weeks of vacation each year, and I figured I'd satiate my craving for travel and adventure then—heading wherever I could go, for as long as I could, combining public holidays and weekends to maximize my time off. I'd spent the second Christmas of my time at Bain hiking the famed Angkor Wat temples in Cambodia with one of my best friends, Dan. My coworkers gave me kudos for finding a way to cobble together three whole weeks off whereas my fellow travelers and the local guides we met in Southeast Asia asked why we bothered traveling for such a short sliver of time. For my part, I believed that three weeks in Southeast Asia would fulfill whatever I was looking for outside of work. Yep, I thought, I could scratch the itch for adventure between Christmas and New Year's, then get back to the desk without missing a beat.

I had taken the job at Bain because of a genuine enthusiastic interest in the work, but I have to admit also that I had somehow got it into my head that I was supposed to stick to a certain kind of postcollege path—and the job at Bain fit into that kind of path: from college to internship to well-paying corporate job. At Bain, I was on the "right" path, surrounded by smart people, doing interesting work, and enjoying well-paid vacations. What else could I want?

Yet deep down, as time went by, I began to realize that I wanted this life mostly because I thought I should. And all the while, tucked somewhere off to the side in my mind, a very distinct if faint voice whispered an idea of something very different.

. . .

I was in love with the sport of squash.

Squash is a British game and a close cousin to tennis but played indoors against a wall. I had fallen in love with squash as a teenager, just after my family moved to California. It's a niche sport in the United States, particularly in places outside the Northeast. While it's a growing sport, there are relatively few courts and few competitive players west of New York City. This was especially true when I was a kid in California, but when my family joined a gym, the Santa Barbara Athletic Club, I was in luck: there were squash courts.

Converted out of racquetball courts a few decades earlier, the SBAC squash court dimensions were not exactly regulation, but they were close enough to attract a handful of enthusiastic recreational adult players. And SBAC had the only five-court setup for another seventy-five miles, until Los Angeles. So, for the bulk of my teenage years, I lived at this club. Breakfast and lunch from the sandwich bar, homework at the tables in the café, squash on the converted courts with anyone who wanted to play. Day in and day out: dropped off on weekend mornings and after school, picked up at closing. Ferdinand the clockmaker, Dirk the tech guru, Robert the British ex-pat, Debbie the office manager—for the better part of junior high and high school, my other family was the group of adult squash players who met at the courts each night.

Beyond the courts and this other family, the biggest gift the club offered me was its tradition of hosting a tiny professional squash competition each year. That's how I learned of it: the pro squash tour. I was fourteen when the pro competition rolled in, bringing with it players from around the world. Professional squash events usually don't offer much in the way of prize money, and to lighten the expense for the players, most tournaments offer lodging through local players in the member community. I signed up our family to host Shawn Delierre, a young and rising talent out of Canada. Over take-out burgers and fries at the dinner table, Shawn captured my imagination with stories of competing around the world, staying with friends and with host families along the way. From mountaintops in Brazil to cities in Japan to the suburbs of Switzerland, Shawn had me hooked. He told me I too could someday play the tour, though even for an optimistic fourteen-year-old like me that possibility seemed far-fetched: I was new to the sport and hundreds of miles from most of the competitive players my age. After I met Shawn though, I began tracking the website of the pro squash tour, enamored by the tiny lights that sprawled across a spinning sphere, representing the competitions that dotted the globe.

Eight years later, at my desk at Bain Capital, having long assumed that Shawn's visit and the image of the dotted globe would fade from my memory, I was unable to focus wholeheartedly on my "grown-up" professional track. The idea of playing pro squash wouldn't budge.

It feels awkward when a little inner voice talks to you, a voice you're scared to listen to. It feels even more awkward when that voice won't go away.

How do you start doing what you really want to be doing? How do you know when to take a chance? I had no idea. And no one was coming along to hand me the answer. I had the job and lifestyle I had thought I wanted, yet I secretly held out hope—for a knock on the door, for someone to enter my tiny office, walk up to my desk, and give me permission to leave: "Mike, it's July 1, time to go chase your dream, remember?"

There was what my friend Nick called a "circularity" to my life. Weekdays I'd wake up at 7:20 a.m. to "I Think Ur a Contra" by Vampire Weekend, hit snooze once, shower and dress, head left out of the apartment and take a right toward Symphony Hall, left alongside the Christian Science museum, up the escalators and past the manicured shops and blinding white lights of the Prudential Center, and straight through the revolving doors of the glistening Hancock Tower. Ride the elevator to thirty-nine, order eggs and juice from my friends working in the cafeteria, talk football and weekend plans with coworkers across the hall, then quietly close the door to my office. Just me, a wall, and the taped inspirational quote on printer paper above the computer screen. Ten to twelve hours later, I'd walk home the way I came. Monday, Tuesday, Wednesday, Thursday, Friday.

I felt alone as I considered the possibility of listening to that little voice, but when it became clear that the voice wasn't going away, I started to do some research. What began as an innocent Google for "when to go chase dreams" turned into a full-fledged investigation for inspiration and, shortly afterward, a scavenger hunt for stories. I devoured books like Tim Ferriss's *The 4-Hour Workweek* on why, and how, people jump to live a life on their own terms. I made a list of my favorite companies and read about how they started. If the founder had a nontraditional background—if he or she took an unusual risk to start the company—I wanted to know how he or she approached that start-up decision. Every "jump" story made me want to find another one. I began identifying and cold-calling people who did cool things: alumni from my college, siblings of my friends, strangers I read about in the newspaper. In the darkness of my office long after office hours ended, I tracked down other people—ex-electricians, consultants, teachers—each of whom had left a place of comfort to chase a passion. They had all jumped.

I wanted to know when to jump.

The first woman who called me back was an ex-banker turned cyclist. I had reached out after reading an interview with her in a recent issue of our college alumni magazine. When I asked about her jump, she didn't tell me anything about how to ride a bike or how to become an elite athlete. Instead, she explained the behind-the-scenes preparations: how she'd saved up money, how she'd mentally prepared for the possibility of things not working out, how she'd told her boss she was quitting. I hung up the phone and rushed into my coworker's office: he was also planning for something different, and I knew that these tidbits could help my jump and his.

Over the next year and a half, I picked up more when-to-jump insights—from a journalist turned politician, a bond trader turned adventure planner, a brand marketer turned toy maker. I had expected clichéd advice and feel-good fairy tales. Instead I got candid details about how to chase an unknown, honesty about the emotional and financial vulnerabilities of doing so, and frankness about the range of thoughts and feelings that come from taking such a risk. Following a dream is lofty and sounds admirable, but real consequences follow. Those costs were the truths I was searching to know.

After I'd heard about a dozen stories from people who had changed career paths, a pattern began to emerge. A few of the same ideas—even the same words and phrases—overlapped across experiences that, on the surface, had little to nothing in common. A onetime karate teacher in rural Virginia shared the same insights as a single mother in the Northeast. A brewery owner in Boston described a jump philosophy similar to that of an aspiring aviation entrepreneur who was half the brewer's age and lived halfway around the world.

Discovering patterns in a random collection of career-switch stories was bizarre and thrilling. I collected more narratives, and more commonalities appeared. These mapped broadly across the jumping experience to form a curve. There was no surefire way to guarantee a jump's success or predict what would happen post-jump, but the process of jumping began to seem less haphazard and random to me. It became clear that there is a smart way to try for a dream, a certain discipline around responsible planning. I saw that I would prepare myself for the best possible jump experience if I was alert to each of the broad phases of the jump process. The Jump Curve provided by the stories didn't give me exact instructions on how to achieve my dream. But I didn't need exact instructions; I needed a sign that I could make a jump, that I wasn't stupid for trying.

The people willing to share their jump experiences also made me feel less alone in my desire to chase something that mattered to me. No longer was my career move going to be "me against the world." The experiences these "jumpers" shared with me formed companionable case studies of how much determination and preparation changing my path would take.

For twenty-three years, I had chased plainly laid out goals. Goals that were easy to want to chase because they were popular with the older people around me and were even popular among my own peers. Also, more people chasing any single objective creates competition, and I'm competitive, so I felt compelled to run faster toward particular goals—at the risk of forgetting what I was hurtling toward, and why. There existed a baseline to each goal—graduate from high school, get to college, earn an internship—and there were higher-level, bonus goals attached to each baseline: graduate with high scores and excellent extracurricular activities, attend an Ivy League university, intern at Goldman Sachs. In this way, pursuing each goal was a game for me. Reach each new baseline and see how many bonus goals you can score. Who doesn't want to win when playing a game?

So when the predetermined game I had been playing ran out of obvious new levels sometime during my first year at Bain Capital Ventures, my feet stopped sprinting. For the first time in a long time, no one was telling me what I was supposed to do next.

Until this moment, two words had summarized the biggest prize in the game I was playing: venture capital. Venture capital is the perceived Promised Land for anyone who wants to work in investing. Venture capital, it was explained to me during the corporate recruiting process, is what you go to business school to get to do someday, if you're lucky. Unlike consulting or banking, venture capital is the "buy side," the side where *you* have the money, and *you* choose how and where to invest it. Better hours, better pay, better success stories: if there was one uniform piece of advice that I received from my college career services director and from older alumni, from friends, and from my parents, it was that a job at a VC firm was above all else. Once, when I let it slip to an older colleague, who was my direct manager, that I had a dream of traveling around playing the pro squash tour, his reply was blunt: "Don't quit your day job." If you were lucky enough to fall into the rarefied air of a venture capital firm at any point in your career, let alone the beginning, you were to stay put. Period.

I had no background in finance, no inside scoop into the firm or the industry when I entered the doors to the castle. My college didn't offer finance to undergraduates, and I had never taken an economics course. While I wanted to go into business, I had decided to use the time in school to take courses that I'd never get to take again. My degree was in political science and environmental studies. And while I may have been qualified for Bain Capital Ventures based on my academics and genuine interests, so were thousands of other students. Being offered one of the two coveted spots at Bain was, without exaggeration, beyond the wildest dreams of my parents, my siblings, and myself.

Getting chosen for the job felt exactly like that: getting chosen. Like winning the lottery. I felt lucky to be there, lucky to be earning a good living, lucky to be doing something my parents could easily share with their friends at holiday parties. *Mike's a venture capitalist* is a hell of a lot easier to explain, and for someone to digest, than *Mike's making no money while sleeping on couches playing an obscure sport somewhere near Fiji*. As I thought of what I was doing, and what I really wanted to do, the emotion that repeatedly crept back up was guilt. I was the last of six children that my parents had sent to college. My job, and this career, felt implicitly like a way I could return the favor to my parents by taking good care of myself.

But when I tried to settle in where I'd landed, I'd end up staring at my office wall. My friend Emily had given me a paper map of the world, a map from the charity Doctors Without Borders, a map that was wrinkled and well-worn, as if sent from a field office for the organization in a rural village. Emily and I had both taken geography classes at school, and she was one of the few who knew my secret squash aspirations. I think that's why she gave me the creased and fraying map, which I stretched out and pinned along the length of my office wall. Sitting at my desk, directly opposite eye level, were the jagged island contours of Australia and New Zealand. There, every June, a series of pro squash competitions took place for guys at my level. As months tumbled along, a nightmare scenario began to haunt me: this flimsy, creased map would remain pinned to the wall while the seasons cycled by, years rolling into years. I would grow older. And every June, I'd look over at the contours of Australia and New Zealand, and they'd look back at me, and I'd go to lunch and stop off at happy hours telling my colleagues how, at this very moment, I could be across the world chasing a dream. And then I'd go home, and the next day, the fraying old map would still be pinned to my office wall.

That nightmare did not come true. After I spoke with the banker turned cyclist in January of my second year at Bain, my jump was set in motion, a process that would take the next year and a half, an eighteen-month window during which I gathered more jump stories and began to lay out my own. I wrote plans and saved up money. I paid attention to where I seemed to be on the Jump Curve. To be clear, I don't think there is any secret recipe or prescription that releases a person to make a jump. But the stories I heard and the common themes and insights from the Jump Curve helped me make a big change—and I believe these stories and an awareness of the curve can help others do the same.

Timing matters. If you're supporting a family or have pressing debts to pay off, now is almost certainly not the time to quit a moneymaking job for a dream that does not pay. But that doesn't mean you can never chase your dream; it means not just yet—as the Jump Curve will show.

During the time I was itching to jump, my situation was lucky. Throughout most of my three years at Bain Capital Ventures, I was able to divert part of each paycheck to a new "squash" bank account, which I didn't allow myself to touch. For the last two years at Bain, I imitated the training, eating, and living routines of my full-time, professional athlete counterparts. Because I had no family, no kids, no mortgage, I could use all of my extra time to train my body and all of my extra money for healthy foods and wellness programs.

In my final year at Bain, I started to reach out to potential sponsors. I told them my story: my dream and my plan to go chase it. I let them know that, lucky for them, I was *now accepting sponsors* to provide cash in return for visible logo space on my playing jersey. It was terrifying to write down and share my most personal hopes and dreams, but I did it. A few months after making my first pitch, I sat across from a recreational squash player and member of my gym, Amrit, sharing with him the pitch materials that had, so far, collected a few nos and a couple maybe laters. As I flipped through the paper slides before us, my voice picked up in pace and grew into an excited whisper. Even though I had struck out in finding anyone to buy into the vision I was selling, the simple act of reading over my most personal, hopeful dreams made me feel a step closer to achieving them. And after taking a final sip from his beer and setting the bottle next to my scattered slide presentation sheets, Amrit told me he was in. I had my first jersey sponsor.

And suddenly I felt I had no choice. I was really going to do this.

Nine months before leaving for the tour, I began competing as a pro part-time, to make sure I knew the lifestyle I'd be signing up for: traveling alone, trusting strangers, sleeping on couches. To attend my second pro event, I slipped out of the office and flew out to Chicago in the late afternoon, only to find out my opponent for that evening had defaulted. The default gave me my first victory, but it meant I'd be competing the next day, a workday. I told an understandably confused tournament director that *I* would now have to default; then I quickly took a shower (though I hadn't done anything to break a sweat) and flew back to Boston in time for work the next morning, having spent a few hundred bucks and three hours in Illinois, earning my first official tour win without actually playing anyone.

The other thing I had in my favor was working in an industry that valued both risk-taking and compelling personal narratives. The only thing investors love more than an entrepreneur taking a big financial or social risk to start a company is if he or she has a great story behind that risk. And that fit my story line: while I wasn't jumping to start my own company, I was risking significant income in the near term and potential career prospects in the long term, all because I wanted to go for something that I believed I had to try. I worked in a business where we spent every day investing money in people and their passions; my jump meant acting in a similar vein but on my own behalf. When I broke the news of my jump at lunchtimes or over a beer after work, I'd carefully explain to colleagues that my dream was a short-term experience—rather than a lifetime pursuit—in an effort to keep doors open, hoping to work with some of these people again in some way down the road. Many of my bosses were risk-takers and had been high school and college athletes themselves. A few years removed from their athletic primes and settled down with families, they could vicariously think of my journey as their journey. I'd stay in touch by sharing photos and stories from the road. Fortunately, when the time came to officially discuss my jump with everyone, the response from all of my colleagues and bosses was: go.

My jump was daunting, but it was feasible, and as I went about preparing for it, I understood how lucky I was.

But as the journey around my jump unfolded, what also became clear is that the desire to do what is meaningful to oneself and the will to find a way to make it happen was *not* specific to me. Bartenders, fellow bus passengers, brand marketers—many people I spoke to had something worth jumping for. The ability to jump is not limited to those who have a college degree or a certain-sized bank account. Applying for an internal promotion at work, going back to school at night, teaching cooking classes on the weekends—big jump or small jump, very many of us have something that we've longed to try doing. A jump is a jump. If you can't do it now, write it down for later. And if you *can* do it now? Go.

And regardless of whether your jump will happen soon or much later, the stories in this book will offer inspiration and ideas that can help along the way.

By the time I met Scott for coffee on that afternoon in Palo Alto, I had made it through nearly two years and ten thousand little, unsexy steps of planning. An hour later, I officially quit my job at Bain, and very shortly afterward, I began to pack my life into a hulking, baby blue fifty-pound monster of a roller suitcase that I'd bought on sale at Marshalls and an extra wide Dunlop squash bag that I planned to carry slung heavily over my shoulder. In preparing for every climate and attire requirement, I chose three anchor pieces of clothing: a pair of khaki-colored Levi's that were nice enough to pass for dress pants but sturdy enough to do everything else in (camp, travel, sleep—my roommate Catherine helped me pick out these pants); a black fleece with the collar of a nice sweater but the zipper of an athletic piece—I'd use it for both (my other roommate, Mike, had tossed me the fleece, which had accidentally shrunk in the wash and was too small for him but a perfect fit for me); and a knit hoodie from H&M (twenty bucks!) that looked hip but was also warm and heat absorbing, thus making itself useful across a variety of party vibes as well as in chilly climates.

I printed jerseys with logos of my sponsors on all sides and with "LEWIS" printed on the back beneath an American flag. Carefully unwrapping three new Dunlop racquets from the manufacturing plastic, I slid each racquet into a compartment in the squash bag, padding the surrounding space with rolls of socks, underwear, and my jerseys. I unpinned the worn paper map from my office wall, folded it back along the creases, and zipped it neatly inside the front outside pocket of my suitcase. And then I booked a one-way flight across the world.

As it turned out, Scott was right: there is a difference between crazy and stupid.

The difference lies in knowing when to jump.

The Jump Curve

THERE IS NO secret playbook to making a successful jump, no guarantee of how things will end. But after considering the jump stories I heard, across a group of otherwise unrelated narratives and characters, I identified four key concepts that seem to apply to all worthwhile jumps. Trace these common points along a narrative line, and they form the Jump Curve, an arc mapping out the phases that accompany the process of making a good jump. The decision to jump is not scientific, and neither is the Jump Curve; instead, it is a guiding framework that outlines the key insights to consider along the journey.

This book will take us through the Jump Curve and is organized by its four key phases:

Phase 1: **Listen to the Little Voice**

- *You are:* sitting at your desk, with an idea you'd like to jump for. You haven't done much—except possibly try to ignore that idea. You are becoming more willing to consider doing something about that idea.

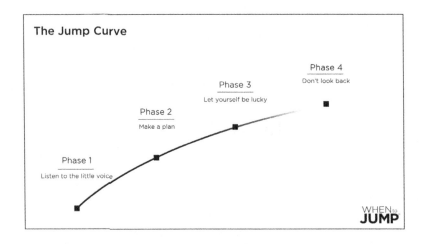

Phase 2: **Make a Plan**

- *You are:* deciding to take action around your idea. From jotting sketches on the back of a napkin to preparing a comprehensive budget, you begin tackling the nitty-gritty.

Phase 3: **Let Yourself Be Lucky**

- *You are:* going for your jump. You have planned, dreamed, and worried as much as you can. No jump can be fully predicted or planned out before it's made, so don't try to nail everything down in advance. You can't. By now, you have done everything you can. To jump means to accept that an unknown outcome awaits. If you've done all the planning you know of up until this point in your jump, and you're ready to run with whatever comes your way from now on, you'll be able to take this step forward. You're going to find your luck.

Phase 4: **Don't Look Back**

- *You are:* clear that this jump was the best thing you ever did. Or you're unclear about whether or not it's going as planned. Or maybe it's become clear that this jump isn't working out. But in every case, you are pushing on, with this jump or toward your next one. You're not looking back.

In the past five years, I've interviewed hundreds of jumpers and have collected their stories—a mere handful of which are in the pages that follow. Not all of these narratives lead to a fairy-tale ending, and I think that's an important reminder: this framework, and the act of taking a jump itself, cannot promise a specific result.

But not one person I've interviewed who followed the Jump Curve framework described remorse for making his or her jump. And to me, this reinforces something bigger: if you follow along this framework— if you are thoughtful and listen to the little voice, if you work hard and plan well, if you put yourself in a smart position and go all in on your jump—you're not going to regret it.

In each section of the book, I'll begin by describing the piece of my own jump story that aligns to that phase of the Jump Curve, before sharing a group of narratives that also apply to that part of the curve. Each section will wrap up with key takeaways to revisit when you find yourself in that phase of your own jump.

Treat the Jump Curve not as an instruction manual but as a steady hand of support. Treat the forty-four different voices that follow not as instructors but as friends and peers. By reading this book, you become part of our crew, a member of our global When to Jump community. Whether you jump now or later, this book will be here, so you won't have to jump alone. Your journey might be crazy, but it won't be stupid.

PHASE 1

LISTEN TO THE LITTLE VOICE

"That little voice . . . it's your true voice."

—Jeff Arch

I HAD JUST polished off a supersized schnitzel outside a youth hostel in Vienna when two traveling Kiwis hanging out in the lobby extended an invite to join their trek heading east to see their friend in Romania. I was twenty-one years old, on a one-week intermission from the steady, firmly planned trajectory of college, internships, graduation, work. Naturally, I leapt at the chance to toss my travel plans. I couldn't say yes fast enough.

We cruised through Slovakia and past the Czech Republic, around Hungary and into Romania, two teachers from New Zealand and their American sidekick. As the overnight train pulled into Bucharest, I stumbled upon what I had been quietly craving. Squash courts.

In the dusty depths of a basement gym in Bucharest, carved out of a couple of worn slabs of concrete, sat three decaying squash courts. Inside the court to the far right, a pair of older men shrieked and lunged, laughed and shouted, barking out game scores in a blur of foreign sounds that I figured to be Romanian. I crept past the men and slid into the court on the far left, spending the next forty-five minutes hitting a series of practice shots against the wall, the ball flying back in a familiar cadence. The grunts from the far court echoed through the cavernous concrete lair, and as I finished my solo practice and headed for the locker room, I stopped to watch the two sweat-drenched Romanians finish their duel. Moments later, their contest done, their eyes suddenly turned my way, a flexed index finger of one player pointed in my direction. It was my turn.

The better of the two Romanians passed me off to his playing partner, watching casually as we went into battle. When I took out his partner in one game and then another, the better player stepped in. A couple hours of body banging and ball bashing later, I had triumphed over both players as the club manager sat watching, waiting patiently with an offer as I walked off the court: Stick around Bucharest. Crash with one of our players. You coach our team; we'll show you life in eastern Europe.

First: shock. I simply couldn't believe it. This was what I wanted: a bizarre, total unknown adventure, a surprise detour from the "path" toward a life of culturally sanctioned accomplishments. This was the sort of story Shawn the squash pro had told me when I was a kid, while he was staying in our house in Santa Barbara. I had reveled in those stories but never thought I would find myself in one of them. And here I was, far below street level, deep inside a dusty Bucharest basement. A friendly Romanian squash club manager was giving me a chance.

Then: reality. My heart burrowed deep inside my gut. My mind began to consider the truth. I wasn't ready to jump. I was in the middle of laying the groundwork for a bigger jump, and that groundwork would only be laid after I completed my internships, wrapped up my degree, and found professional footing. From there, I'd need to start saving money and get a lot better at my sport. There was a lot to do.

I turned back to the friendly Romanian club manager and, with all the self-control I could muster, politely declined the offer.

The next day, I flew to Zurich and moved into corporate housing for a privately owned commodities trading firm headquartered an hour train ride past Lake Zurich at the bottom of a hill in a sleepy Swiss village, surrounded by sheep. The day after that, I put on a business suit and began a monthlong work exchange, quietly commuting to the village by day, returning alone to the silent streets of Waffenplatzstrasse by night. Later, someone told me this neighborhood catered to families and retirees, and that made sense to me as I never bumped into anyone else my age. At work, I shadowed a commodities trader—a world expert in understanding the supply and demand around chemicals like ammonium nitrates. I followed his daily routines while wondering what the guys in the Romanian basement were up to. A month later, I was back in the States, in New York City, unpacking from a box my dad's pin-striped, bell-bottom wool suit from the late 1970s, beginning my first real corporate internship: a summerlong rotational program at Goldman Sachs, a rare opportunity, something that seemed out of reach to me and to my parents. I was moving from one prestigious internship to another, from spring to summer, with graduation less than a year away.

If I had jumped while in Romania during the spring of my junior year, it would have been impulsive and shortsighted. Holding off had benefits. But an inner voice emerged from that encounter. Right adventure, wrong time; but right adventure. A year and a half after I played squash in Bucharest, I was waking up to "I Think Ur a Contra" on my phone alarm at 7:20 a.m., hitting snooze once before getting dressed and heading to the towering castle at Bain Capital Ventures. Out the office windows facing north, runners walked, dogs played, and students napped in the grassy field of the Boston Commons far below.

The scripted sequence rolled along, but the little voice wouldn't go away.

A few years after leaving the dungeon courts in Romania, I looked across my desk to the map of the world taped across my office wall, and two things became crystal clear. First, I still wanted to chase my dream of playing professional squash full-time while traveling all around the world. And second, no one—not parents, siblings, or colleagues—was going to come into my office and tell me when my dream could begin. Instead, a little voice was doing the talking.

I didn't know what to do with this voice. On the one hand, it had to be wrong. My parents provided me with the education and guidance so I could land a job exactly like the one I had—stable, prestigious, lucrative. I enjoyed the work and felt challenged by it. Wasn't this the goal? The thought of mixing things up for any reason—let alone for my grand vision of playing an obscure sport and making no money while couch surfing with strangers—seemed not only disrespectful to my parents but logistically unreasonable and financially impossible.

Yet the voice grew louder.

I pretended not to listen. Rather, I listened, but I tried to forget what I'd heard, to send the thoughts to the back of my mind.

My Boston squash club was located (very conveniently!) across the street from the Bain office, and I started to find myself slipping over to the club anytime I wasn't working. Walking in one day during my lunch break, I caught hold of a conversation near the front desk. Dan was in his late twenties, a lanky, affable, curly-haired Irishman sporting a devilish grin. A former Irish junior champion, now an assistant teaching professional, Dan was on the phone, telling the person on the other end about his experience playing the tour circuits in Australia and New Zealand a few years earlier. I stood awkwardly in the doorway, just out of the elevator, hanging on to every word of advice Dan was giving: when to go, where to play—Dan even knew a few former training partners who could help provide places to stay along the way. When Dan finished, I walked slowly past the desk and to the court, closing the door behind me, pretending for just a second that it was me on the other end of the line. I hit by myself that day, smacking the hard rubber ball again and again against the wall, wondering when it really would be me on the other end of that phone call. On my way out of the gym, I stopped by Dan's desk: "Dan, at some point—you know, not right now, or anytime soon, but at some point, I may go play the tour. Can I get those names and tips you gave the other guy?" Without missing a beat, Dan, replied: "Shaw, mate. Anytime. Jus' lemme know when ya want ta talk." I disappeared back toward the locker room, back toward work.

Through the windows of the Bain Capital London offices, Buckingham Palace looked just like it did in the movies: grand, proper, historic. Six months into my job at Bain, I was riding high, having successfully pitched the idea of spending a few days in the company's offices in London, though no one in our venture capital department was based there. I'd borrowed space from a different part of the firm, and I promised my bosses no dip in productivity. If anything, I'd suggested, perhaps the international business landscape could help me uncover new investment opportunities. My bosses seemed amused by my effort and likely had more important things to figure out, so I was given the go-ahead.

It was March and my first-ever visit to the United Kingdom. I had been determined to inch toward an adventure overseas, even if it meant doing the same job but six hours east and at a makeshift desk and chair inside a bare, white-walled office that could have been mistaken for a hospital closet. I had bent the rules and got to work in London. If I could make this happen, maybe I could bend things even more.

I was squatting in the European headquarters of Bain Capital Private Equity. Leading this office was Dwight Poler, a thoughtful, brilliant investor widely respected both within the firm and in the broader finance industry. As it happened, Dwight went to graduate school where I went to undergrad, and we had been introduced by older colleagues based on this shared connection. Before I left London, Dwight found a few minutes to invite me into his office.

I tiptoed down the elegant hallway, each step taking on significance, as if while I lapped the space used by such a highly regarded businessman, some of his talent might rub off on me. I was in awe of Bain's operations, its sterling reputation, and the leaders like Dwight who had helped sculpt what Bain had become. While the little voice in my head was starting to speak up, I wasn't going to let it out during this visit with Dwight.

But while retracing his memories of business school, Dwight shared something else: he had once jumped to pursue his own dream. "I had a couple buddies, and we always promised each other we'd take a year to travel. So I worked out a deferral to graduate school, and we did it. We budgeted only as much as the lowest-earning traveler, and we left."

I couldn't hold back; I confessed my own wanderlust. And when I gave Dwight a thumbnail of how my little voice was telling me to play squash professionally, he replied simply: "Do it. Everyone will have a reason for you not to go: they'll say you're crazy, you're losing your edge, you could be earning more money. But do it."

My little voice had gotten out, and to receive advice on my jump idea from a role model in business was completely unexpected and exhilarating.

"But," Dwight added, "jump a few years out. You'll value it more. You'll have more money to spend." I made sure to remember that part, and a few minutes later, we concluded our conversation. On my way out, I thanked Dwight for his honest thoughts and for his advice to invest in my passion and to take the chance to jump. He smiled and said, "Life is long."

I walked firmly out of Dwight's office and down the hallway, straight past the palace in the backdrop. Before I made it back to the hospital closet, I messaged my friend Dan: "If I don't go play pro squash, I'm going to regret it forever."

One day at work two years later, in the winter of my third year at Bain, I took a phone call with an executive who was running a business somewhere in Connecticut. We had never spoken before and would never speak again, but for whatever reason, after we'd wrapped up the business portion of our conversation, the stranger on the other end asked about my story. What did I want to do? Was this job it?

It was like he knew.

I laughed nervously and explained how lucky I was to snag the job I had, how I'd have to be crazy to change anything, how I was truly quite happy. He paused, then finished by saying, "Listen, kid, you seem like a nice guy. My advice to you is go where your heart is."

I hung up the phone but broke from my autopilot routine of filing away notes and returning to e-mails. And in that momentary break, I was done. I stopped ignoring the voice, stopped pretending not to hear it. From then on, I was going to turn up the volume.

If there was a subtitle to the subtitle of this section ("Listen to the Little Voice"), it would be "And then tell people what that voice is saying." For too long, I sat at my desk alone and brooding over the validity of my idea, embarrassed to vocalize it, worried that my parents would never understand that I needed to see this idea through so that someday when I was gray and old, at least I could say I tried.

More practically, I worried, what if no one ever hired me again, EVER? I was a few years into a career, and I had thousands of peers capable of taking my job without missing a beat, not to mention the new grads, waiting and hungry. I remembered what my older coworker, early thirties with a wife and young child, had told me when he decided not to make a jump he wanted because it meant leaving the company. "In this job, I'm in line to become a managing director. I don't want to get out of line and miss my turn. I'd have to start over."

If I played pro squash for a while, I would certainly be getting out of line at Bain, but what scared me more was the idea that I wouldn't even be allowed to start over later on.

What if squash didn't work out? What if I didn't win any matches? Or what if it did work out, and I was miserable? There was no promise that my business career could resume—and in my head, I had settled on the possibility that it wouldn't. I'd be the guy my coworkers and classmates would talk about at happy hours or college reunions—what was his name, Mike? Mark?—who got too caught up in a dream and now, poor guy, couldn't get back to reality. If I pulled the right strings, maybe I would be able to start over as an intern, and my friends, now senior associates and vice presidents, would let me work for them, if they could swing such an arrangement with their colleagues.

I knew exactly what I would be giving up by leaving Bain—the money, the benefits, the security, the social status. And if I jumped to play pro squash, I didn't know anything exact about what I'd be getting in return. I feared it would be much, much less than I had at Bain. And in this kind of dark abyss of fear, most jumps die before they are born.

To keep a jump alive, it helps to tell someone.

Nine months into my job at Bain, three years after meeting my Bucharest buddies in the squash basement, and a decade after Shawn sparked my dreams about the pro tour, I first revealed to someone the entire, honest intention that came from my little voice. I ran my own internal vetting process before speaking up about what was on my mind, settling on a friend's dad, a man I considered to be a neutral and objective observer of my life, someone unencumbered by family ties or deep friendship bonds, who could deliver a candid assessment of my idea.

We met for morning coffee at the Blue Glass Café, a grab-and-go food shop tucked into the lobby of my office building. Blue Glass was crowded, bustling in the worst way, with everyone needing to be somewhere else, and no one seeming particularly happy about where it was they had to go. Sandwiched into a table between a blur of moving laptops and briefcases, I pulled my chair in tight. I surveyed the surroundings—the coffee cups and newspapers. Any faces I recognized? Any chances of being overheard? The idea of someone I knew taking notice was frightening. I scooted my chair even closer, chest pressed against the hard white edge of the tabletop. My friend's dad patiently waited for me to begin. After a few false starts, I spilled out my secret.

When it was all out, he said, "Go for it. As I tell my kids: you don't get redos in life."

After that, I allowed myself to share my dream more. Many days later, in the far back table of an empty office cafeteria during a midafternoon snack break, I confided in my coworker Noah. As I peeled an orange and awaited feedback, Noah framed things in a different way: "Dude. Which will be more interesting: another year spent in a job you know how to do or a year spent trying something you love?"

With each new conversation, my voice gained confidence. Another older coworker put it bluntly: "Do you believe in yourself?" I said I did. "Who is responsible for how this jump turns out?" I said I was. "Then you have no risk in trying. You're betting on yourself here. And you believe in that bet. You have no risk."

I was slowly starting to acknowledge that I might actually give my dream a try. In the copy room near my cubicle, I caught up with Paige, a mainstay in our office, a woman in the twilight of her career as an executive assistant. Separated by a generation, Paige and I had often kicked around ideas of jumps we'd like to make someday. As I finished telling her my secret plan, Paige stepped closer, her tone turning serious and her smile disappearing. Wedged next to the printers, in that thick, no-nonsense Boston accent of hers, Paige laid it straight:

"Honey, don't end up like me. Don't wait fah any-thin or any-wun. Just spread yah wings and act. Fear will fail yah. Courage will not."

Four months after sharing the full dream aloud with my friend's father, I'd told another half dozen people what I had in mind. The voice from inside my head was out in the open, and I was going to act on what it said. I just had to figure out when.

JEFF ARCH

Karate School Owner to Hollywood Screenwriter

I WAS CRAZY about the movies growing up. I didn't know, even up through high school, that people actually wrote them. I thought the only kind of writing you could do was books and plays—and even so, those were kinds of writing other people did in other places. But not me and not anybody I knew. I grew up in a community and a culture where the arts were definitely respected, as long as nobody in the family actually tried to be an artist. We were supposed to be professionals and take over the family business or be a lawyer. Something "respectable." Meaning, something older relatives weren't embarrassed to tell their friends about. I have since found out, of course, that this wasn't limited to my community and my culture. Everyone ever born who was called "creative" probably knows what I mean—even when that term is a compliment, it comes with a side dish of worry. Being proud of you doesn't stop them from hoping you'll grow out of it.

I was the youngest of three boys, the youngest of seven cousins, and everything rolled downhill to me as a kid. I had zero influence; I could talk till I was blue in the face and nobody would listen. Strangely, though, I noticed that if I wrote something down, they would stop and read it. If it was funny, they'd laugh, and if they showed it to someone a week later, that person would laugh. I discovered that I could write something down one time and continue to get reactions from it days and weeks later. It could be funny, it could be serious—as long as the writing was good, the payoffs kept coming. I didn't know anything about money at the time, but that's the exact same way royalties work. It was a great discovery.

By the time I got to high school, I could write my way out of a math class. Really: I had an algebra teacher who cut me a serious break one time because she liked a poem I had in the school magazine. When I went to college I took nothing but film courses and was in heaven. I learned every aspect of putting a movie together—except for screenwriting, because there weren't any courses in it. My junior year, I started getting camera and editing work on productions in and around Boston: documentaries, educational films, industrials, and a commercial here and there. I had a great mentor who taught me movie lighting, and I was really getting good at it.

After graduation, on a whim I cold-called my cameraman hero, Conrad Hall, out in California. I couldn't believe it when he picked up the phone. He invited me to visit him if I came out to LA, and so I did. I showed him my work, and he offered to help me, but he also gave me some cold hard advice about where the movie business was going at that time. He said, "If you can write, that's what you should do." The spec script era was really starting to gather steam, and writing was a faster track. So that was the end of being a cameraman and the beginning of being a writer. I moved to California and got started. There was a legitimate way into the movie business, based on something I was determined to learn how to do.

My dad had died when I was fifteen; otherwise, I might never had gotten away with a decision like that. After I'd been in LA a few months, my mother asked my dad's brother to call and talk sense into me, because of how impossible all this was and because I was going to get hurt, because you don't just decide you're going to make it in movies and then go do it.

Instead, though, my uncle told me a story about my grandfather, who I had never met. He told me that my grandfather had left Russia for America in the early 1900s, but he hadn't headed west, through Europe and onto a boat to Ellis Island like everyone else; for reasons we will never know, the man decided to go east—all the way across Russia, then China, on to Alaska, through Canada, and down to Harrisburg, Pennsylvania, because he knew somebody there. To go that way must have involved a level of hardship unimaginable even to the people in the holds of those immigrant ships. He was the son of a rabbi, traveling alone, through territories that were inhospitable in every possible way.

Instead of talking me into coming home, my uncle gave me what's possibly the most valuable thing you can give a person: an identity. He told me that it's in my blood to go my own way, to not do the thing that everybody else is doing. And to trust that part of me instead of running from it. You do what's in your blood, even if it's crazy to everyone else. You just have to really do it well. If I thanked him a hundred times a day for that, I would not have thanked him enough.

I spent the next few years working on scripts. I was growing as a writer, but not getting anywhere in the business and getting more and more frustrated. Then when I was twenty-eight I got an idea for a stage play—one of those comedies that takes place on one set with lots of doors opening and closing and people coming in and out, and finally all hell breaks loose. I found people who believed in it, and it took two years to pull off. And then I got to be one of those people in theater history whose show opens and closes in the same week. We got killed in the reviews. Even by today's standards, they were savage. But it was a really strange disconnect, because in previews and even after the reviews came out, we were sold out and everyone was laughing and enjoying it. I had seen for myself that I could connect with an audience, and that was the thing I was in this to find out. Still, with reviews like that we couldn't stay open.

I was thirty, married, and with an infant daughter. I had just been run out of New York on a rail. *"Go home. Don't come back. This is not your game."* It might as well have been written on the billboards on the way out of town. I will never forget what that felt like.

But worse than the failure of the show? I didn't like the person I was becoming. Back in college I had promised myself that I wasn't just going to do this; I was going to do it without turning into an asshole. But when I got a little distance, two things became apparent: one, that as a writer I was still on a pretty decent track. Regardless of the critics, I did get to see what works with an audience and why. I had to admit, though, that the show was only okay. It wasn't great; it was good, maybe okay to good. And you don't get anywhere with okay to good. I wasn't upset with my progress in that department; it's all about learning, and I had learned plenty.

The other thing that was apparent was that I wasn't nearly as okay with who I was becoming as a person, and that was where the real work had to be done. There was a character issue that needed attention, and the writing could wait.

For the first time ever, I was at a loss about where I was going and what I needed to do. It was a very low time—and everyone's advice, no matter how well meant, was miles off the mark.

Then, once again, the movies came and saved me. *The Karate Kid* had come out a year earlier, and that whole experience lit up a path for me that I had always been interested in but never got around to. I didn't just want lessons; I needed to find a teacher and really learn from him. I checked a bunch of schools in my area—it was all Tae Kwon Do, not karate—and when I met Master Park, a bond happened immediately. It was like we both saw the same movie, and both had the same need—me, for a teacher like him, and him for a student like me. He said, "If I tie a black belt on you, you can do anything." I decided to believe him, started training the next day, and dedicated myself to making that black belt happen. In the meantime, I had gotten a job teaching high school English, so I balanced that with my training, and before too long I had my black belt and had opened a karate school of my own, in the northern Virginia suburbs. My daughter was in preschool, I had a son on the way, and my life seemed pretty damn good. Maybe I wasn't supposed to be a writer after all, I thought; just because I didn't spend my whole life dreaming of being a martial arts instructor didn't mean that it wasn't what I was supposed to be.

Here's the thing though: all your life, you hear people talk about that "little voice inside" that all of us have. And that little voice, they say, is never wrong. It's your true voice. Even if what it tells you to do doesn't work out, it doesn't mean the voice was wrong. So while I was building this new career, and when it looked like the writing thing might finally be behind me, the voice came back. "This is not what you were meant for," it said. "You're good at it, and you can do very well. But it's not your destiny." And it was really hard to hear that. Did this voice not know what I had been through already? There's only so much disappointment a person can take. I just wasn't interested this time. Enough was enough.

So I pretended not to hear the voice. I was committed to the world I was in. I was making real change, helping families, improving our community, and I was proud of that. I was seeing results every day, and there was nothing indirect about it. You sign people up, you teach the classes, you see the changes, the word goes out, more people sign up, they see the changes, and all is well. Still, the voice kept drilling its way in: "This is not what you were meant for. You're hiding from who you are, and making excuses. You need to stop that."

Around this time, my son was born. I was rocking him to sleep late one night when a Tony Robbins infomercial came on. He was talking about personal power and how you could change your life in thirty days. It was a tacky, ridiculous infomercial, but I kept watching. If I had all the answers, I thought, I wouldn't be up at four in the morning rocking my kid and wondering what I was doing with my life.

It was just one of those nights you get sometimes. I was teaching. I had my school. Things were settled. My family had adjusted to the fact that I was determined to be in show business; then I was teaching tae kwon do in a little town—not doing what middle-class Jewish kids are supposed to do, but they were finally okay with it. And my daughter, she was four and a half, and she seemed to love me without preference for what my vocation was. But I looked down at my son, and somehow I felt there'd be a reckoning with him one day. He'd wait until the perfect moment, halfway through some future lecture, and then the words would come out: *"You were gonna be a writer, Dad. You were gonna be a writer."* And I would lose all credibility that I had with him before then. And he'd've been right. What could I tell my kids about going after their dreams if I didn't go after mine? And I decided that night, it was time to turn up the volume on my little voice, and turn down the volume on everything else. I ordered the tapes. I felt ridiculous, but I did it.

The next morning, I went to Master Park and told him that I was done. I sold the school back to him, rented an office in our town, and began writing again. Six days a week, home for dinner with my kids each night. I brought out an unfinished script from a few years earlier, and finished it in record time. A combination of those tapes, a second-degree black belt from the man who promised me what I could do with that, and the determination to be authentic for my son. I broke every personal record for how quickly that script came out, and how good it was.

I made only one mistake: the script was a buddy comedy with a Cold War theme, and the Cold War had ended while I was writing it. So it didn't matter how good the script was. People liked it—a lot—but no one was going to buy it, and I couldn't blame them. All interest in the subject had passed.

That should have been it. What bigger sign did I need? I had thrown myself at this completely, and nothing changed. But one thing I had learned from those tapes was that often all we have to do is ask a better question. So instead of asking "Why can't I write something that sells?" I asked, "What can I write that *will* sell—what kind of story is timeless and immune to current and changing events?" And the answer was a love story. And my agent backed up this thinking. "If you write a good love story," he said, "I can sell it." And I said, "That's it then. That's what I'll do." A week after that conversation, I got the idea for *Sleepless in Seattle*. I knew right away, I could feel it; if I get this one right, it's gonna be a monster.

It wasn't like the path was all smooth and creamy from there. No one had ever thought of a love story where the two characters are on different sides of the country, leading completely different lives. You must be crazy, people said. A woman who just got engaged hears a widower and his kid on a late-night radio show and upends her whole life to find out if he's for real? They're supposed to fall in love and they don't even know each other? You can't do a love story where the people don't meet. You just can't. No one'll want to put up the money, no one'll want to be in it, and no one'll want to go see it. Why can't you just write the kind of love story that everyone else writes? Every meeting you have will be met with laughter, and not the kind you want. Why do this to yourself?

That's when I understood why my grandfather went east when everyone else went west. It just wasn't in him to do otherwise. And so I had to follow the voice inside me, not all the ones outside. Because I was pretty sure the one inside me was coming from him. Why the hell else did my uncle call me up all those years ago to tell me what my grandfather had done?

When you talk about a leap, it all converged that night—rocking my son to bed with an infomercial at 4 a.m.; thirty-four years old, looking hard at my life. If I wanted success, I knew I had to define it on my terms. Succeeding at what somebody else wanted for me wasn't going to be success. It felt more successful to fail, if I had to, at what I wanted to be doing—at what I finally agreed I was meant to be doing—than it would have been to succeed at what somebody else wanted for me. If I didn't follow my own voice, if I listened to the other ones instead, I knew I'd be doomed. I knew a lot of people who were successful and miserable. I also knew that I had already learned everything you can possibly learn from failure—and that success had lessons too, and those were the ones it was time to learn.

So I wrote this very sweet, sensitive movie where none of the details were true in terms of my own life, but all of the subtext was right on the money. One character is living a very good life she can't quite settle for, another is doing his best not to drown in disappointment for the sake of his son, and a little kid is insisting that something can be true if you believe it hard enough. In the beginning of the story they're in three separate universes, even though two of them live under the same roof; at the end of the story, an elevator door slides closed on the same three people, who finally and gloriously feel whole.

That was me. I didn't realize it at the time, but that was my autobiography. There was something out there and I had to go find it. There was something even bigger inside, and I had to meet it and honor it. My kids are all grown now, and I still don't win any arguments with them. But they know they're not dealing with a phony. They know this old man is for real.

There are steps, and there are jumps, and there are leaps. In every case there will be resistance, and you should absolutely listen to it and respect it. We're not here to be idiots and make stupid and costly mistakes, but when you weigh it all—when you know how to listen and know when your heart is really speaking and know when your heart is telling you that the ground you're standing on just isn't enough—then the only thing left to do is jump.

JEFF ARCH, a former karate school manager and English teacher, is a writer whose script for *Sleepless in Seattle* was nominated for an Oscar in 1994.

TERESA MARIE WILLIAMS, MD

Nurse to Doctor

TIMING IS ACTUALLY not everything. And don't let anyone tell you otherwise. I was a late starter in making my jump, and my journey to the finish line was different than most. Looking back, I wouldn't have had it any other way.

I grew up the oldest of four daughters to a pair of wonderful, hard-working parents in small-town Indiana. We were taught to be humble, kind, respect authority, and work hard. When I would express ideas about doing anything other than remaining in my small town, I was met with inertia: neither my parents, nor my grandparents, nor (at that time) any of my cousins had gone to college. My father came of age at the end of the Depression, my mother during World War II; they were focused on working hard and getting through the day-to-day and taking care of their family.

In high school, I worked the front desk for a local dentist. That got me hooked on health care. Knowing that pursuing education in health care was unknown territory for my parents, I worked up the courage to bring up the subject to an important adult in our school. He said, "What do you think you're going to do?" And hesitantly I said, "I think I'd really like to try to go to college." His reply stuck with me: "You know, Teresa, you do not come from a family that goes to college. Maybe you should think about doing something else."

That was the last time I ever spoke to him. His words burned. I managed to come up with the funds to take the SAT, took out my first student loans, and headed for Indiana University. I found some success in the classroom, and that's when I decided, "I'm going to be a nurse." Predictably, funds fell short so I moved back home, got a job, and commuted to nursing school at an Indiana University satellite campus.

This was a time when there wasn't much creativity around what women could do. Generally, the most upwardly mobile women in health care were nurses—that was my ceiling. During nursing school, I had flashes of an idea: it would be very neat to be a doctor. But I never took it seriously because it seemed too big.

Like so many of my peers, I got married during my training. After graduating from nursing school I soon learned that I was expecting my son. I wanted to be a good mother and a good wife, and I needed to make a living. After my son was born, I began working in a doctor's office and found myself taking on more than my nursing role. One day, one of the physicians turned to me and said, "You know, Teresa, you really missed your mark. You are smarter than most of the people in my medical class, and you already have the mind-set of a physician. You should have been a doctor." That one sentence from a man I deeply respected meant a lot to me. For the first time, I thought, "You know, that might be possible."

But I didn't feel ready yet. I didn't feel like I was capable or confident enough to jump. In the back of my head, words from my past returned: "Your people are not people that go to college."

But I couldn't help myself. I have always been hungry for knowledge and fascinated with how the body functions and with medicine in general. I started taking college courses. The more courses I took, the more my confidence rose. I earned a master's in counseling education, then worked as a vocational counselor for people with disabilities. It was around this point when my marriage fell apart. In a way, it was liberating: I could form my own individual identity without trying to fit what I thought I was "supposed to do." I continued to chip away at my learning. I kept thinking, "You know what? Becoming a doctor is possible. And I have to decide when and how it's going to happen."

I quietly continued moving toward my jump because I wanted only to be supportive to my son as he headed toward college. I remember specifically thinking, "Henceforth, in my family, children will be told that education is of highest importance, that they are bright, that they can do whatever it is they choose to do."

It was a beautiful day when I dropped my son off at college in northern Indiana. Afterward, I was driving back home, down I-65. When you take your child to college, it's a really big deal. I was overwhelmed with emotion. I pulled over to the side of the road, and I just started crying. I sobbed and I sobbed, and once I finished sobbing, I said a prayer. I said, "You know, God, I want my son now to take his wings and fly. But I'm going to take my wings too. What would you have me do?" And at that moment, I listened to that still, small voice, and that voice said, "You're going to go to medical school." I set off driving again and decided to take the steps to make it happen. I was thirty-nine.

I had a lot of negatives in my mind, starting with the obvious one: the timing is off. Nevertheless, I told myself: "Timing is not everything. Not everybody goes from A to B to C—not everybody takes just that one path. If you don't follow that and you're different and you're not like everybody else, it's okay. And you know what? When you get there, you find out you're not the only one who took an unusual path." Approaching my jump, I believed that, ultimately, I would not be alone.

I decided not to give anyone the opportunity to tell me I couldn't jump. I wasn't going to hand my fate over to someone else. It was important to seek others' opinions and perspectives, but my encounter with my guidance counselor taught me that no one is in a better position to make decisions for me than I am for myself. I had to embrace being the decision maker. And if things didn't go well, guess what? I was responsible. It's far sweeter to own your decisions and take responsibility when things don't go as planned than to remain at the fancy of someone else.

When I speak with younger folks, I tell them, "Seek advice, but don't dwell there. Listen to yourself. No one can really know what is inside of you. Nobody fully understands your strengths or what you might be hiding about yourself that's superawesome." I rarely relied on anyone else, and when things got lonely along the way, I'd share my jump only with those who knew me best. A good friend, a physician that I had worked with, told me, "We always knew you should be a doctor. Just make it happen." And so I pushed forward. I went to the library, learned Algebra II, physics, chemistry, studied for the MCATs. The time to learn to be more trusting of others' opinions would have to wait.

I found a nursing job at the one hospital that would allow me to work full-time on weekends and study and go to school during the week. When the time came, I told the hospital, "I can't work this weekend because I'm going to take the MCAT." They thought I was kidding, and I said, "No, I'm ready. I'm going for it." By then, I was met with much less resistance because I had proven myself at work. No one was going to stop me.

I visited a medical school admissions officer to make sure my age wouldn't hold me back from honest consideration. Soon after, at forty-four years young, I was accepted into the medical school at the University of Louisville. In one of the last few weeks of medical school, I sat with a highly respected surgeon who knew me well. He said, "When your application came through four years ago, I voted you down. I thought you were too old, and we needed to give that position to someone younger. You proved me wrong."

I applied to the Mayo Clinic for residency because I felt I had nothing to lose. That's a whole different girl than the twenty-four-year-old me. The Mayo Clinic receives three thousand applications. They interview three hundred, and they take thirty. They took me with open arms as one of their oldest residents ever—around fifty years old.

Listen to the words playing inside you. Remember the person in the best position to decide something for you is you. No one else has the information that you have about yourself, your abilities, the talents that you might be hiding, the secrets that you have in your heart, or the experiences that have helped you or hindered you. Jumping is good. It's euphoric, it's scary, but the fear is outweighed by the joy of owning your own actions, taking responsibility. When you hit tough times in your jump, don't look at it as a hard time. Look at it as one more step.

Sure, the timing might be off according to society. Or sure, in your mind, you might be thinking, "Gosh, it would have been so much better if I could have done this when I was younger and more energetic, or if I was smarter." But it's okay to be different.

In fact, it may be better that way.

TERESA MARIE WILLIAMS, MD, a former registered nurse and graduate of University of Louisville Medical School and the Mayo Clinic Graduate School of Medicine, is a practicing internal medicine physician.

NATE CHAMBERS

Mechanical Engineer to Fitness Entrepreneur

I AM NOT a trainer. I won't count your reps, and I certainly can't force you to change your life. But I can tell you how it felt to chase a crazy idea into a car and then onto a couch and finally toward a gym; and perhaps more importantly, what I learned from listening not to the loud voice of reason but instead to that smaller one, that voice buried somewhere deep in my gut. I may not count your reps, but I can tell you about when I jumped.

I grew up in a town of about ten thousand people, in the heart of wine country that stretches through Northern California. My mom worked from home as an accountant; my dad was a mechanical engineer. Along with my two younger siblings, I was homeschooled through middle school. Homeschooling showed me it was okay to take the path less traveled to get what you needed to get done. And it showed me that if you work hard on your own schedule, you can enjoy the freedoms that come from that work. Our homeschool curriculum was creative and spontaneous; if a local history lesson related to some place nearby, we'd pile in the car and go check it out. It was a cool way to learn, a cool way to grow up.

I fell in love with fitness through playing community team sports— soccer mainly but also basketball and baseball. Sports taught me about hard work and integrity and provided all of my social interaction during the homeschool years. I cherished the feeling of being on a team, of working alongside teammates.

In college, I studied mechanical engineering, following in my dad's footsteps. I didn't really have a plan other than going to school to get a good job. We all have dreams, but at some point, it's easier to kick them aside to pursue things the way that everybody else does. After college, I took an entry-level engineering job at a high-tech glass and display company. Over the next couple years, I worked my way up to program manager, and then became the engineering sales manager for my division.

As I rose through the ranks, somewhere in the back of my head I wondered if I needed to be playing my life so safe. The engineering job paid well. I learned a lot and worked with good people, but I wasn't passionate about what I was doing. The more I worked there, day-to-day, and the more I interacted with the people in the industry, the more I knew this work wasn't for me long-term.

Outside of work, fitness became my escape. I loved what training hard provided: it kept me positive, kept me in shape. Team training demanded leadership and integrity; in return, it gave me a broader purpose. I connected with like-minded athletes. We'd hike and surf, play volleyball. These were my people, and our workouts became my outlet from everything else.

That's when I first listened to my gut but in a small way. On my own time, I started designing fitness backpacks that could get your gear from work to the gym using an efficient, all-in-one product. Designing these backpacks was a way to combine my passion for fitness with my knack for making things. I mocked up the designs but was struggling to navigate production processes when I caught a break: a friend introduced me to the former head seamstress for the outdoor clothing and gear brand Patagonia. We got to chatting, and she told me she'd just retired and would be happy to help set me up with the right people for my production line.

Just like that, I went from an idea that was in my back pocket to a production route for my backpacks—and with this product, I thought could help people improve their lives through fitness.

The only catch? I needed more capital to produce the backpacks. At that very moment, I was set to sign the papers for my first home. By most measures, buying a house is a great milestone, a good investment for the future, something that sets you up for a longer-term success. But buying the house would have tied up any free cash and kept me at the engineering job for the foreseeable future.

I knew the cost of owning a home; it was about the same amount of money needed to launch a production line of, say, backpacks. The question became: Do I invest in the house or use that money to fund my project?

I was confronted with the first of what would be many decisions that pitted logic against emotion; choosing between the big voice of reason or the little voice of emotion.

Around this time, I had been reading a book called *How We Decide* by Jonah Lehrer. In it, he describes how people tend to overthink things and value logic over emotion in decision making, yet studies show that people who make emotion-based decisions actually tend to be far happier than those who make logic-based decisions. For example, he writes that in buying a car, there's an endless supply of questions: leather seats, four-wheel drive, Bluetooth? That line of questioning focuses on trying to nail down exactly which choice is right for you, rather than simply asking, "How does the car feel to you? Does it make you happy when you're going to drive it?" I took this question to heart while thinking about buying the house versus putting the money into starting this backpack company.

I talked to family and friends and others whom I trusted, and they were unanimously in favor of me going the route of buying the house. The conversations were logic based. But at the end of the day, it really came down to an emotion. I believed that if I could pursue something that was more meaningful to me, I would be happier than I'd be owning a house—even if the result became detrimental to my financial standing over the next five years. I pulled out of escrow and put the house-buying funds into starting my backpack company, Fit Factory Gear.

My hope with the backpack was to give people a way to take fitness on the go, whether it's before the workday, on lunch break, or for a weekend adventure. The features, the price, and the style supported a healthy lifestyle. That's what I wanted to package and sell: a fitness-based lifestyle.

I prototyped the product over the next six months, while still working at the glass company; then I hit another roadblock. Cash, again, became the issue. Even though I hadn't purchased the house, most of those funds had gone into product development, and now we needed to launch the product with capital I didn't have. I saw three options: one, go for outside funding, two, self-fund, or three, drop the project entirely.

Bringing in outside investors would mean returning to a culture and workplace I was aiming to break away from, so that was out. I turned to the prospect of self-funding.

I looked at a budget of all my expenses to see if I could find a way to shave savings from somewhere to self-fund. I learned that my monthly apartment rent was my single largest expense. The timing was interesting: at this point, I had been dating a woman who was graduating from medical school, and around that time, she was placed in Detroit for her residency. We decided that because of her upcoming move and the things that I was trying to do, it was better if we parted ways on good terms and didn't try to pursue a long-distance relationship.

I viewed the breakup as an opportunity rather than a life disappointment or roadblock: newly single, I wondered if I should move into my car and take that monthly rent money to fund the backpacks.

I returned to my family and friends for guidance, and this time the feedback was much stronger than it had been during the conversations about ditching the house purchase. When I decided not to buy the house, my family and friends still supported me. But as I started talking about moving into my car while working a day job, and also trying to launch this company on the side, my parents and most of my friends reacted emphatically: "You're crazy, Nate. Why would you do that? It's not worth it. It's not safe. Where are you going to shower? Where are you going to cook and eat?"

But there are always a million reasons *not* to do something. If you believe in something enough, that alone is the reason you need to go for it. Again, I sided with the little voice of emotion over the bigger one carrying logic. Against better judgment and input from friends and family, I decided that I was going to move out of my apartment, put the majority of my stuff into a storage unit, and move into my car. I was betting on myself, with the thought that if I didn't believe in myself, who would?

My new accommodation was a compact sedan, a 2014 Volkswagen Jetta. I moved in with some work clothes, workout clothes, laptop, toiletries, and a few other things.

The very first night, trying to figure out how to sleep, I folded down the front seat, and a bunch of stuff was racing through my head: "What am I doing? My parents were right; this is crazy." My nerves spiked any time a car drove by and I saw the headlights. Can they see me? I tried to make it work, tried to fall asleep and get some rest so I could go to my day job the next morning. After tossing and turning some more, I gave up. I said, "You know what, I'm going to go get a hotel room. This isn't going to work."

And then I thought: "I just went through all this effort to get to this point in making my jump work. Is it still worth it?" And I decided that it was still worth it, that I wanted to at least give it a try, just make it through this one night. One night. At worst, tomorrow night I can go get a hotel room. Just do the one night, and see how it goes.

In doing that, I turned this massive undertaking of living in a car for as long as I possibly could to doing it for just one night. Just make it through this one night. And when I got my head around that, I was actually able to get a little bit of sleep. Definitely not the best sleep I've ever had, but I was able to get some rest.

I woke up in the morning. I'd survived. I said, "Okay, time to go to my normal day job." And guess what happened? Nobody thought different of me. No one knew that I was sleeping in my car. It's easy to think that you're the center of the world, the universe. But at the end of the day, there's a bunch of other people that are doing their thing, and you're just a small piece of all the action; all the other people are going through life at the same time, in their own way. My jump was scary for me, but everyone is confronting their own fears in some way, or hiding from them. I almost forgot all about sleeping in the car by the end of the workday and went to the gym, but then showered at the beach. It was cold water from the ocean, but I thought, "You know what, you can survive." Maybe it's good recovery from the workout, like an ice bath.

. . .

I did it again. And on the second night, I found a better sleeping position. I folded down the back seat of my car, slept toward the trunk. I got a better night's sleep. And I'd done it before so it now felt less foreign, like it could work. Sleep a little bit better, get into work the next day. And now it's, "Okay. I can do this." It was about taking one step at a time, one night at a time, trying not to freak out about stuff that you can't handle, focusing instead on what you can. Baby steps, small things that add up over time.

That's what made it work. I trained five to six days a week at a small gym that my buddy Eddie owned and operated. I believe fitness can help you through just about anything, and it saved me here. It gave me a healthy body, healthy mind, while living out of the car—showering at the beach in cold water, brushing my teeth out of the trunk, using Starbucks for the restroom.

Seven months later, I had saved up enough money for the biggest part of my jump. I was in a position where I could survive almost a year without an income and work solely on my company. My friend Peter in San Francisco offered me a couch. So I quit my job and drove to San Francisco, leaving a life of logic for the passionate voice in my head, going from inside my car and onto a couch.

It was thrilling but incredibly scary to finally remove the safety net of steady income. Now I had no choice: this jump must work. It was exciting to start, but excitement fades, and you realize that you have to nail each piece each day just to keep everything running. This is the less sexy part of the journey. Living in the car obviously was not sexy, but at the same time, I had income. At any point, I could have moved back into an apartment and been okay.

Just before I left for the couch, my local gym held a seminar about becoming a certified trainer through this group called Gym Jones. I had to do it. As an engineer, I value structure and techniques; as a person, I crave fitness. And I love to learn. My idea of the backpacks helping people become healthier, more active, better versions of themselves felt tied to learning more about working out itself. So I took a level-one fundamentals seminar, loved it, and signed up for the level-two intermediate training. Between the backpacks and now the gym training, there were a lot of moving parts, but all were pointing toward helping people become better through fitness.

And so I moved onto Peter's couch—actually, an air mattress in the living room behind the couch. Tons of privacy. As I settled in, the backpack business hit some hurdles. What I started to see was that by not taking outside funding, I was sacrificing certain parts of the business— marketing efforts, promotional shipments—and it meant I wasn't able to grow the business as fast as I had hoped.

Around this time, I was introduced to my now good friend and business partner James, a South African gym owner who was certified through this same Gym Jones group and interested in opening a gym in the United States. We really hit it off, and the idea of opening a gym, to me, was still very much in line with helping people become better through fitness. We chatted more and more. We shared the same philosophy and passions. And I decided I could help him launch his gym. My jump remained in fitness, but it took a different form. Plus, I didn't have to abandon the backpacks: I was going to use the gym as a retail front for this product that I loved and believed in.

My budget didn't provide for more time without an income, so to spot myself a few more months of cash, I took a one-week consulting gig in my former life as an engineer. I went in, did it for a week, and it was with very good people, and I received very good pay. It would have been a good experience for most people, but it was probably the best experience I could have had because I hated it. I ended that week thinking, "I cannot go back to working a day job that I don't care about." It felt like it was crushing the passion and fire that I had.

That was a turning point. I went from this low point where I was almost out of money, had been out of a job for nearly a year, to getting reinvigorated in one of the strangest ways possible: by almost going back to work and reminding myself very clearly why I had jumped.

James and I were rejected in just about every way before finally landing on a space, ten months later, opening the doors to Roark Gyms San

Francisco in April 2016. We started with unpainted walls and limited equipment, with classes where literally no one would show up. Today, we've hit our initial membership goals and are selling out some classes and adding caps to others. On the wall of one corner of the gym is a display of my backpacks for sale. The motto of our gym is "Building better humans." We're doing everything we can to provide a space where like-minded people can work hard and build their confidence, break mental barriers and start to believe in themselves, and take that confidence with them outside the gym—to fuel their own passions and their own jumps.

I ask my members, "What are you passionate about in the gym, out of the gym? What do you want to do activity-wise? What do you want to do with your job and your life?" And then I use the fitness itself to build confidence that they can translate into these other areas. A positive mind-set is critical to fulfillment in daily life and especially jumping; it impacts your work, your friends, your relationships. It inspires accountability; it advocates for working hard when no one is watching. And it's precisely when no one is watching when you'll strengthen your footing to jump.

If you don't know how to find your little voice, start by believing in something. I'm not hoping to convince people to go to the extremes that I went to. Instead, I'd like others to simply know that it's okay to believe in something bigger and to follow your passions. Once you know that it's okay to pursue what will make you happy, and once you find out what it is that you believe in, then you have something that, even if it's not logical, will be worth jumping for.

You have to apply a work ethic alongside your voice, and then believe in yourself. If you don't believe in yourself, no one else will. That's why I moved into the car. If I wasn't going to commit 100 percent, who else would? I like to say, "Show me how you spend your time, and I'll tell you what your priorities are." Either the things that we value and the goals that we work toward are important to us and a priority, or they're not. If something is low on your priority list, well, then it's not a priority.

Start simple: list all the goals you'd like to hit that relate to your jump. Then cross off all the ones that you aren't spending time on. You might find that you cross off everything but the top two or three goals, and that's okay. Take the top goals and write out what they will ultimately lead you toward. What will your life look like when you hit them? Now you can look at what you do each day, then look at your big picture vision, and ask, "Is what I'm doing today bringing me closer to this vision or further away?" And if it brings you closer, then awesome, do that thing, and pursue it with 100 percent energy. But if it takes you further away, revisit how you spend your time.

If you're searching for your little voice, I say start your search in a gym. It's one of the few places where life is pretty fair. The results in a gym are directly proportional to your effort. If you work hard, you're going to get results. You will build discipline, strength, and confidence.

A gym is a good place to discover what you're capable of, and over time, you may find something that you're passionate about that could be completely unrelated to working out. But in the gym or outside of it, I truly believe that the best things in life lie on the other side of fear. You just have to trust your gut in order to reach them.

NATE CHAMBERS, a former mechanical engineer and founder of Fit Factory Gear, is co-owner of Roark Gyms in San Francisco.

LAURA MCKOWEN

Marketing Executive to Writer

I DIDN'T REALLY know what I wanted to do, so I did what I thought I would be good at, what people told me I was good at. And, to be completely honest, I was influenced by things unrelated to the actual work: how cool an office looked, the people at the job, and the drinking culture. I could say that I built a fifteen-year career in marketing, but that implies a lot more intent than the reality. A decade in, I became a director, had a high-profile job. My drinking had become really bad by then, and a lot of that was tied to my work culture. I was drawn to marketing because of the "work hard, play hard" ideals. There was drinking everywhere, and I loved it.

But about two and a half years ago, I had to get sober. I had followed the rules of my industry. I had bought into all of it, and I had developed a real drinking problem. It wasn't the industry's fault, obviously, but it certainly didn't help. Suddenly my job, my career, my path—none of it fit me anymore.

I was trying hard to get sober, and it took everything I had. I desperately needed an outlet, and the one that I found—the one that helped me most and honestly saved my life—was writing. It helped because I was finally able to tell the truth about my situation and say things I had kept quiet for so long. During the quiet and sober moments throughout my career, I knew I didn't love my job—but the twentysomething me ignored this fact. Now, in my writing, this truth was exposed. I discovered small cohorts of online strangers with whom I could share my secrets. They weren't connected to my work life, they weren't connected to my personal life, and in some ways that's what I needed. I started posting about my struggles and not watering them down in any way because the audience was nobody that I knew.

I had always wanted to write, always talked about writing, always dreamed of writing. I read all the time. Or I used to, before the drinking took over. My whole career I had been so caught up in everything else that I really never wrote. When I was thirty-seven, a single mom, and finally sober, writing rescued me. It was clear that this was what I should be doing—even if I never made a living from it.

But one of the hardest things to say out loud is what your dream actually is. I wanted to be a writer, but it felt so out there, so far away and like such a pipe dream that I was afraid to even say it out loud. I was fifteen years into a career; I'd never published anything. I doubted myself. I thought: "I'm just another girl with a blog. There are thousands of us." My friends pushed me to keep going, and that was really encouraging, but what ultimately propelled me was that I couldn't not write. It was clearly rescuing me and connecting me to all these people and opportunities. It was expanding my world when every other thing was shutting down—my social life, my work. I was spending less time on them, feeling less connected to them, but this other life was opening, expanding.

So I kept at it. At work, I blocked off every possible sliver of time for writing or doing something to support my writing. Every day at noon, I took an hour to go downtown for an AA meeting, which is blasphemy in the corporate world—at least in my industry: you don't just leave for an hour to go anywhere during lunch. I started waking up regularly at 4 a.m. so that I could write without distractions. I was doing it, and I was loving it—and this coming from someone who had never been conscious that early in the morning before.

I started publishing more pieces online, contributing to different publications. I decided to start a podcast about writing with my friend Holly. We had no time for it, but we made time. It was just something that we wanted to do. (We've now produced more than one hundred episodes, and it's really taken off.) People always say that if you do something you love, you never feel as if you're working. Writing and doing the podcast never felt like work. I was making no money with either one, but I still wanted to do them.

Meanwhile, it became more apparent to me with every meeting I had, every client trip I took, that my day job did not suit me anymore. Another two years went by, and things unfolded with my writing in an easy, natural way. I began to feel this second heartbeat growing inside of me. There could really be a different path for me. I could do something with this passion. I could jump.

The biggest, biggest, biggest concern for making the jump was money. One of the side effects of my earlier journey with drinking—through all those years of irresponsibility—is that it left me with a ton of debt. I also got divorced around the same time that I got sober, so I'm supporting myself and my daughter. Her dad's very involved, but at the end of the day in my house, it's still just me. I don't have a financial safety net.

But the more I write, the more support I receive. I was with a friend who asked straight up what was holding me back. I told her the truth: I can't pause my living expenses, and I have very little savings, so this jump is a huge financial risk. She offered to help, to loan me what I'd need for a while. I was taken aback and felt totally uncomfortable: here was a woman saying, "You're worthy; I truly believe in you." I couldn't get that out of my head. I also secured some contracting work that would keep me working and bringing in income after I left.

A critical roadblock to making a jump is the perception that you need to ask for permission. I am almost forty years old, and after that conversation with my friend, my immediate reaction was to call my mom, dad, and then my ex-husband. But I soon realized that I didn't and don't need their permission to jump. I want their support, but I don't need their permission. This jump is so special to me, so close to my heart that I had to protect it from an onslaught of doubt that could drown it immediately if I sought permission. Ultimately, I did get encouragement and support, although not across the board. But it didn't matter because I wasn't asking for permission anymore, and that was a huge, huge step. I was saying, "This is me. I think I can do this."

It's so hard to jump because it goes against many things that we learn growing up. My outside was very successful: great job, beautiful daughter, newly sober. All these things look great, but something didn't feel right. That tiny internal whisper just kept getting louder, and it got deafening once I got sober. The linchpin was knowing that I would regret *not* jumping. That regret was something I knew I couldn't live with.

Jumping is scary. I didn't sleep for four nights before I went in to resign. I'd have nightmares that I got evicted from my place or that I went back to drinking. I built up irrational fears: What if the banks stop working? What if phones stop working and I can't reach anyone? They were completely irrational fears, but big ones.

I got over the hump by stepping back from the feeling and checking in rationally: these things I feared could happen any day, jump or no jump. They could happen while I still had my job. But it's truly amazing the length to which our subconscious will go to try and pull us back from taking a risk. I have had a little training in being scared—with getting sober and leaving my marriage. Things turned out okay in those cases; I was held and supported. I could risk being scared again.

There were a few nonnegotiable pieces that I knew I needed to have in place so that deciding to jump would not be totally illogical. One was money, and the loan and the contracting work that gave me the little bit of a safety net I needed. The other was that I needed my ex-husband's support—not his permission but his support—because our lives are very connected through our daughter. And emotionally, I was not ready to accept his lack of support, so the beautiful surprise was that I talked to him about it, and he gave me his support. He saw the good that this would bring for me.

You never actually jump alone. The world has completely opened up to get me started on this path in such an organic, natural way. I work my ass off, but around me, things have started to click. Offers of support, the podcast, heroes of mine reaching out to help. I've always been able to provide for my daughter and myself, and I hold the conviction that I'll continue to find a way to do so. There's no proof of this, and that can be really scary. But I think of the worst possible scenario: if I fail, I go back to the same work I was doing before. Is that really so terrible? No.

Plus, the idea of failure is such a lie. The tipping point for me was counting on my left hand all of the risks in jumping, and then on the right hand, counting the risks of not doing it—emotionally, spiritually, pragmatically. There's a line from the Gospel of Thomas that I kept thinking about over and over and over again: if you bring forth what is in you, it will save you, and if you do not bring forth what is in you, it will destroy you. I know that this jump is something that is in me.

The idea of stability in our society is just a facade anyway—anything can happen to me even if I never jump. I could die today; my daughter could get deathly ill tomorrow. Things change that you can't control. Events like 9/11 happen, and even much bigger things than that. Our lives are all transient; there is always going to be a coming and going, regardless of whether we jump or not. Don't avoid jumping because of the illusion of a stability you think you have. Because that, too, someday will change.

The truth—with a capital T—of what you need to do is somewhere in your belly. Listen to it, and proceed carefully. For too long, I hid from my jump. Today, I'm tackling it head-on.

We each have a story. Mine isn't all pretty: newly sober single mom heading toward forty with a big risk on the horizon. But I handed in my resignation, and my new story began. I will no longer ask for permission to live it.

LAURA MCKOWEN, a former marketing executive, is a writer, speaker, and teacher; she is currently writing her first book.

TOMMY CLARK

Medical School Research Fellow to
Nonprofit Founder and Executive Director

IN ZIMBABWE, SOCCER is religion. What if we could use soccer to improve global health?

For a long time, I figured this little question in the back of my mind was too far out and that the best way to address health care was to become a doctor. But sometimes you just can't ignore what's being whispered in the back of your head. I was steps away from finishing medical school when I finally listened to that whisper.

During my childhood, our family followed my dad through his career as a professional soccer player and coach. When I was thirteen, we left Scotland and landed in Zimbabwe, where soccer was everything. It was hard not to fall in love with it. I played in college, and sometime during my junior year, I stumbled into health care. A few friends were doing premed work, and it made me think, "Huh. Maybe that's something I could do." I went to my guidance counselor and said I was interested in pursuing a career in medicine. She told me it was too late, couldn't do it, should've thought of it earlier. So I said no big deal, and turned my attention elsewhere.

. . .

I majored in English and after graduation went back to Zimbabwe and played for the team my dad had coached. I played pro all over the world for the next five years, without any great success but good enough to keep going. During one game, I went up for a header, and my head split open. As I'm sitting in the emergency room getting sewn up by the doctor, my mind went back to medicine. In soccer, my fate was in other people's hands, and not always people I respected. I was tired of being subject to other people's opinions. In medicine, I could bet on myself. If I worked hard, I would be rewarded; my fate would be in my own hands.

I was in California a little while later helping my dad coach his college team when the idea came together. It had been a couple of years since I'd left Zimbabwe, but I still couldn't move past the health crisis that the country had found itself in. The population was being decimated by HIV. Nationwide, soccer had provided a unique pedestal. We'd have thirty thousand fans at our games, and all the guys on the team were famous. Yet people were succumbing to the disease left and right—including some of my teammates.

I felt that soccer could have a role to play in combating HIV. A friend of a friend was a doctor and an expert on behavioral change, so I told him, "Look, I want to use soccer and its role models to fight HIV." He told me to go for it, and I took that to mean, "Go be a doctor."

I picked up a secondhand MCAT prep book, applied to a couple of schools, and, some way or another, got into a med school. Now I was on the steady path of structure, one where you invest a ton of time and money and expect a consistent career in return. I was very excited about my soccer concept, but it never seemed realistic to imagine that I would actually get to spend all my time doing it or that it would actually provide an income. All of that seemed preposterous. I figured I'd become a pediatrician, and that would be the best I could do.

I was plowing through my residency in pediatrics some years later when the director of the program asked me, "What do you want to do with your career?" And I answered truthfully. "Well, I've got this idea about soccer and HIV." Rather than say, which some people did, "Well, that's far-fetched," or "That sounds like a good idea and maybe something to pursue when you're finished with your residency," he replied, "Great. Let's make it happen." That was the first step, taking the voice out of the quiet silence inside me. The next was to file the papers to form Grassroot Soccer, a nonprofit organization. During elective time and on weekends, I poured myself into it.

Still, I stayed the course toward becoming a doctor and was accepted as a research fellow at the University of California, San Francisco, for my postdoc. I kept up my nonprofit work on the side, becoming the volunteer CEO. Instead of using the postdoc solely on major research studies, like most of my peers, I used it as a chance to keep hacking away at my idea.

Eventually, things came to a head. A well-known foundation had learned about Grassroot Soccer, and its founder was ready to make an investment to fund the organization for three years. The only catch? The CEO had to be working full-time. No more medicine.

I remember getting the news, and it seemed like I should've been celebrating. Our nonprofit had just received $300,000. But I was sweating. I polished off a whole bottle of wine in the course of one evening—just thinking and sweating and doodling and worrying.

I had heard that some 90 percent of nonprofits go out of business within five years. And of the 10 percent that make it past five years, only half of them are in business at ten years. The money wasn't a long-term guarantee—it was $100,000 a year for the first three years. It was stability but only for now.

Suddenly, I was having second thoughts. I was bashful and scared to death. One day, your dream comes true, and you freak out. I didn't know if it was the best time to jump. My wife, who is generally risk averse, said to me, "Look, why wouldn't you do this? This is what you've always wanted to do. You'd be crazy not to do it." She reminded me about things that, deep down, I already knew. I had to listen.

I was worried what my peers would think. My postdoc was at a prestigious place, and I was lucky to have one of the few spots in the program. But my colleagues were supportive and believed really strongly in what I was going to try to do. We were now going to have different roles in combating HIV, but we remained part of the same movement.

. . .

It's implied that a jump anytime is the right move, but remember to consider the "when." Weigh what you're jumping from and what you're jumping to and if the time is right on each end. For me, getting to the brink of becoming doctor was huge. I worked out a deal where I could still see patients one day each week. Emotionally, this helped me keep one type of identity. Pragmatically, it made me feel that if the jump didn't work, I had something else under me. I don't think it would have been smart to jump before that point.

That being said, there is danger to jumping too late or not at all. People seem very aware of the risks associated with making a jump but are less aware that there is a risk to not taking a jump at all. It could just be the risk of being unhappy, but it's a risk nonetheless. Even if whatever you jump to fails, there is an upside to it. You can say, "Hey, I went for it." You can learn more from the things that don't work out. We all know this, but it's still hard to put yourself in a position where you might fail.

Today, Grassroot Soccer has raised over $50 million, graduated almost two million participants, and has leveraged the power of soccer to educate, inspire, and mobilize youth in developing countries to overcome their greatest health challenges. I may not be listening to a heartbeat or tapping on a reflex, but my work still feels in line with what I set out to do as a pediatrician. Ironically, starting a nonprofit focused on altering human behavior meant changing mine first. And it was my jump that made this possible.

TOMMY CLARK, a former professional soccer player, is a pediatrician and founder and CEO of Grassroot Soccer.

ELLE LUNA

Technology Designer to Painter

I WAS BORN and raised in Dallas, Texas, surrounded by a wonderful, incredibly spiritual community. As a child, I watched my grandmother play on her rosary, running her fingers over the beads and repeating these little divine messages, and I loved to read books that included first-person accounts of experiences with angels. At a very young age, a fourth-dimensional world became very real to me. But the older I got, especially into college, the more I began to feel pressured to get my stuff together, figure out what I would study, and determine how I would make a living.

My senior year in college, I decided to become a lawyer. I come from a long line of lawyers, and I knew firsthand that becoming a lawyer could provide the lifestyle that I wanted and that I had been fortunate to receive as a kid. Even though I detested studying for the law school exam, and even though the applications were so dreadful that I would burst into tears as I was trying to write my admissions essays, I applied to nine law schools. To my shock and horror, one by one, the responses began to arrive. Lo and behold, the universe gave me the greatest gift by denying me admission to every single law school. Because if I had been accepted at one—even my safety school—I would have gone. I totally would have gone.

As the rejections started to pile up, I began to ask, "Well, what else can I do?" And of course—this is how it always goes, right?—the answer was right under my nose. I was painting nonstop, sleeping in the art studio, and skipping meals and eating candy bars just so I could keep making art. What if I pursued a life of creativity? For some reason, however, choosing to step into my creativity and my art never felt possible. I thought repeatedly, "That may happen to someone else but not to me."

This moment was what I later called a "crossroads" moment. In my book, *The Crossroads of Should and Must*, I write about how we arrive at a crossroads between two really different paths over and over again throughout our lives—*should* and *must*. *Should* is all of the expectations and obligations that we feel other people put upon us while *must* is our own intuition and deepest knowing.

Looking back, years later, I can see all of the *shoulds* that I believed to be true: *should* go to law school, *should* be a lawyer, *should* play it safe, *should* go this way because my dad did it, my brother did it, my grandfather did it. My parents supported my desire to be a lawyer because they wanted me to be safe and supported. After all, the term "starving artist" exists for a reason. Ultimately, as I stood at that crossroads between pursuing law and pursuing art, I chose art. I wish I could say that I was bold and brave enough to choose it independently of being rejected from every law school, but that was not the case. By default, I was thrust upon the path of art, the one that I really wanted to be on, even as I tried in earnestness to be a lawyer.

After graduation, I went to art school and focused on commercial design, thinking surely *that* would feed my creative streak.

I was very fortunate to get a job at the international design consulting firm IDEO as a "storyteller" after school. Within diverse, interdisciplinary teams, we worked with clients to help tell their stories using film and video, paintings, and graphic design. Four years later, I moved to IDEO's San Francisco office and began to see what was happening right in our backyard with all of the up-and-coming start-ups, from Airbnb to Uber. At that time, both of those companies were fewer than five people. I wanted to take all of the power, all of that knowledge, that we were giving to the Fortune 500 corporations and apply it to a start-up. So I decided to leave IDEO and move into the tech sector. My first gig was working with the Uber team to craft their iPhone app, and then I joined the Mailbox team as their Design Lead. I loved the design process of taking something from an idea on a Post-it note all the way through to an implemented product in the Apple store. The idea that we could build something that could be downloadable on anybody's phone anywhere in the world was astounding to me.

Around this time, I began receiving these rather intuitive feelings about where my journey was supposed to go next. In fact, the signs began to arrive when I was sound asleep in bed.

It all started with a dream—a recurring dream. In the dream, I would walk into a big, beautiful white room, and I would sit on the floor, and I would be filled from head to toe with peace; the most unbelievable sense of peace. I suspect that I received this message in the form of a dream because I was so busy, and addicted to being busy, in my waking life.

This dream felt not unlike the angels of my childhood speaking out to me—I couldn't explain it, but it was a palpable sense of knowing. I started looking for the white room from my dreams on Craigslist. I had this feeling that whatever I was looking for was looking for me too. While I couldn't make logical, rational sense of what was happening and I worried that it might be all hocus-pocus, one day I found *the* room—an apartment for rent in San Francisco—and there was an open house the next day. I got the apartment, moved in, and on my first night, I sat down on the floor and waited for the peace to arrive.

It didn't arrive, of course. And I began to panic. My blood pressure went up. I was berating myself, saying, "What have you done? Why are you here?" And so I decided to ask the room a question—because if angels could talk to me and if my dreams could deliver messages, then why couldn't the room give me some sort of answer? I asked the room out loud, "Why am I here?" And, clear as day, the room replied, "It's time to paint."

Of course I had always loved to paint. I painted as a little girl, all through college, and even into grad school. But somewhere along the way, I had just gotten busy, and here I was, all of these twists and turns later, quite far from my original dream. The next day I went to the art supply store and "got the band back together" so to speak, and I began working with an incredible rush of creative energy.

As I look back at this moment, there was no big jump. There was no leap. There was just taking the next step, crossing the next chasm of space, and choosing *must* in each moment. The more I surrendered to the fact that I loved making art, the more time I continued to carve out for painting, drawing, exploring colors, and all of the things that I just *loved* to do. Day by day, I started tiptoeing back into my creative world.

The only catch in all of this?

I was still working full-time at the start-up. I was exhausted and increasingly felt very anxious. I adored many parts of my job, but the busyness and hecticness and culture of meetings meetings meetings just didn't feel good to me. I looked at my finances and saw that I could buy a little bit of time to make art full-time and play in my studio. And I decided to quit my job and give the creative life a go.

One of the first things I began doing during this "sandbox" of time, as I called my creative sabbatical, was to cultivate solitude. The more I read about people who I admired who had done something amazing with their life—in leadership, innovation, discovery—the more I discovered that they all had a sliver of solitude which helped them to make their giant breakthroughs. I believe that solitude is essential if you want to find your true voice and your own true path. In the absence of solitude, our little voice gets mixed in with all the other voices telling us how to live. We get knocked off our path. I knew solitude was going to be essential, and I began cultivating a more restful mind.

The second thing I began to experience was the circuitous nature of my own creativity. In design, so much of our process was about getting from A to B as quickly and efficiently as possible. But the more I started to tune in to what was happening inside of me, the more I realized that A to B, while efficient, was actually not where my process wanted to flow. With time, my journey in the studio was more like B to X, back to J, down to T—making a handful of microjumps in a day and seeing what happened: maybe a mistake would lead me to resolution, or maybe failure was necessary to begin growing in a new way. When I fully jumped, my path wasn't linear; it was backward and forward and diagonal, hopping and skipping around, crumpling things up and destroying paintings, trying again, and trying again, and again, and maybe one piece would never get resolved, no matter how hard I tried, and maybe that process was the point of the piece.

It's fun to fantasize about the idea of taking a jump or making the leap because it's romantic, but I think it's dangerous to say, "I'm going to just quit everything and finally go write and produce my album!" or "If only I could go to that faraway land, *then* I will paint my masterpiece!" In my own experience, big change happens in small ways, and it happens by choosing one thing after another after another. Some days it's boring. Other days it's a slog. Creativity has winters and droughts. Jumping is basically a giant to-do list with about three thousand items on it. It's not this romantic sparkly idea that's off in the distance; it's getting gas in the car, going to the library, signing up for a library card, checking out books, actually reading them and taking notes. That's how jumps start.

In my "sandbox," I tried to drop all expectations of what I was *supposed* to be doing or making, and began just trying to make the art that I *must* make. Unexpectedly, a gallery owner saw my art on Instagram a few months later and offered me a show in her gallery. I exhibited over sixty pieces of work, and when some sold, I was able to extend my "sandbox" time a little longer. After that, another opportunity arose, and then another, and little by little, baby step after baby step, I kept afloat financially and miraculously began to experience my dream in real life.

Last night, I had a dream.

I am standing next to another person, and we are like angels, watching people's days go by—kind of like Scrooge as he's standing on the sidelines of his life, watching. A man sitting next to me is holding a trumpet, and every time somebody makes a decision to jump, he blows his trumpet, and we all cheer. The trumpet continues to sound each moment someone makes the personal choice to jump—not for how the jump ends up or for what other people think of the jump, but for the courage and bravery of having faith and going for it.

Trust your instincts. Get into your body, feel your way into it, jump, and move forward. And as you go, if you want to course-correct or if you want to roll around or dart a different way, cool, you can do that. The trumpet will sound no matter what.

If you start to see jumping as a good thing in and of itself, the jumps you take will no longer be anxiety ridden or full of panic. Instead, they will be enjoyable and necessary—stepping-stones along your journey through *should* and into *must*.

ELLE LUNA, a former start-up designer and storyteller, is an artist, designer, and author of *The Crossroads of Should and Must.*

RASHARD MENDENHALL

Professional Football Player to Writer

WHEN I WAS a little kid, my mom would tell my brothers and me that we were destined for greatness—and that the only thing that could stop us was ourselves.

Growing up and all through college, I'd get lost in literature; write stories and collect poems; pore over books and immerse myself in creativity. I loved football, and from the very start, making it to the NFL wasn't a goal—it was something I knew I was going to do. I also knew that it would only be one part of me.

Once I entered the pros, the world only saw me as a football player. But I had a craving. In the high-pressure, fast-paced life of the pros, my getaway, my escape, came through putting words on a page. I read books. I wrote stories. I even took dance lessons—anything to feed creativity. I never stopped fueling the interests that would lead me to jump, even if I didn't yet know exactly what my jump would be. I knew that when the time came to make my move, I'd want to make it straightaway.

This meant juggling two different lives. Pittsburgh is crazy for the Steelers. Those fans love their team, and they're all about it, which is dope. But as a guy who also held off-the-field ambitions, it felt almost impossible to escape to this other persona, this other world.

So I created the separation myself. I'd get into the training room by

7 a.m., get out by 6 p.m., and as soon as I came home, I would dive into books—history and philosophy, spirituality, fiction, stories taking me to Africa and Spain, on adventures of all types. Once I was done reading, I stayed up into the night writing stories, writing what I felt, what I thought. A few hours later, I'd wake up and do it all again.

With what my salary afforded, I set my standard of living to be as basic as possible so that I could save as much as possible. Eventually, it became harder to see my day job as the best way to spend time. I'd read about adventures, write about my experiences, and express how I truly felt as someone different from my public persona as the football player. I'd go for a walk, and I'd sit in a park and think, "What if I could just sit in this park forever?"

Those thoughts are indicators that it's nearing time to jump. At the start of my final season, during training camp, I remember sitting in the hotel room feeling it was time. I knew a lot of people wouldn't understand. After one game, I told a friend, and he just couldn't follow: "What do you mean? You can sign more contracts; you can keep this going." So I kept it quiet, sharing only with my girlfriend. I learned the importance of sharing your jump only with those who know you the best.

In the final stages of prep, I would tell myself, "Okay, pretend football has ended. Football is no more. Who am I? What am I? If I never make this much money again, will I be okay? If I have to stand on my own without being in the NFL playing, will I be okay?" Rehearsing these questions gave me comfort to move forward. I had a separate voice, a separate personhood—I would not be lost. When the cheers went away, and the fans disappeared, I would not be lost.

I still gave football everything that I had because that's who I am. I wanted to finish without any regrets and without taking my foot off the gas. But when that season ended, I jumped.

The toughest part was telling my high school coach. When I was growing up, he took my mom and me in for a period of time—my mom didn't make a lot, and our church was far away, so in order to stay in our school district, we ended up moving in with my coach and his wife. They were family to us.

Coach helped me grow so much as a man, and I knew he understood my decision as a person, but I also knew he was my biggest fan. He wanted to see me be everything that I could be in the NFL. And here I was leaving early, at twenty-six years old. He understood, he supported me, and he still does, but it was tough.

My strategy was to finish my college degree and continue my personal writing work. By the time I jumped, I had a collection of expressions and poetry that I wanted to put together and publish. So I knew the steps I wanted to take and the path I wanted to walk down. I knew that the writing life wasn't going to be laid out as cleanly as my life in football, but I was okay with that.

If your body's telling you something, it's not lying. If you feel like you want to do something else or be somewhere else, and that feeling stays in your body, and it's not going anywhere, listen. Your body doesn't lie. Build around that feeling. I approached my passion for writing with the same level of work I put into football. I read so many scripts, wrote so many pieces. When you jump, leave it all out. You don't want to look back and wonder if you could have put in more.

People look at a jump as diving into something uncertain. I see it the other way: I was *certain* that I didn't want to be a professional football player anymore. Even if I couldn't get back into school or couldn't get a job, and I was sitting around at home watching the NFL, and I wasn't in it—I knew that I would still be okay because that chapter was complete.

I am a writer, and my calling is to write. Failure isn't part of my thought process. There's no way to fail at this; I'm a success regardless of what happens with one of my stories or books. If it takes me ten years to write one book, and three people buy it, I will be cool with that because this pursuit is my calling, this is what I want to be doing, and this is who I want to be.

RASHARD MENDENHALL, a former running back for the Pittsburgh Steelers of the National Football League, is a writer and staff member of HBO's *Ballers.*

JHOVANY CASTANEDA

Warehouse Worker to High School Student Supervisor

I WAS BORN in Apaneca, El Salvador, a little town near the border of Guatemala. My mom passed away giving birth to me, and my dad was never in the picture. Most of my family had moved to the States to find a better life, so I was raised by my grandma. There was a bit of violence and desperation in our town, and when word got out that my relatives had gone to the States, I became a target for kidnappings; the bad guys figured my relatives in America would have cash to send as a ransom. After a few threats, my grandma wanted to get us out, and we found our way to the States too.

When I arrived, the first thing I did was begin to learn English. I also played soccer. I was good, one of the top players in middle school and then high school. I thought, "This is what I'm going to do with my life." I started high school with straight As, but quickly got distracted. Soccer was going well, so I gave up everything else. Started hanging with the wrong guys, making the wrong decisions. I'd lie to my grandma about my grades, and because she didn't know how to read or write, I could slip by without a hitch.

And then I got injured. After high school graduation, a week before I was to start city college classes, I blew out my ACL and meniscus. Because

I was going to be on a soccer scholarship, the money went away, and I couldn't afford tuition. My club coach, who I had trusted with my life, vanished, moving on to his next player. My immigration papers weren't ready, so I couldn't apply for student loans. I was stuck, and I wished so badly that someone had straightened me out during those high school years, helped me to make a backup plan. That was when a little voice made its way into my head, in the form of my own desperation: I craved a mentor, someone at school who could show me the way. I didn't have that. I just had a bum knee.

By then, my grandma had moved back to El Salvador, and I was staying with my auntie. She told me straight up that I had to get a job and move out of the house and do something. I got my papers in order, and when my green card came through (I was eighteen), I moved out of the house, moved in with my girlfriend, and started working in a warehouse.

My uncle got me the job; he was working in a warehouse as a driver. The company imported Italian products like pasta, oils, and wines. They hired me to "pick orders": open the order, collect the items, and place them ready for the driver to pick up for delivery. From there, I bounced around warehouses: customer service here, a stint with Cisco there, working night shifts and inside the industrial freezers, training new employees and stocking and picking.

A few years in, I landed at a warehouse where I would spend the next fifteen years. A dozen years in, the cousin of one of my best friends from childhood, Antonio, was shot and killed in a drive-by as he was leaving a flea market with his children. It had been a few years since Antonio and I last spoke when I attended his cousin's funeral. Even after so much time, Antonio was like a brother to me; a former teammate on the soccer field, the godfather to my middle child.

Last I had heard, Antonio was a produce delivery driver, but at the funeral he told me he was now the dean of a school. The story stuck with me: he had started out as security guard, then become the athletics director, and now was the dean. That little voice came back, now in the form of a wild idea. Maybe I could help him help his students, or something like that.

That fall, I moved my son to Antonio's school. My son had begun to lose his way in school, as I did in his shoes before him. But this time, the story would be different: a better school environment, and his dad telling him the dos and don'ts. I was nervous that he wouldn't listen, but that wasn't the case. I sat him down and said, "This is the time in your life when you decide your future." Soon, his friends were asking for advice too. The voice that craved a way forward for myself came back: "Maybe I have something that I can offer these kids."

After that, every new day at my job felt harder to get through. I was slowly convincing myself there was more I could do with my life, more to me than just being in the warehouse. This voice began to get the best of me. I started asking more questions, like, "What else is there available for me at the warehouse?"

And the response from management was a shrug, "Not really much; this is it." I'd say, "How come? The company is big. You guys got different offices and different opportunities." But my bosses wouldn't give me the chance to get to the office. I guess that was their policy. Maybe it was because I was an immigrant. Who knows.

Over the next year and a half, I started telling Antonio more about this voice. He could relate. One day, he calls me and says straight up: "You're looking for something else, right?" Without missing a beat, I said, "Yes, if something else comes up in education, I'm willing." That was it. We just left it at that harmless question and answer.

Jumping didn't seem possible. I was hesitant to leave the warehouse job because it was safe. With three kids, I had to make ends meet.

Two years later, Antonio called again: "There's an opening at the school." It was for a campus supervisor: part security guard, part mentor to the kids.

My first reaction was, me? Working in a school? I couldn't believe it was possible. This was exactly the role and impact I wanted to have. But I was so scared. First off, I'd be the adult they'd talk to when they were in trouble, and you never know how the kids are going react to you when they're in trouble. When I was in high school, we didn't treat the campus supervisors well; we talked back to them. What if that happened here?

And how would my son react to having his dad at school? And Antonio, we grew up like brothers; I didn't want to let him down.

I had done my warehouse job for so long. To give that up and jump for something that I didn't know anything about at the time—it was a hard decision. There were nights that I couldn't sleep, thinking, "Am I making the right decision? Am I going to be able to provide for my family, and is it going to be the right opportunity for us?"

The decision came back to that voice, back to my bum knee and the things I had wished for when I was in school. I knew for sure that I could add something positive to the students. I could tell the kids what I wish someone had told me: that if you stay in school and prepare yourself for a career, you can do whatever you want with your life. Even more, I just couldn't see myself retiring from a warehouse. I was meant for something else.

I was going to jump.

I went in to give my two weeks' notice to my warehouse job. I said, "This is a life-changing opportunity for me, and for my family." My boss asked what I was going to do, and when I told him campus supervisor, he said, "Are you sure you wanna take that position?" I said, "Yes, why not?" He replied, "'Cause those campus supervisors don't get treated right," as if to use my biggest fear to scare me out of trying. But I didn't budge: "I'm pretty sure I can make it work." And then I added, "I know I'm going to be okay because I'm going to make sure of it." Saying that out loud right there, I *was* sure of it. The voice in my head was now out in the world. The words gave me the extra little strength needed to believe this was the right time and the right moment to jump. I wasn't going to let my old boss, or anyone else, think otherwise.

And that's the thing: when you jump, you can't second-guess yourself. As I walked out of the warehouse, I pretended the warehouse page of my life was completely turned. Sure, if things didn't work out, I probably could go back someday and squeeze back into that job. But I made myself believe I was done. I erased all the contacts from my phone. I promised never to go back and visit, never to talk to my manager again— and that's what's happened.

It took a couple of months for me to get adjusted to being campus supervisor. I'm pretty shy and don't socialize a lot, especially with three hundred kids. It was hard. You've got to learn how to adjust yourself to the different backgrounds of each kid in the school, so they'll get the message that you're there to enforce the rules, and at the same time, you're looking out for him or her. It hasn't been quick, but the kids are starting to see me as someone they can come and talk to. They come look for me, and I give them advice. My son has warmed up to having me around school, and he's getting back on track with his grades. Some of the seniors who graduated last year come back to talk to me. That's a great feeling, to help shape the future of the school and the kids' future. If I can impact one student from my jump, it is worth it. That would be more than what I would have done had I stayed at the warehouse.

Anyone can jump. Sometimes your life experience prepares you for a jump just as much as a book or a fancy education. And there is more to life that you'll only discover once you jump. When you jump, you'll find your true colors.

I'll tell you what I told my son and what I told myself leaving the warehouse: this is the time in your life when you decide your future.

JHOVANY CASTANEDA, a former warehouse employee, is the campus supervisor for a high school in California.

MERLE R. SAFERSTEIN

Education Administrator to Author and Teacher

WRITING AND TEACHING are my passions. I grew up in Cleveland with relatives spread all over the country, and I constantly wrote letters to them. That's what got me hooked. I remember telling myself at a very young age that if I'm going to write, I must lead an interesting and meaningful life so I have something to write about. I began keeping journals and recorded my life experiences through the years. At some point, I thought I would eventually write a book from my journals.

I started my career teaching third grade, and after a series of jobs in education, I transitioned to administration and became the director of educational outreach for a Holocaust center in South Florida. At that time, my intention was also to start writing a book, inspired by a beachside hotel I walked past every morning at sunrise.

But life sped up. I had two children, and between helping to support my family and raising our children, I did not have time to write the book of my dreams. The years passed, and the book slipped away. But I never lost sight of my desire to tell the story of the hotel.

Periodically, I'd try to kick-start the book, but I could never clear the space to write it. For the most part, the writing I did was in my journals.

The kids grew up and moved out, and I stayed at the Holocaust center for a total of twenty-six years. A cold reality began to settle in. As much as I enjoyed my role at the center, I needed to write. By neglecting the latter, I wasn't allowing that part of my soul to shine. More to the point, if I didn't jump now, I was never going to fulfill that deep yearning within.

Not so easy, though. Not only was I earning a significant portion of our household income, but the economy was in decline. I was concerned that we might not have as much to live on as we had planned. As the time came to jump, my husband and I knew it would put us on a razor-thin budget. But I could no longer back down. We reined in our expenses as firmly as we could and prepared to hold tight.

Also difficult was the emotional decision of walking away from a job that I loved. Leaving the Holocaust center was difficult because I felt so many people depended on me. The survivors were like family whom I loved and adored, and here I was abandoning them. One survivor had told me that I was doing sacred, holy work—God's work. How could I ever leave that?

To address this big question, I challenged myself to answer a series of smaller ones: What am I most afraid of? Am I willing and ready to give up my paycheck? What do I need to do to finally take this leap of faith? How will I realize my dreams, and what does that mean to me? What will my life look like once I make the jump?

From these questions, I discovered that what I feared most was the lack of control in getting my book out. I needed to put my fate in my own hands, and so I began to inquire about self-publishing. Sure enough, e-books sales had picked up, and self-publishing had become a mainstream form of publishing. Had estimable self-publishing not been available, I never would have jumped.

I'll always remember the day I made the decision to jump. I had been having sleepless nights. My emotions were laced with all the anxiety, fear, excitement, and sadness that would come from leaving my job. That day, instead of having lunch, I went walking and bought a big bowl of ice cream. As I sat eating, I told myself that all these feelings—good and bad—are real. I was not going to push them away. Instead, I decided to focus on what I would be gaining. I imagined that this jump would set me free. I would be my own boss and follow my dream. Somehow, some way, I would make it work.

Shortly after that, I gave my notice. I knew it was time to start my life as a full-time writer. I was about to turn sixty-seven and knew I couldn't wait any longer.

It took me over a quarter century, but I finally jumped. I only wish I had done it sooner. I finished the book I wanted to write and now am working on the next one. The new book was inspired by my jump and will be the culmination of my life's work.

I share some of my life lessons in the Living and Leaving Your Legacy classes I have created and now teach. I volunteer with a hospice organization and talk to people who are dying. Their main regret is over the things they didn't do. We need to jump for what speaks to us, and then we must trust ourselves. It is important to follow our gut feelings.

How we live our lives becomes our legacy. People watch us and observe us, and when we die, our impact stems from what people have learned from us. To live, to be truly alive, we must jump for what we believe in. This will guarantee that each of our legacies will be meaningful and purposeful. Who doesn't want that?

After a class the other day, one of my students came up to me and said, "I want you to know that you are the rock that first jumped into the water, and your little ripple was sent to us, and now we're making a ripple that reaches to our family and to other people we know, and they will send more ripples."

This is what I want from my legacy—a ripple that will continue on over time. My children will learn something from my jump and will pass it on to my grandchildren and loved ones, who will someday share it with the generations to follow. Our jump sows a seed. We may not see it grow into a tree, but our children, and their children, will.

I encourage people not to talk themselves out of a jump because of their age. Instead, hopefully they will find a way to make each day, month, and year count—to live in the moment and do what speaks to their heart and soul.

I share the virtues of a jump in meet-ups with people of all ages, both young and old, in a writing group I facilitate at a cancer support center with women who have or had cancer, and at workshops for various organizations: we all can learn something from jumping.

I'm seventy-two now, and with the time left to me, I will keep writing and teaching. I've never been happier, and I've never felt more fully alive. Today, and every day, the ripple from my story grows.

MERLE R. SAFERSTEIN, a former director of educational outreach of a Holocaust center, is an author, speaker, and founder of Living and Leaving Your Legacy instructional courses.

KELLY O'HARA

Advertising Professional to
Advocate for Sexual Assault Survivors

MAJORING IN AMERICAN studies and drama doesn't do much in the way of preparing you to choose a job after college. As a kid, I dreamed of changing the world, but as college went on, I thought those ideas seemed far-fetched. I settled on what made sense, and that was a job in the advertising industry. I was good at it and, maybe more importantly, it was accepted in our house: I come from a family of engineers, accountants, and doctors—my academic interests didn't make sense to them, but a career in advertising did. It felt good to be on a track that everyone was on board with.

Then, at the beginning of my junior year, I was studying abroad in Dublin when I was sexually assaulted by another person in the program.

I was in another country and didn't know how the laws worked, didn't know who to tell. I was afraid of the general fallout, and I didn't do anything about it until I was back in the States. When I got back, I went to therapy and all that, but trauma is a hard thing to solve, especially when you have spent so much time not talking about it. So I turned to theater writing. I was about to start my senior year and begin work on my thesis, and I kept thinking, "What if I looked at sexual assault in an academic setting?" It wasn't something I knew much about, but I thought I could use theater as an educational tool to connect people emotionally to the issue.

Unfortunately, writing a one-person show became isolating for me as I revisited traumatic memories over and over again. I ended up getting depressed and thought of hurting myself. It was an unhealthy situation.

So I restarted with a whole new style, this time writing the show to include three characters. This brought in other women and allowed us to address more issues and perspectives, making the play truly educational. This show created a special community of women supporting each other, a network of people who were there for each other and who were working on making an impact together. The end result of the project was not only a production that I was really proud of, but was also a healthy way for me to move past the assault.

Now I wanted to do more: to speak out louder on the topic, help build stronger support systems, work personally with other survivors. I had a decision to make, and time was short. It was the end of April when the show wrapped, and I was graduating in mid-May. I always thought I wanted be in New York, and I had interned at an advertising agency there the previous summer. Suddenly, there was this other thing I really cared about—but did it have a career path? Professionally, I didn't know what pursuing sexual assault advocacy looked like, and emotionally, did I want to do that to myself?

I had already been through a really dark place in dealing with the subject, and I didn't want to be depressed, or upset, or put pressure on myself to help others if it turned out that I couldn't help myself. Not only did I fear for my own well-being; I also questioned my abilities: How good could I be at something that I couldn't handle on my own? So I stayed the course for advertising in New York, with an aim toward finding a balance: I'd take the advertising job and volunteer with sexual assault survivors on the side.

The real world began, and I set out to volunteer as a rape crisis counselor through a hospital program that trains volunteers to help survivors of sexual assault when they come to the emergency room. We would guide people through what was happening, but we were mostly there to be a friend for the survivors as they came in. The training program was exactly what I wanted: a concrete, meaningful outlet for my passion. I said, "Okay, now I can focus on my day job because I have this on the side." In retrospect, I already knew what my priorities were, but I tried not to take notice. Meanwhile, everyone at the office said, "You're doing a good thing. As long as you're getting your work done, it's fine."

Those first seven or eight months were a difficult juggling act. I was handling a new city with a new job and a very new context for dealing with a tough subject: it's one thing to talk about sexual assault on a policy level; it's another to get into the nitty-gritty of being told, "Someone has been sexually assaulted and is sitting in the emergency room and needs you now." Again, I doubted myself and my emotional capacities. But the work that I was doing felt important, and I'd leave the hospital exhausted but happy: satisfied that I was playing a small part in helping people.

It was St. Patrick's Day. I was on the night shift and at 11 p.m. a young woman about my age came in. I was assigned to help her. As a rape crisis counselor, sometimes your job is just to distract the survivor, and so we spent hours together just talking, laughing. At one point, a nurse came in and said to me, "I thought you were the advocate." I told her I was. "Oh, do you two know each other?" We had met that night, I responded. "That's so wonderful! It just seems like you two are such good friends."

That was when I knew. It was 8 a.m. when I left my shift and went straight to the office for my advertising job, in my same clothes from the night before. I hadn't slept, but I didn't care. I felt like I had actually made a connection with someone—I had made a real difference in that person's life. I helped her get through a time that was very difficult. I showed up to work, and everyone was yelling about advertising, and I just sat and watched, absolutely exhausted in my yoga pants. I thought, "I can't do this anymore. I just can't do this anymore."

It's not that I had a problem with anyone in my job or in the industry. I think people mistake that part of the jump process—as if there is always some clear adversary or bad guy that you jump from—but that's not accurate. The truth is, whatever it is you've been doing, it becomes really hard to keep doing it when you identify a new value system and new priorities. If you then find yourself surrounded by people, on a day-to-day basis, who don't share those priorities or values—it's not bad or anyone's fault—it just makes it very hard not to jump.

As I sat there at work, my jump crystallized. I was going to leave advertising and go to law school so that I could become a full-time advocate for sexual assault survivors. The area in the hospital where I was most helpful and where I was most productive was teasing out the legal part of what was happening. In terms of making an impact, knowing people's legal rights was a really big deal—especially at a public hospital where you work with all types of underserved populations. And I realized that as nice as it was to support people emotionally, leveraging the law was an important tool for actually improving their lives.

My parents were supportive of law school, but they were concerned. I hadn't told them that I was assaulted until long after the fact, and when I did, it troubled them—I don't think any parent can hear that and feel good. And now they were worried I'd be setting myself up to hurt even more. I probably would have shared that sentiment had I not planted the seeds prior to jumping: by now, I knew what my jump would look like. I knew what I could do, what I would feel. The volunteering, the brainstorming—it was helpful for my parents, but most important, it was helpful for me.

Telling everyone at the office was hard. For many people who work in advertising, that industry is the pinnacle of professions. For most of my colleagues, this work was all they wanted to be doing. They were confused that it wasn't what I wanted. When I announced I was leaving, the response was, "Okay, good luck, but I don't know why you're leaving."

The one exception was my former boss. She is French, and her understanding of work/life balance and chasing down a passion is very different from the traditional American perspective. In the months prior to my jump, she would say, "You do a good job, but I can tell when you're passionate about something and when you're just doing it. And I know that you're not passionate about this." And when the day came to hug her good-bye, she whispered in my ear, "You're absolutely doing the right thing."

Walking out of the office, I felt relieved. I had started to resent myself for not making a move. I had the urge to jump, but in my head, I would think, "Well, they say that in the real world you're supposed to stay at your job for at least a year, and how will it look on my résumé if I left before then?"

Turns out the answer is, who cares? I hated getting up in the morning. I hated going to work. I hated staying any amount of time past 5 p.m., which in advertising, you just do. I was putting all this time and effort into this thing I didn't care about. No part of it was fun anymore. Whatever you're doing, when it gets to that point, do yourself a favor and jump. It is only scary until you leave.

Everyone thinks about a jump differently. Personally, I think at the end of the day, you have to be honest with yourself about what's going to make you feel fulfilled. I think that we get comfortable because it's the easiest thing to do, and being honest with ourselves is sometimes the hardest thing to do. I think that if you've got a little voice telling you something, the best thing you can do is not shove it down, but just sit with it and listen to what it's saying. And ask, "Where is this coming from? Why is it here, and what does it mean?"

Then you can start to think, "Okay, what would it look like to make this transition? Yes, there is an unknown, but what are the actual details leading up to it?" When you let an idea remain a vague dream, it's tough to act on it. But if you start putting the pieces together and thinking through what it means to go forward, it's a lot easier to get excited about it because it's not a pipe dream anymore; it's not foolish anymore.

No part of me is grateful for what happened or feels good about my experience being sexually assaulted. But it did shake up my priorities. I thought, "Okay, this shitty thing happened. Now what am I going to do about it?" I'm only looking forward. I enrolled in law school with many question marks still ahead. But I have spent a lot of time and effort trying to be honest and authentic with myself—honest about where my head is, what I want, and what I care about.

I think that process of self-reflection has been really helpful. It's helped my decision. It's helped me realize that it's okay to jump, to change things.

And, perhaps most important, it's helped me believe that it isn't crazy to want to have an impact on the world.

KELLY O'HARA, a former advertising associate, enrolled in law school in the fall of 2016, with plans to become an advocate for survivors of sexual assault.

Listen to the Little Voice

Section Takeaways

Tune in

- "In retrospect, I already knew what my priorities were, but I tried not to take notice." (Kelly O'Hara)
- "It feels awkward when a little inner voice talks to you, a voice you're scared to listen to. It feels even more awkward when that voice won't go away." (Mike Lewis)
- "That little voice . . . it's your true voice." (Jeff Arch)
- "The truth . . . of what you need to do is somewhere in your belly. Listen to it, and proceed carefully." (Laura McKowen)
- "If you've got a little voice telling you something, the best thing you can do is not shove it down, but just sit with it and listen to what it's saying. And ask, 'Where is this coming from? Why is it here, and what does it mean?'" (Kelly O'Hara)
- "It was time to turn up the volume on my little voice, and turn down the volume on everything else." (Jeff Arch)

You are not alone

- "You never actually jump alone." (Laura McKowen)
- "We all face moments in our lives when we have to decide: To jump or not to jump?" (Sheryl Sandberg)
- "Tell people what that voice is saying. . . . To keep a jump alive, it helps to tell someone." (Mike Lewis)
- "The director of the program asked me, 'What do you want to do with your career?' And I answered truthfully. . . . Rather than say, which some people did, 'Well, that's far-fetched . . . ,' he replied, 'Great. Let's make it happen.' That was the first step, taking the voice out of the quiet silence inside me." (Tommy Clark)

There will be a moment when you know

- "That was when I knew . . . I had made a real difference in that person's life." (Kelly O'Hara)
- "That was a turning point. I went from this low point where I was almost out of money, had been out of a job for nearly a year, to getting reinvigorated in one of the strangest ways possible: by almost going back to work and reminding myself very clearly why I had wanted to jump." (Nate Chambers)
- "If your body's telling you something, it's not lying. If you feel like you want to do something else or be somewhere else, and that feeling stays in your body, and it's not going anywhere, listen. Your body doesn't lie." (Rashard Mendenhall)
- "That tiny internal whisper just kept getting louder, and it got deafening. . . . The linchpin was knowing that I would regret *not* jumping. That regret was something I knew I couldn't live with." (Laura McKowen)
- "An inner voice emerged from that encounter. Right adventure, wrong time; but right adventure." (Mike Lewis)

Embrace the difference between crazy and stupid

- "When you let an idea remain a vague dream, it's tough to act on it. But if you start putting the pieces together and thinking through what it means to go forward, . . . it's not a pipe dream anymore; it's not foolish anymore." (Kelly O'Hara)

- "There were a few nonnegotiable pieces that I knew I needed to have in place so that deciding to jump would not be totally illogical." (Laura McKowen)

- "Timing matters. If you're supporting a family or have pressing debts to pay off, now is almost certainly not the time to quit a moneymaking job for a dream that does not pay. But that doesn't mean you can never chase your dream; it means not just yet." (Mike Lewis)

- "There is danger to jumping too late or not at all. People seem very aware of the risks associated with making a jump but are less aware that there is a risk to not taking a jump at all. It could just be the risk of being unhappy, but it's a risk nonetheless." (Tommy Clark)

Think "support," not "permission"

- "A critical roadblock to making a jump is the perception that you need to ask for permission. . . . I want their support, but I don't need their permission." (Laura McKowen)

- "Some people I really trusted told me I was making a mistake. . . . They might have been right. But my heart told me otherwise. I wanted to jump. And I've never looked back." (Sheryl Sandberg)

- "Telling everyone at the office was hard. . . . They were confused that [the work they were doing] wasn't what I wanted." (Kelly O'Hara)

- "The toughest part was telling my high school coach. . . . [He and his wife] were family to us. Coach helped me grow so much as a man. . . . He understood, he supported me, and he still does, but it was tough." (Rashard Mendenhall)

- "It was important to seek others' opinions and perspectives, but . . . no one is in a better position to make decisions for me than I am for myself." (Teresa Marie Williams, MD)

Words to jump by

- "The question I've come back to again and again in my life is, 'What would I do if I wasn't afraid?'" (Sheryl Sandberg)

- "Anyone can jump. Sometimes your life experience prepares you for a jump just as much as a book or a fancy education." (Jhovany Castaneda)

- "It's okay to believe in something bigger and to follow your passions." (Nate Chambers)

- "It felt more successful to fail, if I had to, at what I want to be doing—at what . . . I was meant to be doing—than it would have been to succeed at what somebody else wanted for me." (Jeff Arch)

- "This is what I want from my legacy—a ripple that will continue on over time." (Merle R. Saferstein)

PHASE 2

MAKE A PLAN

"If you've planned it out . . . the actual jump
isn't as risky."

—Brian Spaly

I READ, REREAD, and, just to be sure, re-reread my pro squash sponsorship slideshow.

Using my employer's slide-making template, I had pasted a squash ball over the Bain Capital Ventures logo. In place of charts and graphs showing market research and company revenue projections, I'd inserted plans to pursue my passion. I labeled the presentation "Sponsorship Opportunity Overview." The titles of the slides included: "What I'm doing," "Why I'm doing it," and "Where I'm going." Following the wisdom of my coworker and confidant Frank from a few office doors down the hall, I had commanded the flickering pixels on my computer screen to display a rough sketch of how I would turn into a pro squash player, leave my desk, and make my jump.

Five months had passed since I had spoken my idea aloud to my friend's father. I had to move beyond speaking the idea toward having a plan.

If you believe what you read in your newsfeed or see on Instagram, chasing your passion is pretty easy: quit your job, fly to Bali, be happy in Bali. But from what I've heard and what I've now experienced, pursuing a passion doesn't exactly work that way. Or at least it isn't likely to work out well that way. To jump well requires a bit of planning first, even if this notion of "plan for your jump" doesn't make for riveting retweet material. When viral videos, ads, and websites looking for clickbait romanticize jumping, they overlook everything leading up to a successful jump—the grit, the provisioning, the hurdles, and the retries. If I could add ". . . and start by making a plan" to the end of the aspirational quotes that flow by in my social media feeds, I would. Follow your dreams . . . and start by making a plan. Trust your gut . . . and start by making a plan. Become a squash pro . . . and start by making a plan.

Way back, two years before I began preparing to jump, I had a brief phone call with my dad that turned out to be useful later in my planning process. The call took place when I was on a break one day during my summer internship at Goldman Sachs. Sweat trickled down my back as I walked out of the imposing glass building dressed in a hand-me-down wool pin-striped suit and smacked into the stifling heat of July in lower Manhattan. As a parent, my dad gave conservative and play-it-safe advice, but as a fellow squash enthusiast he viscerally understood my passion for the sport. He was my coach, teammate, travel buddy, and best friend during my years playing squash as a kid. When I tried to take things to the next level of competition in high school, my dad took time off from work to take me across the country to national tournaments, where my losses far outnumbered my victories. If there is one thing I am most grateful for when I look back on that time, it is the unwavering support from my dad in encouraging me to stick with the sport, even after early tournament exits, regular flight delays, and time away from home. In my pursuit of the game, we were on the ride together. I felt proud that as I continued to improve, my wins were our wins.

Catching Dad on the phone, I paced through the blur of passing suits and briefcases to a quiet corner of the sidewalk near a back entrance to the Goldman Sachs building. A melody of car horns wailed in the distance. I wasn't ready to get into details with my dad. Even as a squash fanatic, he remained a cautious parent, and our shared goal for my competitive squash trajectory was to reach the college ranks, nothing beyond that. From his viewpoint and to some extent from mine, a gig at Goldman Sachs was the next big prize. As I finished giving the general gist of an idea about competing as a squash pro, I expected confusion and hard questioning, but his reply was pragmatic: "Mike, I think that's a great idea. But there are two things you gotta do. One is that you're a good college player, but you're about five standard deviations from the pro level. So you've got to work real hard and hope your game improves. And second, you're about to start earning an income, but you'll need to earn a lot more and save a lot more and get sponsors to create a way to make this work financially." We hung up, and I shoved the phone deep into the front pocket of his vintage suit, then turned and sprinted back to work.

Two years after that conversation, my first attempt at a plan was an epic flop. Maia, a bond trader turned hiker turned entrepreneur (whose story is featured later in this section), answered my cold call from my office at Bain and patiently listened as I launched into my dream of playing the pro tour and my jumble of ideas involving a twelve-hundred-day schedule that would lead me to that dream. Maia cut me off somewhere in the first hundred days: "Take a deep breath! You're planning out the next four years of your life. You can't possibly do that. I'm twenty-eight, and I'm getting married in the fall. Will I be at my current job next June? Probably. But no one knows for sure, and you shouldn't try to know every detail for sure either. Take your dream year by year."

So I stopped trying to plan future minutiae and stuck to facing down one doable goal at a time. I thanked Maia profusely and vowed not to take up her time with any more twelve-hundred-day plans. Before hanging up, she had a final comment: "I do think that this squash idea is great, and something will come out of that, for sure."

I cut out beer and bread to get into better playing shape. Through a friend at the gym, I tracked down the e-mail address of a former world champion who I had heard was starting a technology company. I shot off a cold e-mail, and months later, my office phone rang. With the former world champion on the line, I stammered slightly before diving into my proposal: I'd help the squash legend with his business plan in return for his advice on how best to become a pro: how to budget, how to travel, how to live. After that call, following his wisdom, I returned to my sponsorship presentation pitch, still a work in progress. In the silence of my dimly lit office on a deserted floor 39, I stared at the blank space underneath the title card that read "Why I'm Doing It." Then I typed: "Because a long time ago, I promised I would."

Any jump planning includes three common components:

- financial planning,
- pre-jump practice, and
- safety-net sewing.

On the money side, I was planning a jump from something lucrative to something not at all lucrative, especially at the start. So I opened a bank account and put away a portion of every paycheck to set up a nest egg that could make my jump possible. I asked ex-pros and travel gurus for advice about and models for how to come up with a realistic budget. While I was lucky that my job gave me the chance to save on the side, once on the road, expenses were going to pile up in every direction, from the obvious (everyday breakfasts and bus tickets) to the less apparent but no less real (travel insurance and cellular data plans). This pile of expenses was made larger by the high costs of competing: coaches, trainers, sports medicine experts. So, in addition to getting my nest egg ready, I prepared to pitch sponsors, offering corporate logo placement on my playing jersey in return for cash, which is one of the ways professional squash players make money, along with coaching or playing in exhibitions. For most players, these options are more lucrative than the prize money from tournaments, which rarely tops a few hundred bucks. Thanks to the company presentation template and Frank's advice, I had cobbled together a simple several-page pitch to sponsors. It was the first time I had put my dream on paper, so while I was officially pitching others, I was also pitching myself. Putting words to why I wanted to jump, how I was going to do it, and where I was going to go delivered the confidence I needed to believe this jump could actually be made. After my umpteenth reread of the presentation, I went out searching for sponsors.

By late 2012, I scored a ticket to a lecture on entrepreneurship given by a successful CEO of a travel company that I had long admired. When the lecture ended, I mustered some courage, cornered the CEO at the cocktail bar, and introduced myself. I was nervous but prepared, ready to pitch my first potential sponsor. After rattling off the overview of my idea while standing at the cocktail bar, I sent over my slideshow to follow up. And I waited. I predicted a range of possible responses: at best, complete sponsorship; at worst, a few free flights. And what I got back was something else entirely: "Summer 2014 is a long way away."

That was the unsexy beginning of the new, simple, straightforward steps in making a plan. It would have been nice if the CEO had committed to sponsoring me instantly, but it no longer mattered because preparations were under way: my savings account, my pitch slides, my budgeting. Eight months and a few tries later, the pitch slides worked, and my first sponsor signed on. That first support was on the order of just a few hundred bucks, but more important than the money was this: for the very first time, I had a tangible stake in the ground. Someone was betting on me; someone had read my most vulnerable, mushy, touchy-feely dreams on three sheets of paper and was concretely supporting them. After a dozen years, an idea I had at first only dreamed of was kicking into gear because of a small check. A million unknowns still seemed to loom ahead, but one thing was now certain: this jump was going to happen.

Another absolutely necessary part of my plan was to get better at my sport. As my dad had noted, I had been a good, not great, college squash player. I would have to make athletic strides to compete at the next level. Obviously, I had to practice. But making the big athletic advances actually started in my head. I began by repeating this statement: "I am a professional athlete." A number of behaviors followed from that. I began to live like a professional athlete. What does a professional athlete eat? Gluten was out. What does he drink? Bye-bye, booze. And of course, I had to log many hours on court, honing my skills. To act "as if" I were a professional athlete at a time when becoming one was only a dream may sound nutty—and it did feel a bit nutty—but I stuck to the routine of visualizing my life as an athlete. I made myself believe that I was going to be a pro athlete by telling myself I was a pro athlete every morning and behaving like one, in many ways, every day. This continued until one day, months later, when I woke up a pro athlete—working, for the time being, at a desk, but a pro athlete in mind and body nevertheless.

Another part of my planning was positioning myself to earn the proper pro credentials. So, while still at my day job, I joined the world tour part-time—which may sound impressive (maybe), except that anyone can pay membership dues to become the last ranked player in the world. What tour membership gave me was eligibility. And eligibility cracked open the doors to the qualification spots in the smallest events, the events that would get my ranking off the ground. Using sick days, half days, vacation days; taking night flights to Chicago, returning to Boston before dawn; hopping one express train to New York, and another back to Boston the next morning—my travels as a player began. I didn't score a single point in my first game as a pro, but I had become, technically, a pro.

Finally, there was safety-net sewing: I didn't want to vanish one morning from work leaving a group of people baffled and a career bridge burned. There's a misconception that taking a jump forever destroys your chances of returning to the work you've been doing or to the individuals you've been working with. Sometimes, that's true. With some jumps, there is no going back. But for many other jumps, there will exist an opportunity to jump back, so long as you have shown ability in doing your job well and have built meaningful relationships with the people you worked with along the way.

In the year building up to my jump, I prioritized spending real time with anyone who had invested in me at Bain, inviting them to join me for coffee breaks, happy hours, squash games. I wanted each person to have my most authentic story: why I was jumping, what I was hoping to get from it, the fears I was facing and why I was choosing to face them. The purpose of talking to my colleagues was not to gain permission— by then, I had committed to making the jump—but to share ideas and listen to feedback and create ways to stay in touch. I liked my job, and I respected my coworkers. It felt personally weird, not to mention professionally shortsighted, to abruptly cross them off my contacts list. I was jumping away now, but someday I might very well find myself trying to jump back.

Meanwhile, in spite of the solid advice Maia had given to me, I regularly fell into the trap of overplanning. I thought, incorrectly, that if I made enough slides, the unknowns would go away, and the risks from jumping would vanish. Turns out, it's not possible to make all the unknowns go away. Andy, one of my regular practice partners at the gym, pointed this out one afternoon as he sat hunched on the bench across from my locker. A quick-thinking, number-crunching businessman in his late forties, Andy has broad, husky shoulders, wide blue eyes that dart behind wire-rimmed glasses, and neatly parted jet-black hair. I always enjoyed speaking with him and found it interesting that this man, for whom a known, steady path had served up a highly successful finance career, felt determined to encourage me to give up such a path. On many occasions, like this one between our lockers, Andy played the role of the godfather, choosing his words carefully: "Plan your jump as if you're climbing a ladder. Plan the rungs on the ladder. Set up a few concrete milestones and events. But leave out planning the rest. Embrace the space between the rungs."

With nest-egg saving, training, and safety-net sewing, I planned for what I could control. Looking ahead, I reviewed the competition calendar. The pro squash tour is comprised of several levels of competition, determined by prize money: at the top, a handful of tournaments that offer several hundred thousand dollars in winnings, and at the bottom, a scattering of tiny events where a couple thousand dollars could be split up to thirty-two different ways. In those minor league–type tournaments at the bottom, you find your stories of the high schoolers on the way up, the has-beens on the way down, and every other type of player and personality in between.

As my half-day escapes from Bain scraped me off the bottom of the rankings, more tiny tournaments and their range of random locales— from sleepy farmlands on the edge of New Zealand to village outskirts in Paraguay to hidden beach towns on the edges of Australia—slowly came into view on the tour calendar. I grouped the tournaments by area of the world, and on the bottom of my slide presentation, below boxes explaining me and my jump, why I was doing it, and what I was asking for, I squeezed in one final box: "Where I'm Going." Under the title, I pasted in country and continent outlines of New Zealand and Australia, South Africa, Southeast Asia, Europe, and South America, and below each outline, I listed the names of some of the cities I'd likely travel to while competing in the events.

And so my tournament planning marched along, through small but important steps. For the better part of a year, I was a finance person by day and a 300-and-something-ranked part-time professional squash player by night, training mornings and weekends, at lunch, and after work. I woke up an athlete, and I pitched my jump to those I hoped might bet on me. Occasionally, I still lost sleep over my finances and feared life without a regular paycheck. An older squash friend didn't seem too concerned. "Careers are long," she told me. "You'll have time to grow your IRA." My uncle, a registered financial advisor and my de facto CFO, was more blunt: "You're in that first ten years after college; just have as many experiences as you can."

On the cover page of my presentation slides, I inserted a photo of me dressed in khakis and a button-down taken by a photographer for the Bain website the day I joined the company. Surrounding my awkward stance, I pasted a dozen logos belonging to different squash federations worldwide. At the very top of the page, I placed a final patch of text, a quote often falsely attributed to Mark Twain but actually first uttered by the mother of the writer H. Jackson Brown Jr.: "Twenty years from now you will be more disappointed by the things you didn't do than by the ones you did do. So throw off the bowlines. Sail away from the safe harbor. Catch the trade winds in your sails. Explore. Dream. Discover."

Foundation laid, knowns known—and unknowns still unknown, I had a plan.

DEBBIE STERLING

Marketing Director of Jewelry Company to
Founder and CEO of Multimedia Company for Children

I GREW UP in a middle-class family outside of Providence, Rhode Island. Making it to Stanford from our local public high school was a big deal. Before I headed west, my favorite teacher told me to dream big and also to give engineering a try when I got there. I tried it, I loved it, and four years later I graduated with an engineering degree, determined to change the world. As if I needed more inspiration, our commencement speaker was Steve Jobs, who gave our class that famous advice: "Don't settle . . . keep looking until you find [your passion]."

That's all great, but the trouble is no one tells you how to find your passion. For the first few years, I tried corporate America, and when that felt hollow, I quit and joined a nonprofit doing volunteer projects in rural India. I returned Stateside after six months, more lost than when I had left. I took a job as marketing director of a tiny jewelry business—jewelry making was really just engineering at a micro level, and I did love engineering, so I wondered if it might be my passion.

It wasn't. One Saturday a few months into the jewelry-making job, I got together with friends for an "Idea Brunch"—cooking pancakes and pitching each other on crazy ideas for passion projects. Christy, my friend and engineering classmate from Stanford, stood up during her turn:

"Why is it that Legos are for boys, and dolls are for girls? What about engineering toys for little girls?"

I knew in that instant, sitting there listening to her, that this was what Steve Jobs meant when he talked to my graduating class about passion. I found Christy afterward, and she agreed to team up and try to make her idea a reality. It wasn't until college that I discovered engineering, and my only regret was not being exposed to it earlier. I wanted to create something that would help girls discover their passion for engineering. GoldieBlox would offer toy sets for girls, based around the adventures of a young female engineer, Goldie.

Suddenly, I was scared. I knew, deep down, that I had just found what I had been searching for my whole life. My biggest fear was, what if I fail? This was the first time that I knew what I wanted to do, and I was about to give it my all. So what if I gave it my all, and it wasn't enough, and then I failed? This possibility was terrifying. Imagine you find your calling, and then you go for it, but you aren't successful. What are you supposed to do?

My other big fear was money. I couldn't grasp the idea of working day to day without receiving a paycheck. Ever since I was old enough to work, I had worked, and my notion of what you are expected to do is that you're supposed to work and make money. Even though I spent months saving and budgeting, it was hard for me to accept that what I was going to do while starting up GoldieBlox was "real work" because I wouldn't be compensated for doing it. I remember signing up to participate in research studies on the side so I could make a hundred bucks here, a couple hundred bucks there.

To get the company off the ground, I needed feedback from experts, but I didn't know anyone. So I sketched all my ideas in a notebook and brainstormed with friends of friends and with former coworkers, with anyone who knew anyone who might be able to help. The first person I showed my sketches to was my friend's boyfriend, who had a background in engineering and design. He spent a full hour telling me how hard it is to manufacture a physical product, how long it took for Lego to perfect its bricks, how it was impossible to do what I was talking about. I nodded and took it in. While it was dispiriting, honestly my initial reaction was how helpful it was: the feedback was right on. And in the back of my head, I thought, "This is helpful, and I'm not going to let this guy stop me."

That first meeting launched me into getting more meetings with more experts. This is the trick I learned: mine your personal network for anyone who may know somebody who knows anything on the subject. Then go meet that person, and after you've talked together, ask, "Do you know anyone else that might be able to help me?" So after that cup of coffee, you'll have five new people you can talk to. Then you talk to those five people, and each of them will introduce you to five more new people to talk to. This is how I did it.

Meanwhile, I would come home from work and write things down on the calendar: "Here's the big day when I'm going to leave my job." I'd write something down, it'd be on the calendar, and then the date would come, and I'd always come up with some sort of excuse, like, "Well, I've got this trip coming up" or whatever. I would keep pushing back the jump. And Christy was doing the same thing—she was making good money at a prestigious law firm, on track to be a partner. She'd be leaving a lot of money on the table for this toy company, and so would I. We kept putting off our jump.

After about nine months, though, my interest in GoldieBlox reached the point where I was fanatical about starting the company; the desire became all-consuming. Every day at my jewelry job, I was looking for any possible excuse to sneak out. I'd spend my lunch break walking through a toy store. If my boss didn't come in to work, I'd think, "Yes! More time to do research online." Finally, I marked a real departure date in the calendar, in December. I figured the end of the year would be the most natural end point for my job. Christy wasn't able to commit to leaving, but I couldn't wait any longer.

I was obsessed with my idea. I felt like it was a calling, a life calling. I think you have to be that passionate about whatever it is you go and do because the path is hard. It is so difficult that unless you just feel so strongly about what you'll be doing, it's going to be tough to continue doing it, given the amount of hardship and rejection and second-guessing you are going to face. Ultimately, I told myself, even if I went for it and tried my hardest, and it didn't work out, I would never feel stupid or ashamed or regret trying.

The scariest part was preparing to tell my boss I was leaving. I think it's scary for anybody to make a huge transition and leave a job. By the time I was ready to quit my job, it was apparent to everyone I worked with that my heart was in a different place, but it was still hard and scary because I didn't want to upset people I liked and respected.

Funnily enough, telling my boss turned out to be very easy. He understood and fully supported me. Sometimes I think you build stuff up in your head to be this huge deal, but it's not. Maybe you have an uncomfortable conversation, and it's awkward for a day, but it's way worse to sit around worrying about all the ways it could go. Once it happens, you feel like this huge weight has been lifted off your shoulders; you realize it's not the end of the world. And then you move on, and a month later, you look back and think, "Wow, why was I so scared about that?"

Debbie Sterling, a former brand marketing associate, nonprofit volunteer, and jewelry marketing director, is the founder and CEO of GoldieBlox.

BRIAN SPALY

Private Equity Investor to
Founder of Men's Clothing Company

SO I WAS in business school, having spent a few years in consulting and finance beforehand. I was interested in the apparel business but had never made the jump for it—not because I didn't want to but because the one time I tried snagging a job doing corporate strategy for the Gap, I didn't get the gig. It would have been a big pay cut compared to my finance job at the time—50, 60 percent at least—and when I was invited back for the final round of interviews, my brother had asked me if I would really leave all that money on the table. And I decided I would, and even though I didn't get that job, I like to think it prepared me for what would come later.

I had this idea to start a men's pants company and did a bunch of work on it during a project in my first year in business school. As the year ended, I asked my brother (a key mentor of mine over the years) if I should spend my one and only summer internship working on it. He didn't think that was a good call. "You should definitely get a job. Business school is giving you the chance to get a high-class internship. Take it."

So even though we were both aware that I had found something creative and relevant to me with this apparel idea, the risk-averse thing to do was to stay on the lucrative and proven career path, which is what I did. I interned at T. Rowe Price during the summer, covering stocks. And when I came back to school for my final year, I did corporate recruiting and ended up taking a job at a private equity firm for the following fall. Safe, lucrative, on track.

Then there was this day in March when things changed. A bunch of friends went skiing in Tahoe, and instead of going, I decided at the last minute to drive my car down to Los Angeles, buy fabrics, and move the pants project forward. That was the moment I said, "Screw it; I'm going to go do this," and started spending money—real money—on the process of creating a company. At the time, business school cost about $15,000 a quarter for tuition, so I told myself, "I'm going to make this project my seventh quarter. I'm going to spend fifteen grand on making a product. And if it doesn't work, or if it's a total waste of money, fine. It's just part of the cost of business school."

A week later, I canceled a two-week spring break trip to Brazil. Instead, I drove down to LA a couple more times to buy fabrics, found a factory in San Francisco, and began working around the clock to make great-fitting pants designed to be more comfortable than the status quo, thanks to a curved waistband and a trimmed cut through the thigh.

I realized, "If I don't do this now, I may never do this. I don't want to have that guilt. I don't want to be that guy, the classic MBA joker who has some idea that he talks and writes about, builds a model around, but doesn't ever do anything about after the program ends. I said to myself, "I don't want to be that guy. I'm going to do something about my idea." I called the company Bonobos.

Crucially, this was all a lot less scary to do because I had a cushy finance job lined up for after graduation. The finance job served as the perfect safety net, providing cash flow to pay my bills while I carefully ramped up my project on the side. Four months into the finance job, I was already spending a lot of time traveling to New York for Bonobos. Around the holidays that year, I was ready to jump. I'll never forget being in the city right around New Year's Eve, talking to my father on the phone, telling him there was a really good chance I would quit my job in Chicago and move to New York.

But the toughest conversation was telling the guys at my private equity firm that I was going to leave. I felt loyal to these guys, almost embarrassed to tell them. I couldn't believe I was doing it. They were surprised too; the thinking was, "Hey, no one ever leaves here." But they were supportive. I was walking away from almost certain financial success. I was good at the job, I knew what it entailed, and I was guaranteed to make a lot of cash. Now I was leaving all that, moving to a more expensive city, with no guarantee anything would work out.

I was certainly frightened, but above all else, I was excited. Remember, I wasn't starting from scratch by the time I left the finance job. I had been building my company for a year, and we had raised some money. It was more of a staged, planned transition than it was an impulsive leap. That was critical. I think it's the best way to make one of these types of jumps—create a plan, make some sort of safety net, get halfway started on the idea, and then go. A jump doesn't have to start from scratch. Actually, it shouldn't.

I think one of the big questions we have to ask ourselves is, "Are we passionate about what we're doing every day?" You work hard, you are competitive, and you go to a good school. You care a lot about winning. And yet you are choosing these really low-risk paths that aren't that inspiring to you. I have many friends from business school who confess to me, ten years after we finished the MBA program, that they wish they had taken a riskier path and perhaps an entrepreneurial one. And I have many former colleagues who confide that they are simply not inspired by their work in larger companies and more traditional fields.

When you do decide to jump, the hardest thing is accepting the upcoming uncertainty—the possibility of failure. That's when those traditional, lucrative career paths seem so good: they help you avoid facing this type of failure. What I'd say is this: "You're always going to have some fear that your jump might not work. The sooner you can say, 'Okay, I'll live with it, but I'm going to try anyway,' the better."

If you're passionate about whatever you are going to go do, and you love the process, even if it's not successful, it won't matter because you'll be fulfilled by getting to do what you love. And if you've planned it out along the way, you'll have created a situation where the actual jump isn't as risky, and the stakes aren't as high if it doesn't work out.

• • •

When I finally left my finance job to start Bonobos full-time, it felt liberating. It reminded me of this one night in the fifth or sixth grade. I was at a roller skating event for my elementary school, and there was a romantic interlude where you could invite someone to skate with you. I remember feeling very nervous and kind of shy when it came to asking a girl to skate with me. When I finally did it, we skated around the rink a couple of times and talked, and everybody was looking at us. There were only a couple of others doing the same thing.

And when the song ended, the girl and I said, "Okay, well, that was fun." We separated, and I looked over and saw five other girls just sitting there, waiting to be asked.

By then, asking a girl to skate wasn't so scary. I was ready for a new song, whatever it might be. All I could think was, "I wish there were five more of these songs, 'cause this skating with girls routine is pretty awesome and there is so much opportunity out there!"

BRIAN SPALY, a former private equity investor, founded the clothing brand Bonobos and is the founder and former CEO of Trunk Club.

BARBARA HARRIS

PR Executive to Bishop in the Episcopal Church

EVER SINCE I was a child, my passion has been the church. Eventually, after a few different jumps, I found a way to fulfill my calling from God. It's been over sixty-five years now since I made my first jump, and I can tell you that, overall, my journey was not easy. It was not smooth. But I had a calling, I crafted a plan, and I believed it would work. I just didn't know it would turn out quite like this.

My childhood was modest, filled with choir, the piano, and church activities. My parents made some sacrifices so I could take vocal and instrumental lessons, and I envisioned myself growing up to be a music teacher. But when I left school, I let myself drift away from all that and toward a safer route, as a receptionist in the X-ray department of a children's hospital.

I might have stayed there forever if it hadn't been for the stepfather of a young man I was dating. He offered me an internship at his public relations firm. Twenty-five bucks a week to learn PR. The man seemed brilliant, and I figured I'd learn a lot. I rose through the ranks and some years later was asked by the director of public relations at Sun Oil Company, or Sunoco, to join his staff. I named my position, description, and salary, and they agreed to it. I was set.

But I had a longing for a different life lingering within me.

Beginning with the receptionist job out of school, I made a point to invest in my passion of being involved with the church. Whenever I wasn't working, I was volunteering. That stayed true when I joined Sunoco, and as I moved up in the company, my church participation continued to increase—to the point where I had an opportunity to become ordained. Now *this* was my dream.

Becoming an ordained minister wasn't going to pay the bills. I couldn't afford to give up my position at Sunoco. I was in a significant role, managing a staff of about twenty-six people, making real money. I had to find a way to both proceed toward a ministry and earn a paycheck. So I concocted a plan: my day job would remain as PR executive at Sunoco. At night, on the weekends, and on my vacations, I was a seminary student, working with the bishop of the Episcopal Diocese of Pennsylvania and his team to become ordained.

I got ordained, and things came to a head. My next step with the church was to serve as a deacon—something that would require much more than nights and weekends, but that still wouldn't pay the bills. So I got creative and pitched Sunoco to allow me to consult for them part-time, on my own schedule. In the short term, this deal would bring in cash to make ends meet, and more importantly, in the longer term, it would give me a backup in case the church didn't work out.

Sunoco agreed to my proposal, and I swapped my duties: I began work as a deacon by day, and as a Sunoco consultant on my own time, to make ends meet. A year later, I was a priest, and nine years after that came the biggest surprise: the church asked if I would allow my name to be considered for the role of suffragan bishop.

I thought about that for a while, then said yes because I thought that the people ought to have a woman's name to choose from. That's what gave me the courage to go forward. From the beginning of the nomination process to the final round, I didn't think it would go anywhere. When I met with the nominating committee, I thought to myself, "I'm never going to see these people again in my life, and so I can say exactly what is on my mind," which is what I did.

Shortly afterward, wonder of wonders, I was elected suffragan bishop of the Episcopal Diocese of Massachusetts. I was told I was elected because I gave the most honest answers. I became the first woman in the

Episcopal Church as well as in the worldwide Anglican Communion to be elected a bishop.

If you believe in what you want to jump to, then I encourage you to make that leap of faith and not to be timid. Make that leap, and see what the end may be. That being said, first try and make a plan. Think about a way you can maintain your lifestyle in case the jump is not successful. When I first considered ordination as a deacon, I had to think through how I would support myself. When I became a priest, I could not maintain myself on a priest's salary. I had to have other ideas. I had to have a plan.

None of this was easy. There were many people who objected to my jump because 1) I am a woman, and 2) I am black, and 3) I had not formally gone to seminary as most ordained people do. Then there were objections because I was a divorced person, and there were questions about my sexuality since I was a divorced person who had not remarried. They thought I was a left-wing radical. You wouldn't believe the type of hate messages and death threats that I received. I had to have my telephone number in Philadelphia changed twice and the last time to an unlisted number. On the day of my consecration, the Boston police department offered me a bulletproof vest to wear, which I refused. I said, "If some fool is gonna shoot me, what better place to die than at an altar?" That was that.

From the beginning, my jumps were measured. It was a series of little, practical decisions. Did I know how my jump would end? No. Was it all smooth? No. But all along, I knew it was a jump worth taking.

<hr />

BARBARA HARRIS, a former PR executive at Sun Oil Company, served from 1989 to 2003 as a bishop of the Episcopal Church, the first woman ordained to that position, worldwide.

ADRIAN CÁRDENAS

Professional Baseball Player to College Student

I LOVE BASEBALL. I still love baseball. I think it's arguably the best sport there is. A couple of years ago, I was an infielder for the Chicago Cubs, on track to make half a million bucks a year. So it's always a bit complicated to answer the question, "Why did you leave it all?"

I grew up reading books, asking questions, and playing the piano. I loved to learn. I dreamed of going to college and becoming a writer. Baseball sort of just happened: I liked it, I got good at it, and when I was eighteen, I was offered nearly a million bucks to skip school and start playing it professionally. I couldn't say no. My parents are middle-class immigrants from Cuba; I knew I could make that money go a long way for us. I figured I could put my other passions on hold for a little bit, and later when the time was right, I would pursue them.

So I had spent a few years inching upward through the minor leagues when, in the summer of 2010, my progress slowed, I got demoted, and I decided I was done. I dreaded telling my high school coach, Tom Duffin, because I admired him so much. As a player, he got close to the big leagues but gave up before breaking through, and I feel that he has regretted it ever since. I think that he didn't want me to make the same mistake. He had told our high school team, "My life is now through you guys.

If you guys make it, then I feel like a part of me has made it." Here I was, in almost the exact same position, ready to call it quits too. I feared I'd be letting him down.

Coach Duff was disappointed but not for himself. He said, "Look you've never quit anything in your life, and at the first sign of failure, you just give up like that? That's not you; that's never been you." He reminded me that my goal all along in baseball was to make the major leagues and that if I gave up now, I wouldn't get another chance. He knew I was passionate about writing and telling stories. He told me, "Listen, it's a lot easier to be a writer if you've made it to the big leagues. Nobody cares if you're a minor leaguer and you want to go write. They care if you make it to the top. So make it to the top." That stuck with me.

My parents were blunter: I hadn't thought about the details. I had no planning. I wanted to go to college but had no applications in, and it was now June—school was out. I had set up no alternate streams of cash coming in, no personal health insurance, nothing. Even though I had just been demoted, this was clearly the wrong time to leave.

And so I didn't quit. I doubled down on getting to the majors and at the same time researched schools that were very good in creative writing and philosophy. I started saving up money and investing part of it in real estate, to begin generating passive income for later on. In a weekend, I rethought an impulsive jump and began to prepare, instead, for a much larger one.

For the next two years, I was a ballplayer by day and a college student by night, and it was those midnights spent writing term papers that made me really believe that it was going to be okay to leave because I could point to real, tangible things I'd been doing for two years that I absolutely loved—loved more than baseball. The irony of all this was that it was during those couple of years—while I was balancing both worlds—that I played my best ball.

On May 7, 2012, I stepped up to the plate for the Chicago Cubs, my first at bat as a big leaguer. A few months later, I quit.

What surprised me most was that I was as happy as I dreamed I would be. I was anxious and nervous, but I wasn't fearful. I was ready. After almost quitting in 2010, I had written down a series of steps: finish off this season, go to school, and see what happens. If you don't want to return to baseball, quit. I also wrote down my goal: make it to the majors. I constantly revisited these notes. They gave structure to processes and milestones so that when it actually came down to it, I knew what was coming. By the time I quit, I had spent the better part of two years planning. What came next was a relatively easy decision, or at least one that I wasn't fearful to make.

I had one last person to tell, and that was my high school teammate Brian Fariñas. We were like brothers, and I was scared to tell him because, as with Coach Duff, I was living his dream too. Brian wasn't good enough to make the big leagues, so I felt like he was living vicariously through me when I made it. And now I was leaving the dream. I had no idea how he was going to react.

I spilled out the whole situation to him. When I was done, Brian looked at me. Then he said simply, "Relax. It's not that serious."

He was spot-on. I had spent a couple years thinking about this move, doing all I could to inform the decision, and now as I stepped back, it didn't actually feel that serious. It wasn't a big deal. It was a seamless transition. Brian was all for it.

There's self-doubt that comes with leaving something comfortable. You're doing something out of the ordinary. At least that's what the outside world is telling you, or that people who are not inside your inner circle are telling you. And, unfortunately, sometimes it's people within your inner circle too.

But if you are thoughtful about your jump and try to analyze it and take the time to plan for the different possible outcomes, you should bank on the fact that you've taken the necessary steps to make a well-informed decision. And if it ultimately doesn't work out as you had planned, I'm a big believer in the idea that you will be able to live with that mistake, given the preparation that led up to that decision. If you do plan, then the jump itself is just not that serious.

Because I was fortunate to play baseball at the highest level, I understood loss very well and I understood failure very well, so I never held this romanticized view of success. But I feel like I'm giving myself a chance at whatever life comes next. I'm okay with loss. I'm okay with failure. Baseball's prepared me for that.

———————————

ADRIAN CÁRDENAS, a former second baseman for the Chicago Cubs of Major League Baseball, is a 2015 graduate of New York University and 2017 graduate of NYU Tisch School of the Arts.

ADAM BRAUN

Consultant to Nonprofit Founder and Executive Director

HE ASKED ME for a pencil. As a street beggar in the slums of India, the boy knew that anything of traditional material value would be taken away from him by either an older child or perhaps a gang lord, or even by the family member who had put him on the street. But a pencil—a pencil wasn't of tremendous material value, yet its latent potential could unlock his own sense of curiosity and imagination. I was in college and studying abroad at the time, on the well-worn path toward a career in consulting and business. This boy and his request for a pencil would change all of that.

Fast-forward a few years, and I'm a young analyst for the prestigious consulting firm, Bain & Company—a type of dream job for someone in my shoes. But I couldn't shake the memory of the boy and the pencil. Back in college, I had picked up a habit of working various side gigs to fund my obsession with traveling through the developing world whenever I had the chance. Now I wanted to combine this travel obsession to help children like the boy. On the night of December 20, 2008, I sat down and began writing.

I started writing so that I could get all my ideas and sparks of inspiration on paper. Once they were on paper, I could organize them. The most wasted resource on earth is human intention; for any idea, you need a system to filter that early excitement and emotional momentum into action. I find that documenting ideas on paper often creates that filter; I use the writings to articulate my ideas to others. So I wrote out all of my initial fund-raising plans, the countries in which I had traveled where I might want to try and build a school, and a list of the different people I would need to reach out to for support to get this idea off the ground. And the text I wrote that night became the original charter for what I called Pencils of Promise. The original goal was to simply build one school in the developing world to change the lives of children in one community, but the organization would go on to build nearly five hundred schools around the world within the next decade.

I wasn't ready to quit Bain full stop, so I pitched the senior leadership to let me take a few months off as a special type of externship. They allowed employees to do externships and go work elsewhere, but to work for yourself wasn't part of the rules. I framed it strategically—I explained that the experience wouldn't only benefit me but that it made sense for Bain: they wanted to groom future leaders of the organization, and what I'd learn from starting my own nonprofit would give me leadership experiences I needed to develop at Bain and that I wouldn't get in my junior analyst role otherwise. This is what sold them: the idea that I'd come back more well-rounded and better equipped to serve the firm.

By far the hardest thing came next: when I had to tell my parents. They had both come from total poverty, taking traditional paths to become a dentist and an orthodontist. Here I was in a position to make a lot of money in the career I had chosen, yet I was about to take a tremendous risk. It was 2009. The economy was in a bad place, an especially bad place for starting a nonprofit. It was really tough to persuade my parents that I was doing the right thing; convincing them happened incrementally. Initially, I said, "I am going to start this organization, but it's just an externship. I am going to come back to my job." Once I started, I said, "Look, I am going to return to my job once the externship ends, and later I am going to go to business school, and I can continue to pursue my nonprofit on the side of my business school pursuits."

I brought them along at each stage, saying, "If this doesn't work out, I will have also taken this next step that seems a little bit more safe and on the traditional path." Once I left Bain, I never went or even applied to business school. The nonprofit organization continued to grow, and I continued to promise that I would consider safety nets, or more traditional paths, down the line. That's how I got my parents on board.

When I started Pencils of Promise, I doubted myself, but I never doubted the organization. I think it's really important to not doubt the idea of what you are doing, the value of it, and the fact that it can succeed. I certainly had moments of self-doubt where I thought, "Am I the right person?" My response to this was to step back and distinguish between pursuing an idea out of passion versus pursuing an idea out of purpose. Aside from just raw emotions, I was driven by a fundamental sense of purpose. I felt like I was here in this existence pursuing this nonprofit because I was meant to contribute to the world in this way. In my mind, it had to succeed, and it would.

The thing that has surprised me the most is that people who don't have huge track records of accomplishment can take on incredibly high-level tasks and thrive if they are given opportunities for growth along with meaningful coaching. As an early-stage entrepreneur building this nonprofit without a lot of capital behind me, not only did I have to attract funding, but I also had to tap my personal and professional networks to recruit great talent and the energy and efforts of others. I had to bet on unproven personnel with big upside potential. The result surprised me early on, and I continue to remind myself of it today: if you find the right people, and you invest in them properly, they can go out and do extraordinary things.

There's an external perception that making a jump means going off a diving board into the deep end. But I find that most individuals who are jumping off a safe path don't jump all at once. A good jump is much more like walking from the shallow end of a pool, starting with getting the tip of your toe wet in the first step, and then the next step and the next step. Soon the water is waist high; it comes up to the middle of your stomach and maybe eventually up to your shoulders. Then, at the very point at which you have reached the deep end, are comfortable with the risk, and feel like you have solid footing beneath you, or you are at least comfortable in the uncertainty of being in the deep end . . .

That's when you go for it.

ADAM BRAUN, a former management consultant at Bain & Company, is the founder and former CEO of the nonprofit organization Pencils of Promise and current founder and CEO of MissionU.

AKANSHA AGRAWAL

Internal Jump: Advertising Operations Associate to Market
Research Analyst to Sales Analytics Professional

I ALWAYS FIGURED I'd be happy. I just didn't know how. My
story isn't about chasing a lifelong passion or finally ditching the nine-
to-five. It's about finding confidence within four walls, learning about
myself from side projects and supportive colleagues. Without leaving
my company, I've jumped more than once. And I'm just getting started.

I come from a traditional Indian family; my parents met through an
arranged marriage shortly after my dad wrapped up college in the Midwest. He flew back to India during a school break and met my mom,
was engaged within the week, and wed the next. After that, it was back
to the States, back to starting the dream: a house, a yard, kids, and a
safe job.

My dad didn't have much money starting out but found his footing in
studying engineering. Engineering provided stability, and that was the
goal. From the very beginning, my parents' intention was clear: provide
a supportive and loving environment at home. Our family life was somewhat of a bubble, with a simple goal to make money and play it safe. It
was very simple in that way. And there was nothing wrong with that.

It was a nurturing environment, though over time I felt I was missing
out on critical dialogues at home—conversations around what we kids,
the children, really wanted to shoot for: our own passions, our own

interests, especially anything that might be different from a "safe" job, a yard, and a home. But to my parents, this path was what they knew and what they cared about. And so, by default, it was the path I cared about.

By high school, my goals were their goals: land good grades, nail the extracurricular activities necessary to get into a good college. From there, the logic went, everything will figure itself out.

But then I got to college. I looked around at so many people doing so many amazing things. I thought, "They all have ideas—start a business, form a band, build a school. What about me? Where do I stand?" It was a constant struggle, a daily battle to find out what I was good at and a pressure to discover what I was passionate about. I had never thought about it—I shoved the idea to the side for a long time. I was wired to keep my grades high, not develop a passion. When it came time for summer jobs, I got lost as internship recruiting began early on in my junior year. I scanned the job boards and went to informational sessions for finance and corporate internships. They weren't for me. I kept browsing, trying to find something that could click. After some time, I stumbled across an internship at a big, growing technology company in a role for advertising operations. I had no idea what that meant, though I did know that ad operations likely was *not* going to be my passion.

But I was an econ major, and the job description sounded somewhat data driven, which I thought I would like. And more importantly, the technology company was big and diverse and growing. I pictured the summer job as a foot in the door to other things I might like, though what those things were, I didn't yet know. Trying to quickly discover my passion felt overwhelming, but spending a summer pulling at a thread that might unravel into something interesting—that felt doable.

I applied online for the advertising operations internship, and then I started my research on the job and the company, doing whatever I could to improve my odds for getting picked. I dug up a YouTube video where a manager at the company discussed their various summer internship programs. I bought a subscription to their company business networking website that allowed me the chance to send her a message, and I wrote her a cold e-mail: "Hey, I'm really interested in one of the internship roles, and just applied for it. Could you connect me to your colleague who oversees it, to see if I would be a good fit?"

The woman responded, and after we traded messages, she decided to put my résumé on the top of the pile. That cracked the door open, giving me the chance to actually talk to the hiring manager for my position. Luckily, that conversation went well. I was offered the job. I liked the team, and I knew I would learn a lot. I headed to the company for the summer.

The job was pretty plain, unsexy, and very operational: when you get a request for X, do Y. For every X request, do Y. X, then Y. Repeat.

Was it my dream? My true passion? Of course not, but I didn't mind. I was simply ecstatic to be inside the building. I liked the company, I believed in its culture, and I knew that I would learn a lot and, from there, find out more about myself and my passion. And, to be honest, I was hooked on the free perks that came with the work. Compared to life at college, where I had to pay for everything, even the smallest corporate benefits went a long way.

Sure enough, as the summer started, I picked up pretty quickly on what was missing in the role. I was a numbers person in a role void of analysis. The work bore no relationship to my econ studies. I craved the satisfaction that comes from the rigor of quantitative assignments, but that wasn't part of the job.

This may sound like a lame summer, but it turned out to be the opposite because the business environment and the people I worked with became more meaningful than the job itself. My colleagues wanted to help me find the right fit elsewhere in the company. To do this, my bosses and others encouraged me to have coffee with people on different teams who were in different departments and held different roles. I'm not the most vocal person. I can be pretty shy. But one-on-one I'm great about chasing after something and speaking up, and so when people offered to make introductions, I pushed myself to take them up on the offers. I started to think of anyone else internally whose help I could seek out, making a list of family friends or friends of friends who worked at the company, then reaching out and asking them for coffee too.

As I gained confidence from these meet-ups, I went a step further: when I would read about a person working on something interesting in a different department, I would e-mail a mutual contact and ask for an introduction. Something I learned: don't be scared to send that type of e-mail. More often than not, the person on the other end was willing to make an introduction—from entry-level folks a year older than I was all the way to senior executives. I just had to ask.

At first, it felt awkward to ask for help in this way, until I learned that there is no better method to find what it is you want to be doing. I'd pull up a chair in the company café with these other employees, and they'd ask me to be honest about what I liked and what I didn't about my job, and what I wanted to try to do next. They had all stood in my shoes before. They had once jumped to a new role and wanted to help me jump too.

While I hadn't found a passion just yet, and my day-to-day job that summer wasn't so great, I was supported to jump within the company. The countless coffee chats made me grow confident in the company and what opportunities could come for me later on, if I just stuck around. Which is why at the end of the summer, when I was offered a full-time job in what I was doing, my *not*-passion, I accepted it right away.

Before I started full-time, I began to strategize. Coming back, I wanted to hit the ground running. I thought through what I enjoyed about college to determine what stood out. I went back to my time as an econ major and thought about the real-life applications of what I had learned. I appreciated that way of thinking. I felt doing something analytical and data driven would make me feel fulfilled—and that I'd be good at it too. I decided I'd pinpoint these interests when I started work.

The company preached a culture of transformation: encouraging people to succeed within different roles. There was a belief that they don't hire you for a role; they hire you for the company. I leaned into this mantra on day one, when I began carefully strategizing for my next potential role.

Starting out full-time, I needed hard skills to make a jump into more analytical work feasible. I asked my manager to teach me the ins and outs of Microsoft Excel, and I found someone at the company who taught one-on-one courses for a more advanced computer program during lunchtime. The company offered a computer programming class to learn a coding language that I took after work. I tried learning programs and side projects to get the flavor of this type of work, to see if it was something I enjoyed and would be good at.

Meanwhile, I began reaching out to colleagues in other roles on other teams that sounded like promising potential destinations for my new skills. I wanted to learn what they did in their job, what skills they used, what challenges they faced. I still couldn't nail down what job I was searching for, so I started talking to people in departments I found interesting, like marketing, or in leadership positions that I looked up to, like team managers.

I was in my advertising operations role for about a year, and when I made my jump, I still wasn't totally ready. I was wrapping up one of my regular coffee chats, this time with a manager in market research. By now, I was less shy and more direct, rattling off questions to learn every detail about her job and what it entailed. As we finished up, the manager said: "Actually, I'm hiring right now, if you're interested."

An actual job opportunity threw me off at first. I remember thinking, "I don't think I'm ready for this jump. I don't feel it's the right time." But it hit me that no time is the "right time" to jump. You never know when an opportunity is going to come around again. I knew enough by then to understand the research department and to know the kind of opportunities a job in that area would offer me. Getting that job was a massive step toward what I wanted to be doing, and while the job didn't *exactly* reflect my passion—I was, and am, still figuring out that passion piece— it was a role that would bolster my skill set, play to my analytical interests, and expose me to an exciting piece of the company. All I needed to do was believe in myself.

That was the hardest part. But it was made possible by all the work leading up to that job offer, starting the summer prior. My pile of side projects gave me the skills for the jump, and my chats with others provided a sense for what I'd be getting into. Most valuable was that I had built a support system within the company, so when I shared the jump idea with my manager, he said, "I knew you wanted something like this," and offered his help getting me the offer. Ultimately, I believed in myself because others—colleagues who knew me well, who worked alongside me—believed in me first. That's how my jump was made.

It's those people around you who help make a jump possible within an organization. The odds are it's your current manager who will help pitch you to the next hiring manager. By the time I interviewed for the market research position, that hiring manager knew I was proven and worth the risk: "Look, you don't have as much experience in the techni-cal skills that other candidates have, but we know your performance within the company has been strong. We've talked to your manager, and from our conversations, we can tell you're good at working with teams and in leading projects. And those assets are just as valuable as any rel-evant skills—we'll teach you whatever else you'll need to know."

The research role was a huge leap, a 180-degree turn from ad opera-tions. I'm grateful for that jump in many ways, most of all because it gave me the confidence to jump again.

I was on the research team for a couple of years and truly enjoyed it. But even in that role, I didn't stay comfortable—and it was clear the com-pany didn't want me to, either. Just six months in, other managers were teaching me about positions within research that would further play to my interests and to the company's strengths. My job was overwhelmingly data driven, and that was great, but I began learning about and, perhaps ironically, becoming interested in more client-facing roles within the sales analytics department. Two years later, I jumped again.

Today I can honestly say that this new role, the result of my second jump, is playing to my professional interests: a mesh between using data-driven research and people-facing sales to make a real impact on the com-pany's bottom line. More than the job, the experience jumping has shown me that I can, and I will, jump yet again.

During my time at this company, I've also carved out personal me-time: outside-of-work explorations of what I personally enjoy doing. For a few years, I've centered on wellness and health—someday, I want to find a way to link these interests to a professional pursuit. For now, I'm setting the stage in simple ways; I operate a wellness website that my manager proudly shares with our other colleagues, and the marketing team has allowed me to work with them on certain projects. I earned my certification as a group fitness instructor, and the company has invited me to teach fitness classes as part of our corporate wellness programs. As my personal identity threads itself into my corporate one, my company has encouraged these two halves to coexist, and in this way, there is no pressure to choose one over the other.

•   •   •

Explore the idea of internal jumping; if it isn't an established norm where you work, odds are it will be soon enough. Encouraging internal jumping makes sense for many companies, and it makes sense for you to try things out without the fear and risk of quitting your job first. I think in the first three to five years out of college no one really knows what he or she wants. I used to think you had to leave a workplace to explore your boundaries and continue growing, but when you're jumping among people who know you well, they can see in you what you can achieve, maybe even more than you can.

If you want to jump internally, don't complicate things. I'm all about staying balanced: take a few actions, tinker with the results, talk to others, and continue to refine your jump. While working in your current role, find a small side project to explore what another kind of work is like. Don't be in a rush to take the next step. Slow your steps. Internalize and reflect on what your gut is saying. Talk to people who support you, who know you and can relate to your gut feeling. Seek out the people who have done what you want to do. Study and understand what they do. And when it's time to jump, don't worry about being qualified.

I still struggle with failure and rejection. But with failure, you learn so much faster than if you didn't fail—if you didn't have opportunities where you have to question yourself. Going back to my childhood, I was in a bubble. I didn't reach far for things, and I got them pretty easily. There was no sense of failure in my life before I started working. And now I'm realizing failure really helps you understand who you are.

I couldn't imagine not jumping. I've always wanted my career to make me happy, and I had to reach out of my comfort zone to make that happen. There was no alternative in my mind. I had to jump.

AKANSHA AGRAWAL, a former advertising operations associate at LinkedIn, internally jumped into a sales analytics position within LinkedIn.

MAIA JOSEBACHVILI

Wall Street Derivatives Trader to
Founder of Social Adventure Company

"WHAT'S THE WORST thing that can happen?" I ask myself that a lot. That's the attitude my parents had when they took off from South America to start a new life in New York City. That's also the attitude I had when I discovered the great outdoors, and when I decided to jump for something I believe in. When you get comfortable with the worst-case scenario, you get okay with trying—and that's when things get really fun.

I grew up a first-generation American to Argentine parents. They moved us Stateside when I was eight, to chase the quintessential American dream: the promise of a good education for their children and steady jobs for them. Growing up, the focus was always on getting good grades and getting into a good college. There wasn't much room for risk-taking in that path.

College opened up my world, exposing me to outdoor adventures like skydiving and immersing myself in the world of travel through solo study programs on the other side of the world. And that's where my notion of a career got turned upside down: meeting real people—grown adults—building lifestyles that I hadn't even dreamed of. I met people who were taking yearlong sabbaticals from their high-power jobs, and couples who were spending their parental leave hiking through New

Zealand with their newborns. I didn't think these paths were allowed; they certainly weren't posted in our career services center.

But when the time came to get my first job after college, I stuck with the comfortable path I'd been on: I went to the career fair in the gymnasium. I was swayed by the cool swag and nice guy at the desk of one particular Wall Street firm. I wound up with an offer to work on the floor of the stock exchange for this firm. They offered me a hefty signing bonus and a fall start date. I wasn't really thinking, "What do I wanna be when I grow up?" It was more like, "This is sweet. I can take the signing bonus and skydive all summer."

The problem with seeing other lifestyles is knowing that these alternative worlds exist. Working late and being generally uninspired was bad enough; worse was admitting that, most likely, there were other ways I could be spending my days. About a year and a half in, I got my first promotion. That's when I told myself I was done. Being a derivatives trader just wasn't for me and I had to get out before I got too far in.

My next thought wasn't too original: quit my day job, travel the globe, and come back to the "real world" once I got it all out of my system. My boyfriend and I had been tossing around the idea of taking a backpacking trip around the world, and this seemed like as good a time as any. It'd be a crazy journey, and I knew I would come back refreshed and happier. I went to my boss and told him I was ready for the next thing.

I left on a one-way ticket to India with my boyfriend of four years. At the beginning of the trip, we were pretty sure we were going to come back, buy a house, and get married. We made it about five months. Somewhere in Cambodia, with a suddenness much like when I realized I wasn't going to be a trader, we realized we weren't going to get married. We broke up in the Kuala Lumpur airport, and I had that terrifying moment: What now?

I went to the counter at the airport and booked a new ticket for the same day, leaving him in Malaysia, while I hopped on a plane to New Zealand. "What's the worst that can happen?" I remember thinking. If I didn't feel comfortable, I could always go home a few days later. I ended up staying on the road for another ten months. By the time I finally made it home, I'd been gone for fourteen months and traveled to twenty-two countries.

This was the beginning of my jump. Funnily enough, deciding to quit my job and travel was an easy decision. The real crux was what I was going to do when I got back. I looked in the mirror and saw two very different versions of myself. One version I could put neatly on a résumé: twenty-four-year-old with two years on Wall Street, who took some time off to travel and is ready to get back into it. This made sense to my coworkers, to my peers, and even to me.

But then there was this other version of me: the twenty-four-year-old who rode solo on the Trans-Siberian Railroad from Beijing to Moscow, sleeping in the second-class cabin because it felt more authentic. This was the person who went scuba diving in a frozen lake in Siberia because it sounded cool. Walked across the border into Jordan and spent a few days hanging out in a cave with the Bedouin people in Petra. Befriended Sherpas during hikes in Nepal. I felt like I'd met so many other types of people in the world that the concept of a twenty-four-year-old with two years on Wall Street just didn't capture me anymore.

I felt so different and alone, no longer able to relate to my old life but also lacking a sense of what else I could do. I remember one of my first days back. I walked into a convenience store to buy shampoo, and I was so overwhelmed by all the choices that I had to walk out. If you find a store in Mongolia, there's one shampoo. I went almost a month without reactivating my cell phone. It had been over a year since I'd been so connected, and life without a phone had become so liberating. I was not the same person I was when I left.

The things I now cared about were different from those of my friends and former colleagues. That was the hardest part: feeling like I had transformed but nothing else had changed. Most of my friends were in their old jobs. I stopped by the regular happy hour with my old coworkers. The first question was "How was it?" followed quickly by the second question, "So what are you going to do next?"

In the far reaches of the back of my mind, I knew exactly what I wanted to do next. One night, while passing through Egypt, I had camped on a beach with a group of other travelers. We sat and we talked, and I just thought, "This is an experience that everyone should have: sitting around a campfire with a bunch of strangers, exchanging personal life stories and having a great time together." I want to create experiences like this for people.

This was in 2008. The economy was starting to falter, and starting your own company wasn't really a thing. I didn't even hold the vocabulary to explain what I wanted to do. Every time I started to share the idea, it didn't make sense. So when I answered the inevitable "what are you going to do next" question, I just said what was easier: "I'm thinking about business school," or "I'm interviewing for jobs."

But jobs and grad school were the last thing on my mind. I wanted to bring that night in Egypt to others. I thought back to Ole, the guy who ran a skydiving place when I was in college. He'd always say, "What could possibly go wrong?" which is a little bit ironic for your skydiving instructor to say. But I applied that here because I think it was a helpful barometer. Most big mistakes are recoverable. If this idea flopped, things definitely seemed recoverable.

I decided to jump—slowly and with a safety net. I ran parallel tracks: I put together my résumé, started applying for jobs—all the usual stuff. At the same time, I began to explore my concept, in tiny bites. I was really scared of failing; at that point, I'd never actually had a major failure in my life. Going through the motions on the corporate side made preparing for my jump much easier. When people asked about my plans, I could say, "Yeah, I'm applying for jobs." That answer checked off some social perception box—a box I cared about but wished I didn't—while giving me an opening to secretly chip away at my plan. I put together my MVP (my minimum viable product) in a way that wasn't so intimidating: I would say, "Hey, I'm putting together a couple of weekend camping trips. Who wants to come?" I didn't put a name to it. I didn't say, "This is my company." I just said, "I'm doing it as a small project," and told everyone, "I'm trying this for the summer, and then I'll take the GMAT in the fall and start interviewing for jobs."

Ultimately, I tricked even myself. The honest, honest truth is that there was no moment that I knew I was all in, not until over a year later. I set short-term milestones: get a few trips off the ground and then apply to business school. In the fall, I received some press and started getting inbound interest. My trips were selling out, so I thought, "Okay, maybe I can try this for a year. Why don't I give it another nine months and then apply to business school next spring?"

That winter, someone asked me if they could join the company full-time. All of a sudden I had a much bigger leap in front of me: Was I ready to be responsible for someone else's livelihood? That's when I had to make a decision: Will I keep this as a project or actually go big? By then, that question wasn't so dramatic to answer.

I tricked myself with my timelines. Outlining steps in six-month increments compared to two-year windows didn't actually change the risk I was taking on day-to-day. Yet it made that risk more digestible. It gave me an emotional crutch: I can do this for a few more months; I can bring on one employee. Over time, with enough of these little pieces, the business was built: Urban Escapes grew to four cities with ten full-time employees and over fifty guides. A couple of years in, we were acquired by Living Social and ended up growing the business under their umbrella to a $25 million venture that took 250,000 people per year on adventures around the world.

The most meaningful outcomes happen after your first plans change. If you describe your perfect next ten years today, and you stick to whatever you decide, I believe you will end up underachieving. We're only so creative and so imaginative—how can we possibly know what exciting choices we'll have in front of us in three years? Seven years? New experiences open up your eyes to what the possibilities are. They make you a more complex and interesting person, and they teach you more about yourself. It would be a shame to stick to the original plan that you drafted before all of that personal growth.

My jump wasn't about traveling. It wasn't about quitting my job on the stock exchange and flying to India. My biggest jump happened when I was sitting on my couch after all the dust had settled: single and uncertain, taking baby steps in figuring out how to pursue an idea I really cared about. The concept of taking a jump is doing something that pushes you outside of your comfort zone. And you learn the most about yourself by living in that beautiful, scary, and exciting world outside of your comfort zone.

Jump. What's the worst that can happen?

MAIA JOSEBACHVILI, a former equity derivatives trader in New York and founder of Urban Escapes, is the vice president of strategy and marketing at Greenhouse.

ERIC WU

Investment Banker to Tech Professional to
Designer of an Activewear Brand

WHAT WE WEAR changes who we are. For too long I was a preppy son of immigrants who did what I was told. But what if the chinos and collars aren't for you? What if you're actually a leopard leotard and neon ski jacket kinda kid? That's when you need to jump.

My upbringing was influenced by a certain duality. My parents grew up in Communist China, working in fields and on farms because they were ordered to do so. They ultimately rejected that regimented order by finding a way to the United States. My parents espouse the benefits of following the rules, while having broken them themselves.

In college, I fell for fashion. On campus, dressing with flair for nights out was the thing. It wasn't about looking good; it was about being outlandish and expressing things like deep, weird aspects of your personality. Dressing for nights out was totally excessive and bizarre, and I loved it. I'd never had an opportunity to express myself this way before; it was whimsical and creative, far from the straightlaced path to which I had, until then, defaulted. I reveled in planning out the quirks and novelties. I treasured every part of that experience.

But when the time came to think about careers, dressing up in crazy clothes took a back seat to snagging a prestigious corporate job. The race for a prestigious job was a race worth joining: you got to wear a nice

costume if you got one of those jobs. You got to fit in. It was hard not to
get caught up in that race, and there was a universal sense of relief when
I was given an entry-level job at a Wall Street bank after graduation. My
parents could proudly share this with their Chinese friends and family.

I started work and almost immediately craved a creative outlet. I
longed to return to outlandish fashion, or something along those lines. I
knew I wanted to do my own thing, but I moved slowly. For me, jumping
was a de-risking process. It sounds so bland, but it is incredibly hard to
go from a stable job to "I'm going to go and start my own company." I
don't have that entrepreneur-who-doesn't-give-a-shit-about-what-anyone-
thinks-ever kind of personality, or obviously I would have just jumped
big in the first place.

I'm more the guy who's like, "Yes, I understand that there's a part of
me that wants to make the jump. But how can I do things in such a way
where I'm still able to cover some of these risks?" So I made a small jump
first, to a young and growing technology company that would let me be
more creative and entrepreneurial. This wasn't the cannon ball jump by
any means—just a toe in the water. And it felt right; it felt good, like I was
making progress. I was exploring aspects of myself that I hadn't discovered before. But soon enough, this situation too became limiting: the job
was never going to allow full effort on creative work.

Three months into this job, I went to an arts festival deep in the
Nevada desert. It was 3 a.m. on the final night, and my friend and I went
on a bike ride toward one of the far corners of the fairgrounds. Through
the darkness, we came upon a surreal scene: several hundred people, in
the middle of nowhere, dancing. We slowed to a stop and watched the
scene unfold. After a while, the sun slowly started rising. Dawn was coming. The first piece of sunlight peeked over the mountain just as the final
beat dropped.

And in that moment things cleared for me.

Shortly afterward, I was commuting to work when I saw an ad for
a textile fair being held in China. I could no longer ignore the questions: "What if you just went to that? What if you just quit your job and
you just went to that? What if?" Familiar constraints were manifesting
themselves in my work life: the staleness, the ceiling, the constriction
on creativity.

That same day just so happened to be my quarterly review with my boss, the company CEO. We sat down, and he asked me if I was truly happy at the company, if this was something I was truly passionate about. I replied with genuine honesty: I love the people here and I believe in the mission, but it was time for me to do my own thing and start this clothing brand.

Our CEO had jumped from a consulting job to start this tech company, and he cautioned me: "Are you sure, dude? Starting your own company is really hard. If you want, maybe we can figure something else out, or you can get a job at another start-up." I told him thanks but no thanks: that this is what I should be jumping for—that I should be my own boss, working on my own ideas. That day I quit and bought tickets to the textile fair in China. There was very little ruminating, very little thought. It just felt right.

I called my parents from under an awning that rainy November afternoon. I said to them, "Remember when I was working on Wall Street, and how much you approved of that and how much I hated it? You have to realize that you want what's safe for me, but what's safe for me isn't necessarily what's best for me." They struggled to understand. They tried to support me while clearly still at odds with what I was doing: my mom traveled with me to the textile fair, while telling me along the way that she didn't approve. Even now, my parents still harbor considerable doubt. At times, my mom will nudge me and say, "Maybe you should get a real job, you know?" And I reply, "Mom, you've got to realize that I'm having so much fun doing this. And it is going to work."

I'm rationally irrationally optimistic about my jump. It's irrational because failure is obviously within the realm of possibility. It is a very real potential outcome. But early on, I reasoned that thinking about failure—apart from thinking about ways to mitigate failure, which is different—is not valuable. Thinking about failure, wondering, "Is this going to succeed? Is it not going to succeed?" is not helpful; it's only stressful. So I operate under the day-to-day assumption that I won't fail. And that helps me cope with the natural stress that comes from a jump.

When I jumped, I wrote down a few notes to keep in mind, for the moments when intense doubts and panic attacks would come my way. The most critical note that I wrote to myself was: "Those who succeed do not have the privilege of escaping hopelessness; they simply endure the whimsical whisperings at them. There is a way to make it work; you just have to find it." I read that to myself every single day. If you read something like that to yourself enough times, you sort of embody it. That's my hope at least.

To me, jumping means believing. Sure, I'm going to feel hopeless at times, but this fear will enter my consciousness, and I just have to acknowledge it, then put it aside. I have to believe that the only way to power through is just to hear the fear, then let it go and keep working.

Even the most courageous jumpers faced the same doubt and the same fear that we all do. You cannot escape those thoughts. There's no way, at any point in your life, to wait for that fear to subside before you make a jump because that fear will never go away. You just have to say, "I feel fear. And of course I'm going to keep working," and accept that these are simply thoughts that you have; they are not who you are.

I don't think I'd be making this jump without the collection of my past experiences. Making a jump is like riding a bike: you don't learn how to ride a bike solely by reading about bikes, right? You have to make small, real steps. You could be the smartest person in reading about how to pedal, but that is completely separate from actually pedaling. A lot of people—and I was guilty of this—think, "Well, I'll just keep reading about how to jump. There's always more I can learn, right?" Now I'm not saying you should skip the prep, but after a few pages, it's worth it to start small: get out and try some laps around the street.

Don't know your jump yet? Go out and find something you enjoy doing, and do more of it. Start off with training wheels: explore the activity; maybe start a small project. Not even a business, just a small project. Maybe something as simple as volunteering or starting a side hobby. Just start doing something that interests you, and once you begin to go down that path, I think you'll realize that not only have you built a new skill, not only have you gained expertise, but you will have found something that you're likely passionate about. And when you work at something you're passionate about, it ultimately becomes a manifestation of who you are.

Whatever your jump may be, put down the book and pick up a set of wheels. Then start pedaling. And when you do, come find me in lower Manhattan. I'll be that guy in the leopard leotard and neon ski jacket, trying to ride my bike too.

ERIC WU, a former analyst at Morgan Stanley and business development associate at Hinge dating app, is the designer/founder at streetwear brand Public Space (public space.xyz).

PAIGE JOHNSON (PSEUDONYM)

Internal Jump:
Customer Support Representative to Sales Engineer

BALLET IS IN my blood. It's part of who I am. The lights, the crowd, the nerves. I live to perform. As I entered the working world, I longed for those thrills that came with dancing. And when I jumped, it was to get back to those old feelings but on a very different stage.

I grew up in a small town in the Rustbelt of northeastern Ohio, where hard work was what we knew. But it was never something that was synonymous with happiness or fulfillment in any way. People worked to live, and there wasn't really that much else to it.

My dad's a lawyer, and from what I can tell, he's good at it. But it always seemed to me he wasn't truly happy. He told me once that his only goal was to provide, and that he was always willing to forsake personal fulfillment in his job to fulfill that goal. He regularly complained of his "golden handcuffs" to the family. My dad was not living the professional life that he wanted, and based on how he pushed me into my passion projects, I could tell he didn't want that for me.

When I was a teenager, my dad confided in me about his one true dream—to be a history teacher. He said there wasn't a day that passed by that he didn't think about it. Despite everything that came out from making a nice living as a lawyer, and despite how cushy my childhood was because he was a lawyer, I had to wonder: Would he have been a happier, more fulfilled person, if he had pursued teaching? Did happiness outweigh the comforts of his handcuffs? I don't know. But I know that his dissatisfaction affected me in some ways.

Ballet and I have a long history. I started tap dancing when I was three. My mom loved the idea of getting me into dance. She was never athletic and never considered herself artistic, but she felt that dancers were of the utmost beauty. She said that when I was young, I became almost like a drill sergeant, calling out for more training and telling her which classes to take me to. By age ten, I was taking classes with twelve-year-olds; by age twelve, I was taking fifteen classes a week. By fifteen, I moved away to train with my coach for two years before college. I was totally obsessed. Being onstage, I think, above all things, was really why I got hooked. It wasn't necessarily the class or its repetitive nature. I just absolutely loved being onstage, and there was something about being nervous and having that interplay and then that reward after a performance that really hooked me.

In the ballet world, you have to make decisions fast—it's a young person's art. I made a crunch-time decision between going straight to a company and going to college. It was then I decided that ballet wasn't going to be my career. It just wasn't something that I felt was sustainable long-term for me personally. I learned a hard truth: not everything you're passionate about should be your full-time job. When it came time for a first job, I found a role on the marketing team for a nonprofit, and while I was there, I became more and more interested in the marketing tools I reviewed and purchased for our team. While evaluating one product in particular, I got to know the company behind it, and they offered me a job on their customer support team. It was a standard customer service role, and the day-to-day duties wouldn't be anything sexy, but the company seemed interesting, and I said yes.

In customer support, you're in charge of being a product expert, training all customers on how to use it, and then making sure they're happy and remain customers for the long haul. You also have to learn the technical side of the product for when complaints come in—and, boy, do they come in—to decide if the issues are due to user error or product malfunction. I had to know the ins and outs of the product, while also playing a client-facing role for each new customer coming on board.

For me, customer support was a thankless position. I felt as if I never went home satisfied with my work—as I was at the mercy of external relationships twenty-four hours a day, in a position where most of the feedback was expressed when people were having a negative experience. It started to get maddening. And for someone who really wants to do well at whatever I'm working on, those circumstances were not something that I could let go of easily at night. I couldn't let go of the fact that somebody was unhappy with our product. I wanted to go in and work on the product hands-on and help solve these problems flowing past me. I started to sketch out ideas in my head for a position where I could work more on the things that I liked in my current job but not to have to grapple with all the things that I didn't.

It was in the middle of our weekly Monday morning meeting within my first month at the company when a colleague announced a new role on the sales team, called a sales engineer. The role combined the deep product expertise and technical understanding of the tool with presentation skills and a need for really strong internal relationships with the product team. And in my mind, this was exactly what I needed to do.

I was only a few weeks into customer support—I barely knew the company, let alone the industry. So publicly, I pocketed my jump. But in ways I could control, I acted from that day onward toward that jump. I focused on the aspects of my job that would prepare me for the other role, which meant showcasing my relevant skills to my peers. I was strategic about self-promotion, in a way; you have to be. I stayed authentic to my personality, while professionally, I began orienting myself to be in line with a candidate that would fit in the sales engineer role. Even my most minute actions were premeditated: carefully crafting the types of questions I asked, and to whom, so I could show my peers that I cared and took their answers seriously. Everything was new to me, so I naturally had a lot of questions, but I framed them to show I could grow and adapt into the sales engineer responsibilities.

I needed to impress two groups: sales and product. On the sales team side, I needed to make myself invaluable to new client pitches. When a salesperson is pitching a new customer and hopes to expand the pitch and talk more about the product, sometimes they will ask for a customer support person to present with them. I volunteered to fill that role on

every single pitch call, every day, even if it was more work. It didn't feel
that different from preparing for a dance recital: I studied the slides and
rehearsed the calls so that I could step in and nail the part. I made it my
goal to have every one of my colleagues ask for me in the pitch, even
though I wasn't on the sales team. I knew that these folks were crucial
for me to, number one, feel comfortable enough making the jump, but
number two, have my back when I wanted to jump.

I knew the engineers on the product team were notoriously wary of
working with salespeople because they questioned how well the salespeople understood the technical specs of the product. So while still sitting on the customer support team, I built my own friendships with these
engineers and asked them to teach me what they knew—well before I
would be labeled a salesperson. And it worked: at that time, product managers felt comfortable with me because I was coming from customer support, not sales. I built crucial relationships with the engineers, and this
would become an integral piece of my ability to jump.

I hustled on the sales pitches and met with engineers for the next
eleven months. In my company, it was very well known that you're not
going anywhere new until the one-year mark. And at that year mark, I
returned to my search and found the sales engineer role still open. Honestly, it was a no-brainer to try and jump.

But while product and sales may have supported my internal jump, it
wasn't the case company-wide. That was when I hit the hard part because
there's always a bit of politics involved in switching teams and roles
within a company. On my customer support team, the leadership was not
necessarily happy about the idea of my leaving them. While they were
mostly supportive, there were still those comments like, "This is a big
move. What if you're actually not good at it?" I thought to myself, "You
think I haven't thought of that?! Thank you for stating the obvious; that's
my number one worry: What if I'm actually not good at this? What if I'm
actually not that good at it, and I make that jump, and my original team
doesn't take me back?"

And while that was tough, something bigger clicked with me in this
process. I went back to what I loved about ballet. In order to feel fulfilled
in a role professionally, I had to experience the underlying aspect that
drew me to ballet, and that was the performance aspect, the nerves, the

pressure, and the grit. And I had to experience those same things if I was going to be satisfied in my professional career. In my mind, those emotions are found in the presales pitching and in the closing more than the post-sales supporting and troubleshooting.

I jumped. And where I landed was better than staying where I had been. The opportunity far outweighed the murmur of a worry that I might not be good at the job. I knew that the position was worth jumping for; I also knew that I had built a safety net by being in my old role for a year. I believed then, and believe now, that people who build a safety net will have the skills to get another job. I also understood that in moving internally, with the politics that are involved, some people might not be looking out for my best interests, and there might be naysayers. I just had to remind myself to act against that negativity. Because honestly, this jump was for me: it was about proving to myself that I could do it. And no one was going to stop me from trying.

I've been in my sales engineer job now for eight months, and I can honestly say it was the best decision I've made thus far in my adult professional life. Across the good and the bad, it's everything that I expected. I didn't have any delusions about it. I didn't imagine this job would be utopia—and it's not. Every job is hard. I simply believe that this one truly plays to my strengths, and it pushes me where I need to be pushed in order to go home and be satisfied at night. Now I'm ready to go to work in the morning, and I'm satisfied when I return home to go to bed.

When you internally jump, your main focus should be to make those internal relationships with folks who will not only go to bat for you but who will also supply you with confidence that this is the right move. That's the most crucial part: the people around you. Without those supporters, I would have jumped externally. At the time of my jump, I was interviewing with four other companies for a similar role. I didn't want to leave my company because I loved the culture, and I loved the product; I loved the people. And ultimately, that's what kept me from leaving: my relationships with the people.

In the long run, this decision serves more than just me. For my company, the fact that it was possible for me to jump without leaving means

I'll likely stay here much longer than I would have otherwise. For my colleagues, the visible nature of my jump has inspired others to consider one themselves: anything from sales into support, to support into product, or even product into sales. It's rewarding to see my colleagues find that it's possible, and that it's even okay, to jump.

Some people feel the need to make a big jump because they're so far from where they want to be. But for some, like me, it was just a matter of finding that underlying factor that made me tick, that made me passionate about something. That's what my dad was missing, and that's why he's so proud that I was able to jump.

And here's the key to fulfillment: rather than jump to a thing, jump toward a feeling that you get when you're working.

For me, it's the feeling of getting onstage.

PAIGE JOHNSON (pseudonym), a former professional-track ballet dancer, nonprofit marketing associate, and customer support representative at a technology company, internally jumped to become a sales engineer within the same company.

ALEXANDRA STEIN

Investment Professional to
Coxswain of the US Paralympic Rowing Team

I GREW UP in Connecticut with a mom and dad who were adamant that athletics would always be an important part of my life. Ultimately, this belief was spot-on—in a way none of us could have imagined.

I ran track in high school but couldn't compete at the college level. My track coach told me to try rowing, so freshman year I wandered to the boathouse. At 5 feet 4 inches, 110 pounds, I was surrounded by giants: 5 feet 10 inches, 150 pounds; 6 feet 2 inches, 180 pounds. When we got to the boats, Coach put me in the coxswain seat. The coxswain is the person at the front of the boat who commands the boat, bringing order and strategy. I had no idea what I was doing, but I felt completely invigorated.

When I'm asked what I studied in college, I often tell people I majored in rowing because that's really where my heart was. After graduating, I thought about how to pursue it further but had a lot of pressure from my parents to get a master's degree in business. I wasn't really feeling it but applied to graduate programs anyway and landed a scholarship to attend a school near my hometown. How can you say no to that? You don't, and so I went.

I learned a bunch and was set up with a job in financial services afterward, moving right along the corporate track at a blue-chip firm, working with really smart people while finding a way to row when no one was looking. I'd be in the office until ten at night, then wake up at five in the morning to practice or coach a local team. I should have felt overwhelmed. But the truth is I craved the early morning swing rows and weekend regattas.

Back at my desk, the work was never intuitive or interesting to me. I'd often ask myself, "What am I doing here?" I wasn't sure at the end of the day what I was achieving. I was making new loans, and companies were able to pursue things because of the work I was doing, but it just felt like shifting money from one place to another.

In rowing, the fulfillment was so clear. And after a while, all my early morning practices turned into an incredible opportunity to jump. I had been competing and practicing with an athlete who was training with the US Paralympic Rowing Team, and he connected me with the coach, who invited me to try out to be the coxswain for the team. I don't happen to have a physical disability, but, according to Paralympic rules, a boat's coxswain need not have a disability.

I was in awe through the tryout but did pretty well, and the coaches came to me on selection day. It was a Sunday morning, and they said, "Alex, we want to choose you as the coxswain, but you're the only person in the boat who has a job outside of rowing." It was June, and the world championships weren't until November. They'd need me to go full-time, and if I couldn't, they'd move on to the next cox in line.

This was what I always wanted. I had just accepted a new job at my company in a different department, to work in equities, and because it was a Sunday morning, I couldn't call human resources to ask for permission. I thought, "Oh, my God, July to November—that's five months of being away from my job, and I don't know if I can do that." I never thought this would become a possibility; it was a naive mistake on my part to have zero plans. So very quickly, I said no thanks and passed up my chance to jump. It was one of the worst things I've ever done.

I regretted it almost immediately. For the entire year after I declined their offer, I sat in my cubicle thinking, "Why did I do that? How could I have passed up the opportunity to train with these incredible athletes and to represent the United States in world competition? What if that's my only shot to jump, and I just let that pass by?" I sat in my little cube night after night, just suffering. "How could I have made that call? How could I have done that?"

I knew why I didn't jump. Up until that point, I had worked so hard to be winning in the game that I thought I should have been playing: I had accepted the new job within the company and recently completed the leadership training program; people were looking at me, saying, "This woman's a leader." My work life looked like smooth sailing ahead, like I was headed for the Emerald City. And even though deep down I wasn't feeling so fulfilled by the prospect of the Emerald City, I thought I ought to keep following those golden bricks.

On that Sunday morning, when my rowing coach gave me a chance to peel off, away from the bricks, I wasn't prepared. I didn't consider the possibility of stepping off this path, didn't consider it would be possible to return to it later, didn't consider that senior colleagues within the company may have actually thought that going to chase my dream in rowing was a great opportunity that I should pursue. So in that moment, it was really easy to say no because this would-be jump didn't make sense on the one path I was on. And I didn't know if any other paths existed.

In the days that followed, I could see a clear contrast between what those five months would have been like, representing the United States alongside world-class athletes, compared to what actually transpired, a lot of fluorescent light and late nights in front of spreadsheets. I could feel the loss, the missed opportunity. Sitting under those lights, in front of those spreadsheets, I began to take the time to try again, this time with a plan.

I went to human resources and talked to them about how, if I tried out again and if I made the team, it would take me away from work for four months, starting in May. My approach was friendly but firm: let's figure out how we can make this work because if I'm given the opportunity I'm going to do it. I realized I actually had a bit of leverage; the company had invested in me for a few years, so it was in their interest to keep me around. That gave me confidence.

I finally reached out to coworkers for support. Fortunately, I had some brutally honest colleagues who said, "Alex, who cares if the company's not going to give you time off? If they won't, then you go do it anyway because it is worth doing." And to think this whole time I had kept to myself, believing no one else would understand.

I did my homework within the company: I'd have to ask for a leave of absence and wouldn't have an income for four months. But if they could accommodate my request for a leave, I'd have the security of coming back. I would have to make a plan and save money over that nine-month anticipation period so that I could get through four months without income.

My parents saw my heartache from giving up the opportunity the first time, and for that reason, they felt more understanding when I needed to try again. I realized I couldn't please everyone anymore: the first time I decided not to jump, I felt like I was letting my team down, and then the second time when I decided to jump, I was letting a different team down—my coworkers. It's tough to realize that you can't please everyone in a jump. But that's all the more reason to do what's right for you.

About a year after *not* jumping, I scraped together the chance to try out once again, and this time, I came armed with a plan. From tryouts, I was chosen to cox the US Paralympic Rowing Team in the upcoming World Championships in Slovenia. This time, I jumped. Our sixth-place finish qualified the boat for the London 2012 Paralympics the following year.

I'd always had this opportunity to jump. It had been there the whole time. Had I done my homework and some relationship management, I would have had the pieces in place to jump a year earlier. Sometimes you dream of seemingly crazy dreams, and when the opportunity appears, you keep the dream inside. I wish when I was first invited to try out, I had told my colleagues my crazy dreams because they wouldn't have let me go at it alone—and certainly would not have let me say no when the offer came in.

Find support through others, and start by finding those who share your values. I had a colleague whose wife competed on the University of

North Carolina national championship soccer team with Mia Hamm, and I started sharing my own athletic ambitions with him. Even though he was on the yellow brick road, had graduated from Harvard Business School, and was navigating a twenty-five-year career at the company, he had the same value system that I had about athletics. And when he learned of the caliber of my competitive ambition, he was the most encouraging supporter I could have asked for. Plus, he had the life experience to put my jump in perspective when I was unable to.

If you look carefully, these types of people are around you. Corral them into your jump because they can serve as your sounding board when you are feeling hesitant or pessimistic, or when you are wading through that unknown territory right before you jump, thinking, "I'm too scared. What's in that murky water?"

After the World Championships, I went back to work when a job opportunity came up at my alma mater, in athletic fund-raising. It would call for a massive pay cut and a permanent diversion from everything I had set out to conquer after business school. I asked to learn more, and I told them about my rowing responsibilities coming up in London.

They offered me the job, and I took my second jump (along with a 50 percent pay cut), a move that remains my biggest jump and the best decision I've ever made, off the yellow brick road for good, on a river toward somewhere else.

———————

ALEXANDRA STEIN, a former investment professional and coxswain of the 2012 US Paralympic Rowing Team, is an alumni development officer for a small college in New England.

RAHUL RAZDAN

Financial Services Professional to
Social Impact Entrepreneur

I MOVED TO the United States to escape violence and threats of terror, only to confront it when the marathon bombings hit Boston. Up until the marathon bombings, my career goal had been to reach the safe road, but that day put forth a different path. I don't know what will come of it, but I'd rather risk facing failure than regret not facing anything at all.

My family comes from the Indian side of Kashmir, a state that was torn apart during the partition of India and Pakistan. It's an area riddled with violence and shadowed by terrorism, and when things got particularly ugly, our family picked up and fled, leaving our property, our assets, and our friends in order to find somewhere safe. We settled near New Delhi, and when I was old enough for college, I got out of India for good.

I landed alone in the United States, got myself through school, and spent the next ten years trying to navigate the road toward that American dream. After two master's degrees—in applied mathematics from the University of North Carolina and an MBA from Columbia Business School—just as I was getting my footing, just as everything was coming together the way my family and I had hoped, the bombings hit Boston on Marathon Monday.

I felt overwhelmed by a feeling that I needed to do something bigger than earning a paycheck. And there was a larger question I couldn't escape: Why are you doing the work you're doing? I had an idea to help, and I couldn't ignore it. I couldn't convince myself that money was all I should be going after.

Around that time, I was training for my first half marathon. Races nationwide were canceled for security reasons. But people across the country wanted to help; in every community, folks were organizing runs in honor of the bombing victims. That got me thinking: "Can there be a way to channel this energy toward actually helping?" It gave me the idea for my project, Charity Footprints, a user-friendly online platform that enables individuals to run, walk, bike—any sort of physical activity—to raise money for a cause they care about.

My family back in Kashmir had endured my whole journey: leaving everything to move to the United States, putting myself through college and then grad school, struggling to nail down a professional career for the better part of seven years before receiving a ticket into something stable. But the day I finally secured that dream job offer—a full-time position in the financial sector, a situation our whole family had fantasized about for me—was the same day I decided I would jump.

I dreaded telling my family.

It was not easy to explain why I was turning away from that kind of financial security, especially with so many uncertainties ahead. It was tricky to figure out the financials for the organization, and I worried, "If this doesn't work, what happens next?" I talked to another small-business owner, who pushed me to make a plan B. If I wasn't able to return to my industry, where would I go then? More to the point, what about my timing? I had a wife and a newborn. Was this the time to jump?

I set forth to figure this out. On a tactical level, I reached out to potential customers to gauge interest and get feedback. I needed to determine if this project was actually viable. The feedback was positive and justified moving forward. More important to me, however, was to build emotional conviction. I did that by reaching out to all types of people who had made various jumps as well as to those who wanted to make a jump but had never attempted one.

Some of the people who had jumped were successful, and some were

not, but regardless of outcome, every single person was incredibly passionate about what they had done. They were laser focused: this is why
this happened, this is why that happened, this is why I'm doing this, and
this is why I'm doing that. All of these folks, successful or not, felt a clear
purpose and mission behind their decision. There was a conviction I could
see. These conversations gave me a transparent picture of what my path
looked like in both the short and long term, in both the good and the
bad. None of the stories were specific to my personal circumstances, yet
they prepared me precisely for what I would be getting into.

While that was all very helpful, I found it even more impactful to talk
to those who had an idea for a jump but had never made one. Each person had a concept, perhaps even had started working toward it, but for
whatever reason—time, money, personal situation—had decided against
jumping for it. In nearly all of these conversations, it was evident that
each person now resented the inaction. The reasons differed, but the sentiment was the same: uniform regret.

And that is what pushed me over the edge. Coming out of all the
conversations, I had been given some feedback that my idea had potential, and I had received some interesting advice from those who had
jumped, but more than anything, I realized that I really didn't want to
find myself in that last group of almost-jumpers. I didn't want to end up
in a situation where I would be telling someone, "Hey, maybe this would
have worked, maybe it wouldn't have, but I never tried." That seemed like
a much worse outcome than to have said, "Hey, I gave it my best shot,
and here's what happened."

So I went ahead and made my jump, when I was thirty-one, married,
and with a six-month-old. There's never a perfect time to jump, but while
this was far from ideal, it wasn't going to prevent my movement forward. I first had the idea for my jump a year and a half earlier and was
preparing to go for it then when my wife learned she was pregnant. Suddenly, the equation shifted, and the timing didn't make sense: a baby on
the way, a family to support. I didn't want to jump irrationally. So I
started working on the product on weekends and at night, developing a
small prototype that I could fine-tune and test out for months going forward. Later, after our child was born, and as he neared his first birthday,

the timing was right. Or maybe not right but doable. It wouldn't be perfect, but it was good enough to try.

In making a jump, a lot of people think about the what and not so much about the why. I think knowing *why* you are making a jump is more important than *what* exactly you're doing in your jump—because that will all change. There are very few cases where the flight of a jump goes smoothly. Most of the time, the path is like a choppy wave: up and down, up and down. Having a very clear conviction for *why* you are jumping is what will help you rebound from the downs and back toward the ups as you move through your journey.

Along the way, get feedback. And as you go, it's actually okay to look back. It's part of being human. But only look back through a lens of understanding, using the feedback to improve for the next day. As I try to push forward in my jump, I look back and say, "Let me understand what is working, and what is not." The life of a jump is not measured at the start, on day 1, or at the end, on day 1,027. It is measured by how you improve through every day in between.

I still think back to my conversation with my friend about making a plan B. To be entirely honest, in the back of my mind I still think about a plan B, C, and D because I don't know where my venture will end up. If things are successful, everything looks good in hindsight. But there's always that little bit of doubt that it won't be, and that doubt can be okay, maybe even a good thing, because it pushes me to try even harder. If this venture doesn't work, then I can say I tried. You might fail a hundred times, but that doesn't define you; what defines you is whether or not you get back up.

RAHUL RAZDAN, a former financial services professional, is the founder of Charity Footprints, a technology company that combines personal fitness and charitable giving.

Make a Plan

Section Takeaways

Wade in

- "There's an external perception that making a jump means going off a diving board into the deep end. But . . . a good jump is much more like walking from the shallow end of a pool, starting with getting the tip of your toe wet in the first step, and then the next step and the next step." (Adam Braun)

- "From the beginning, my jumps were measured. It was a series of little, practical decisions." (Barbara Harris)

- "I moved slowly. For me, jumping was a de-risking process. It sounds so bland, but it is incredibly hard to go from a stable job to 'I'm going to go and start my own company.'" (Eric Wu)

- "I had written down a series of steps. . . . I constantly revisited these notes. They gave structure to processes and milestones so that when it actually came down to it, I knew what was coming." (Adrian Cárdenas)

- "Don't be in a rush to take the next step. Slow your steps. Internalize and reflect on what your gut is saying." (Akansha Agrawal)

Save dollars to make sense: start your financial planning

- "Think about a way you can maintain your lifestyle in case the jump is not successful." (Barbara Harris)

- "I was planning a jump from something lucrative to something not at all lucrative, especially at the start. So I opened a bank account and put away a portion of every paycheck to set up a nest egg that could make my jump possible. I asked ex-pros and travel gurus for advice about and models for how to come up with a realistic budget." (Mike Lewis)

- "I did my homework within the company: I'd have to ask for a leave of absence and wouldn't have an income for four months. But if they could accommodate my request for a leave, I'd have the security of coming back. I would have to make a plan and save money over that nine-month anticipation period so that I could get through four months without income." (Alexandra Stein)

Put in the time: get some pre-jump practice

- "Making a jump is like riding a bike: you don't learn how to ride a bike solely by reading about bikes. . . . Get out and try some laps around the street." (Eric Wu)

- "I started to sketch out ideas . . . for a position where I could work more on the things that I liked in my current job but not to have to grapple with all the things that I didn't." (Paige Johnson)

- "While working in your current role, find a small side project to explore what another kind of work is like." (Akansha Agrawal)

- "I started working on the product on weekends and at night, developing a small prototype that I could fine-tune and test out for months going forward." (Rahul Razdan)

- "I put together my MVP (my minimum viable product) in a way that wasn't so intimidating. . . . I didn't put a name to it. I didn't say, 'This is my company.' I just said, 'I'm doing it as a small project.'" (Maia Josebachvili)

Keep your options open: sew a safety net

- "I talked to another small-business owner, who pushed me to make a plan B." (Rahul Razdan)

- "I had built a safety net by being in my old role for a year. . . . People who build a safety net will have the skills to get another job." (Paige Johnson)

- "There's a misconception that taking a jump forever destroys your chances of returning to the work you've been doing or to the individuals you've been working with. Sometimes, that's true. . . . But for many other jumps, there will exist an opportunity to jump back, so long as you have shown ability in doing your job well and have built meaningful relationships with the people you worked with along the way." (Mike Lewis)

- "I wasn't starting from scratch. . . . It was more of a staged, planned transition than it was an impulsive leap. That was critical. I think it's the best way to make one of these types of jumps—create a plan, make some sort of safety net, get halfway started on the idea, and then go." (Brian Spaly)

Get feedback

- "Seek out the people who have done what you want to do. Study and understand what they do." (Akansha Agrawal)

- "I needed feedback from experts, but I didn't know anyone. So I sketched all my ideas in a notebook and brainstormed with friends of friends and with former coworkers, with anyone who knew anyone who might be able to help." (Debbie Sterling)

- "I'm not the most vocal person. I can be pretty shy. But . . . when people offered to make introductions, I pushed myself to take them up on the offers." (Akansha Agrawal)

- "Get feedback. And as you go, it's actually okay to look back . . . using the feedback to improve for the next day." (Rahul Razdan)

- "Mine your personal network for anyone who may know somebody who knows anything on the subject. Then go meet that person, and after you've talked together, ask, 'Do you know anyone else that might be able to help me?'" (Debbie Sterling)

- "Corral [others who know you] into your jump because they can serve as your sounding board when you are feeling hesitant or pessimistic, or when you are wading through that unknown territory right before you jump." (Alexandra Stein)

- "He spent a full hour telling me . . . how it was impossible to do what I was talking about. I nodded and took it in. While it was dispiriting, honestly my initial reaction was how helpful it was: the feedback was right on. And in the back of my head, I thought, 'This is helpful, and I'm not going to let this guy stop me.'" (Debbie Sterling)

Commit to what you believe in

- "I doubted myself, but I never doubted the organization. I think it's really important to not doubt the idea of what you are doing. . . . Aside from just raw emotions, I was driven by a fundamental sense of purpose." (Adam Braun)

- "Overall, my journey was not easy. It was not smooth. But I had a calling." (Barbara Harris)

- "I liked the company, I believed in its culture, and I knew that I would learn a lot and, from there, find out more about myself and my passion." (Akansha Agrawal)

- "In making a jump, a lot of people think about the what and not so much about the why. I think knowing *why* you are making a jump is more important than *what* exactly you're doing in your jump— because that will all change. There are very few cases where the flight of a jump goes smoothly. . . . Having a very clear conviction for *why* you are jumping is what will help you rebound from the downs and back toward the ups as you move through your journey." (Rahul Razdan)

- "If you believe in what you want to jump to, then I encourage you to make that leap of faith and not to be timid." (Barbara Harris)

- "I was obsessed with my idea. I felt like it was a calling, a life calling. I think you have to be that passionate about whatever it is you go and do because the path is hard." (Debbie Sterling)

- "Rather than jump to a thing, jump toward a feeling that you get when you're working." (Paige Johnson)

Go ahead and feel the fear

- "When you do decide to jump, the hardest thing is accepting the upcoming uncertainty—the possibility of failure. That's when those traditional, lucrative career paths seem so good: they help you avoid facing this type of failure. . . . The sooner you can say, 'Okay, I'll live with it, but I'm going to try anyway,' the better." (Brian Spaly)

- "Even the most courageous jumpers faced the same doubt and the same fear that we all do. You cannot escape those thoughts. There's no way, at any point in your life, to wait for that fear to subside before you make a jump because that fear will never go away. You just have to say, 'I feel fear. And of course I'm going to keep working,' and accept that these are simply thoughts that you have; they are not who you are." (Eric Wu)

- "You might fail a hundred times, but that doesn't define you; what defines you is whether or not you get back up." (Rahul Razdan)

- "I still struggle with failure and rejection. But with failure, you learn so much faster than if you didn't fail—if you didn't have opportunities where you have to question yourself. . . . Failure really helps you understand who you are." (Akansha Agrawal)

- "There's self-doubt that comes with leaving something comfortable. You're doing something out of the ordinary." (Adrian Cárdenas)

- "I remember thinking, 'I don't think I'm ready for this jump. I don't feel it's the right time.' But then it hit me: no time is the 'right time' to jump." (Akansha Agrawal)

- "What surprised me most was that I was as happy as I dreamed I would be. I was anxious and nervous, but I wasn't fearful. I was ready." (Adrian Cárdenas)

- "To me, jumping means believing. Sure, I'm going to feel hopeless at times, but this fear will enter my consciousness, and I just have to acknowledge it, then put it aside. I have to believe that the only way to power through is just to hear the fear, then let it go and keep working." (Eric Wu)

Relax, it's not that serious

- "If you've planned it out along the way, you'll have created a situation where the actual jump isn't as risky, and the stakes aren't as high if it doesn't work out." (Brian Spaly)

- "I still lost sleep over my finances and feared life without a regular paycheck. An older squash friend didn't seem too concerned. 'Careers are long,' she told me." (Mike Lewis)

- "If it ultimately doesn't work out as you had planned . . . you will be able to live with that mistake, given the preparation that led up to that decision. If you do plan, then the jump itself is just not that serious." (Adrian Cárdenas)

- "If you're passionate about whatever you are going to go do, and you love the process, even if it's not successful, it won't matter because you'll be fulfilled by getting to do what you love." (Brian Spaly)

- "Telling my boss turned out to be very easy. He understood and fully supported me. Sometimes I think you build stuff up in your head to be this huge deal, but it's not. Maybe you have an uncomfortable conversation, and it's awkward for a day, but it's way worse to sit worrying about all the ways it could go." (Debbie Sterling)

LET YOURSELF BE LUCKY

"Put yourself in a position to get lucky."

—Ethan Eyler

I CONTINUED TO slide across the circular restaurant booth until all five of us, high school buddies, had squeezed in, side by side, at our favorite neighborhood Mexican spot. It had been more than two years since we'd been together. I was two years into my job at Bain, home for Thanksgiving, and sitting with the same faces around the same worn wooden table that had defined my Friday lunch routine as a high school senior. On my plate was my regular half-steak, half-chicken burrito with guac; on my mind was the growing conviction that moving to New Zealand and Australia to begin a full-time professional squash pursuit was possible. The four others in the booth hadn't left California for college or for work, and while I already felt unusual for venturing east to college and then staying east for a job afterward, at least I'd been able to explain those choices in a few words: got into a good school, got a good job. I felt that the idea of describing my next move, even to my closest childhood friends, would be difficult to do and to defend. As the conversation turned to life updates, I debated what to share. Alex was working at a gym, the other Alex was starting a company, and Greg was coaching high school lacrosse. What was Mike doing? *Thinking of moving to Australia.* I fumbled with a stack of chip plates as eyes shifted toward me, waiting for my update. I crunched up the remaining burrito foil wrappings before tossing out the shortest blurb I could muster: *still at Bain, enjoying Bain . . . and, at some point, want to travel more.* For my own sanity,

I had to let out something that related to what I really wanted to do, but I cut myself off from introducing much more.

Next to me, Adam, who offered the fifth and final update of our group, began with, "I just joined a new company, and they may send me to Sydney."

As the conversation moved on, I stared at Adam in disbelief. First, jealousy: *Why does he get to move to Sydney?* Then, hope: *If he can move to Sydney, I can move to Sydney.* The group chatter continued while I waited for a free moment to grab Adam. Minutes later, the crew shuffled out of the booth, emptied trays, and pushed out through the single door of the shop, five childhood buddies beginning to break off into the darkness. I hung back and pulled up next to Adam, trying to keep my voice casual as we trailed behind the others, heading toward the parking lot. "Hey." I did my best not to show my excitement at the scenario forming in my head, an idea that seemed at once both improbable and inevitable.

"You know, if you end up moving to Sydney," I said, "well, I was thinking of playing the pro squash tour at some point, and it stops in Australia!"

I'm pretty sure Adam had never heard of a pro squash tour. But he said, "Yeah, dude! If I get moved down there, and you go play your tour, let's live together."

And I felt a pure sense of joy.

My brief chat with Adam was one of those aimless, otherwise forgettable conversations you have with an old friend, a little dream hatched up on a Friday night. But for some reason, it felt different. I slapped Adam on the back as we caught up with the rest of our group.

Once you know what you want, once you've started to plan, you're just steps away from running into some luck. You might not collect on that luck until you actually jump; but once you've started to plan, favorable coincidences begin to appear. Leaving the restaurant that night, neither Adam nor I imagined that a couple of years later on the other side of the Pacific Ocean, we'd meet outside Adam's corporate apartment overlooking Bondi Beach in Sydney and then live together during my three trips there, trading ideas and back-of-the-napkin brainstorms that ultimately helped me form the framework to this book. But it all came from jumping and letting myself be lucky.

*   *   *

Ironically, I reached a point in my jump preparations where the planning process had become a comfortable, safe set of motions. From the budgeting spreadsheets to the morning gym workouts to the weekend competitions, the new tactics I was using to help break up my old life routine had quietly meshed to form a new routine. The act of preparing to change your life can turn into one of the world's most seductive procrastination tools. Talking about travel and adventure makes for great cocktail conversation and, dangerously, can go on forever. It was at this point in my jump—the end-of-the-diving-board point in the process— where I struggled most. I wanted to jump. I was going to jump. But *when*?

I'd begun to tell others that jumping was a matter of time. Which, technically, was true. I just didn't know how much more time. Complicating my decision was that, as if on cue, my job turned slightly more engaging; I got a promotion, a cross-country assignment, a new group of coworkers. In moments of doubt, each of these new aspects of my Bain life made it easy to justify staying a little longer. There was never going to be a "best" time to leave.

Two critical forces pushed me forward. On the corporate job front, leaving aside the new title, the new geography, and the new team members, I had to admit to myself that I had tackled the core work. My learning curve at Bain had steadied. I had formed real friendships, received references, and built a reputation. That was my baseline, and I had hit it, and someday I might find my way back to venture capital investing and spring forward from there. Yes, there was more to learn, but there was always going to be more to learn. And I was at a suitable stopping—or, at least, pausing—place.

The second force pushing me forward was this: in my jump preparations, the stage was set. I had hit my savings account requirements, used the part-time tour matches to climb the first hundred spots in the world rankings, and was sitting just outside the top 300. I was in shape and injury-free, only a bag to pack and a flight to book away from actually jumping. Six months later, a tournament circuit would open across New Zealand, ideal for guys like me clawing their way off the ranking floor. In shape and even sponsored, I knew, deep down, there wouldn't be a better time to get out on tour.

That all made sense, but it did not remove the fear factor. For many jumpers, making the big leap—facing so much future uncertainty, placing a big "TBD" around your finances, career, and lifestyle—is almost too terrifying. We tend to react in one of three ways:

- by planning more to try and fully solve all uncertainties,
- by pushing back the jump date, or
- by deciding not to jump after all—concluding that the job we have and the life that it provides simply aren't worth jeopardizing.

Pick your poison, each of these three reactions prevents a jump.

I dabbled in all three responses before ultimately zeroing in on the second: delay. I casually floated the idea to my mom that maybe, just maybe, it could work out nicely to jump *after* the summer season. My mother is a mother—watching her sixth and youngest child prepare to take off on a one-way ticket wasn't exactly the experience she had thought raising me would offer her. But to her credit, she, who has never been one to sugarcoat anything, kept me honest. She said "Mike, delaying your decision to jump by three months isn't going to solve anything. If you're going to go, go!" She was right.

Still, that final step is where most people turn back, and it's where I wanted to turn back too. Even the best jump planners will only know a little bit about what's about to happen. It is human to crave knowns, and by definition, the act of getting up and taking a jump will rob you of those. You have to jump and believe that some good luck will come to you.

This sounds crazy—and as I mentioned, it sort of is—but if you've done things right until this point in the curve, your jump won't be blind. It won't be stupid. The writer Michael Lewis (whose story is featured in this section) is the person who first told me that this phenomenon was "letting yourself be lucky." And I love that phrase. If you've planned as well as you could, if you've softened the landing in case you fall instead of fly (through financial planning, pre-jump practicing, safety-net sewing), and if you've set up connections with good people and opportunities to head toward when you take that first full step, then it is quite possibly time to go. With the backdrop you've created, your jump is hedged, and with the pieces you've put together, your jump is ripe to find some luck.

But is this luck?

Isn't luck when you win the lottery or find a five-dollar bill: random, complete instances of chance? You, after all, have planned your jump, have carved away some of that randomness. In making those preparations, you've actually set the stage to bump into things (I call these "collisions"). Once you've done all the planning you can, you're ready to let yourself get lucky.

I looked at the tour calendar: three tournaments in a row across New Zealand, bringing together players just like me from a dozen other countries, in a nation with numerous players and host families willing to offer up a couch. I figured if I could get to New Zealand for that first month, I'd collide with some helpful hosts and supportive players.

No amount of PowerPoint slides or spreadsheets, expert interviews or time spent crossing my fingers could further predict what would happen after the first New Zealand tournament. There's a leap of faith component to this. After all, it wouldn't be a jump if you were moving along solid ground. It'd be a walk or a run or something.

The time had come for me to make my move. I bought my ticket to New Zealand.

I decided to believe that I would get lucky from there.

MICHAEL LEWIS

Finance Professional to Bestselling Author

I TELL MY seven-year-old all the time: "Allow yourself to be lucky." When I was his age, I used to think, "I'm so lucky that if I just look around, I can find money on the ground." And I often did. Because grown-ups drop it everywhere. It's in seats, on the sidewalk, everywhere. It's amazing what you can find if you're looking for it. Sometimes I'll tell my son, "Let's just go find valuable stuff." And you wouldn't believe what we find. All you have to do is keep yourself in a frame of mind to be open to what's dealt to you.

To back up a bit, I grew up in New Orleans. There was not much of an orientation toward careers, certainly not for kids, and I didn't start thinking about college until I was in my junior year of high school. At that time, my ambitions amounted to getting up every morning, going to school, playing baseball, and when I graduated, going to Princeton. Nothing beyond that. I thought that once I got in I was done, that I didn't have to do anything else, so I didn't think much about what happened after.

I majored in art history because I liked it. There weren't really career tracks at Princeton. I mean, if you wanted to be an engineer, you majored in engineering. And there was premed, of course. Neither of those interested me. So the only implicit career choice I made was not following all the people who majored in economics because it could possibly get you a job on Wall Street.

Junior year, I started getting involved in my thesis composition. Princeton's senior thesis is a really big deal. Your whole senior year is basically organized around it, and it's a book. I think mine was forty thousand, maybe fifty thousand words. It was 130 pages, and it took forever. But the writing of it was what changed everything for me. I loved it. It transported me. I thought, "This is what I want to do."

At first, I thought that meant I wanted to be an art historian. But my thesis advisor told me that was crazy. There wouldn't be any jobs. Told me flat out that I just shouldn't do it. So it took me a little while, but I realized that what I wanted to do was write books. Actually, to be specific: I wanted to write senior theses.

But I didn't dive into writing full-time. I remember thinking that too many writers don't ever do anything else, so I should go have lots of adventures that would give me material. My first adventure was in finance, starting with a pass/fail class my senior year in the econ department that interested me enough to get a master's in economics. While getting my master's, I was at a dinner party sitting next to these women whose husbands ran Salomon Brothers International. I got along quite well with one of the women, and she made her husband hire me after the dinner. It was just about the best possible place to land on Wall Street at that moment. They were extremely successful, and I would have been crazy not to do it.

By the time I started at Salomon Brothers, I had begun writing and submitting unsolicited magazine articles on the side. They were rejected a lot. Eventually, I got a foot in the door at a few places, and they started publishing my work while I was still on Wall Street. Even though I was doing pretty well at Salomon Brothers, I knew that writing was what I wanted to do full-time and that getting published was my first step toward leaving.

I remember when I told my dad that I wanted to quit. I had just gotten my bonus, and it was big. I think it was something like $160,000. My salary was around $60,000 at the time, and I was twenty-seven. My dad thought I was crazy to walk away from that kind of money. He said, "Stay ten years and you won't have to work any longer. Then you can write your novels till you die." But when I looked around at the guys who were ten years older than me, I saw that none of them could leave. If I'd stayed, I would have been trapped by that success; the money would have gotten too big, and my life would've changed.

I also didn't have any kids then. Once you have children, it changes everything. It's not just your own life you're affecting. It's a family's life. I was really lucky in that regard. I didn't have any student debt, and I didn't have any other financial responsibilities, like taking care of sick parents or anything like that. So I didn't have to let money rule my decisions. Some people don't have that liberty. Quitting that job felt like going out on a tightrope, but with a really nice safety net underneath it.

The people at Salomon Brothers were actually charmingly indulgent of my literary ambitions, letting me write about Wall Street as long as I did it under a pseudonym. I used my mother's maiden name, and it was those pieces that got me my book contract. When I told my colleagues that I was quitting, they thought I was nuts. They were very sweet about it. They were concerned. They took me into a room and said, "You're sure you wanna do this? This is a mistake." I knew what I wanted to do and just thought to myself, "None of these people are qualified to tell me what to do with my life."

They thought I had a big future there because I had done well the first couple of years. But I knew a lot of my success was somewhat fluke-ish and that it would dry up the moment I was exposed as someone who was basically not interested. It's very hard to keep up with anything you're not really interested in. It was interesting for a little while, and then it got boring. Once it did, I seized the first opportunity to leap out of it.

Looking back, it seems like a giant risk to quit a job that paid me all kinds of money at Salomon for a fairly unknown future as a writer. But I knew I really wanted to do it. There wasn't a shred of doubt, and I was getting so sick of going to work there every morning. So it was not a terribly hard decision, and it didn't *feel* like that much of a risk.

When I left, I had scraped together enough writing to get a book contract, which meant that someone was publishing a book I'd written. I thought, "Hell, if someone publishes a book by me, I can make my way as a writer." I was twenty-seven when I quit my job and almost twenty-nine when the book came out. During that period, I did not feel like,

"Oh, my God, if I don't make it here, if this doesn't succeed, I'm screwed." It was more like, "I'm doing exactly what I want to do, and I'll just figure out a way to make it work." I knew that as long as I allowed myself to be lucky, I would find some money on the ground.

MICHAEL LEWIS, a former finance professional, is the *New York Times* bestselling author of more than a dozen books including *Liar's Poker*, *Moneyball*, *The Big Short*, and *The Undoing Project*.

JUAN ROMERO

Curator of National Marine Aquarium and BBC
Field Producer to Sailing Explorer

A FEW YEARS ago, I was the director of Husbandry and Engineering at the National Marine Aquarium of the United Kingdom. It took a few jumps to get there and an even bigger one to get out.

I was born to Spanish immigrants in Caracas, Venezuela. We lived alongside untouched forest and mountains. Growing up, I'd take my backpack and get lost in that wilderness, dreaming up great expeditions and reading my dad's books about worldly adventures. As a kid, I never really knew exactly what I wanted to do; I just wanted to be outside.

And then I discovered the Cousteau films. Jacques Cousteau was a famous French oceanographer, explorer, and filmmaker. A legend. He and a bunch of crazy guys in a boat and a helicopter, going around the world, making films. I got hooked on adventures of sailboats and the open ocean. I thought, "This is the lifestyle I want."

After high school, my grandmother gave me a plane ticket and some money to hitchhike Europe for a year. My parents figured this trip could afford me one special life experience before returning home to Venezuela. At the end of my trip, I headed for the Oceanographic Museum of Monaco—everything related to Cousteau took place there at the time.

I was just about out of cash after the train ride. I slept in the station and later at a bus stop outside of the museum until it opened. When it did, I wasn't allowed in: entry was twenty francs a ticket. I had only ten. As I turned to leave, I saw a woman across the road trying to fix her car, and in my broken English, I offered to help. I got it going, said so long, and turned to walk away when she pulled out ten francs. I tried to decline, but she insisted I take it. So I turned right around with my twenty francs and used it to get into the museum.

I was the last one out of the museum that night, and when I left, I said to myself, "One day I'm going to come back and work here."

And that's what I did. In college, I studied the obscure subject of aquaculture because it let me be outside, and after graduation, the museum in Monaco just so happened to be in search of an aquaculturist. I didn't think I'd ever be considered, so I didn't submit an application, but my friends sent in an application for me. A few months later, I was back at the museum: twenty-four years old, ripped jeans and long hair, working for my idol, Jacques Cousteau.

That should have been it. In the years that followed, I would report to my hero, develop skills in filmmaking and aquarium management, and ascend to what I thought was exactly what I wanted: director of Husbandry and Operations at the Genova Aquarium in Italy, the largest aquarium in the world, and host of my own Italian television program; then director of Husbandry and Operations for the National Marine Aquarium of the United Kingdom while serving as a field producer for the BBC's *Blue Planet* and *Planet Earth*. I was living what should have been my dream.

But what if your dreams change? Or rather, what if you have lots of them?

I knew all along that my passion for the outdoors came from my fantasy of someday setting sail on the open water—inspired by those first Cousteau films I watched as a kid. Now I was behind the camera, not in front of it, filming staged adventures and finding reasons not to take one myself. Things had settled down: I was married with three kids, living in the suburbs with everything looking fine on paper. I tried telling myself that the time had passed for my other jumps, my other dreams.

Our family spent the next eight years in England. I pretended to ignore my sailboat idea, but it lingered: at the end of conversations at the dinner table, in the car, in the bedroom with my wife, Diane, before bed.

Diane and I watched life slowly become more and more a routine, our world drifting into a comfortable cocoon. And when things became so predictable—when every day started to look exactly like the one before it—that's when we knew it was time.

We didn't want to be fifty, sixty, seventy years old, getting older with gray hair, going to the same supermarket every week, saying hello to the same people every week, parking in the same parking spot every week. Life has much more to offer than that. We should be able to go to a different supermarket, talk to different people, and we should show the kids that the world is theirs to explore. We decided that we would.

I put together notes on the details: boats and itineraries, schooling and safety. In six months, we sold the house, moved everything out, and began searching for a boat. In six months, we changed our lives from being a steady forty-year-old couple with three kids and great jobs in the United Kingdom to having nothing more than savings in the bank, living with Diane's aunt in Florida, looking for a boat.

People ask, "How can you do it?" Everyone can do it. Truly. We knew what we wanted, made a plan, sold everything we had, and went as far and for as long as money would take us. There's a trap of trying to plan it all out—and if you do, you'll never leave. We have friends that will spend their lives dreaming of sailing around the world, studying the routes, researching the gear, but will never leave. People who spend years rigging their boats in the marina, thinking they're leaving next year but never do because they listen to the wrong little man in their head who's saying, "Don't do it. Don't do it. What happens if? What happens if? If you don't get a job when you come back? If you get sick along the way?" At some point, you just need to jump.

I did my research so I could shut up that wrong little man. It was not easy. I spent a long time looking for the right boat, places to go, what to do, how to do it with kids. I put all the possibilities on the table: "Okay, what if we don't like it? What if somebody gets sick? How much money do we have for how long? What is the budget?" Diane worked wonders getting homeschooling set up for the kids.

Nothing about this was spontaneous. We spent almost a year planning, and then we gave ourselves a place and date. We would start in Florida, where the waters were friendly and warm, and we'd leave one day in mid-January. That's the date we were to set off with the boat, and if the boat wasn't ready then, we would finish working on it as we went. If we didn't stick to this rule, if we kept trying to plan a bit more and a bit more, we'd still be stuck in the harbor with everyone else.

On the fifteenth of January 2006, my wife, three kids, and I set sail around the world.

Our family of five hopscotched across islands and around archipelagos, crossed the Pacific again and again, floated and wandered and bumped into the world in every area of sea and every sight of land and person along the way.

Three years later, we docked.

We were nearing New Zealand and running out of money. It was time for me to start looking for work, but things weren't that easy. Passing by the island of Tonga, the boat got caught in a cyclone, and that destroyed the sails. By the time we reached Auckland, I badly needed a job.

My biggest fear was, "What the heck am I gonna do? People will forget who I am."

But when I returned to land, I wasn't forgotten in my field; in fact, it was the opposite: I was the guy my peers wanted to meet, the guy who left with his family to chase their dream by sailboat. I'd be at a conference in China, and my colleagues would say, "You're back! How was the trip?"

People love to live through other lives, so my coming in with this story to tell starts a conversation, which in turn leads to an interview. I knew I didn't have to be brilliant, but if I was smart enough and could carry a good conversation, I would end up in a good place. And that's what happened.

I helped my case by staying in the game. While I was gone, I made a point to stay in touch with old coworkers and friends from my industry so that when my jump was over, I'd be ready to reenter. It was an important lesson: never stop moving. Through these conversations, I had expanded my reach of potential employers around the world, including in far-off places like New Zealand. That came in big.

I don't think people have good luck or bad luck. The luck is there. You just have to jump to experience it. It's a wonderful world on the other side of jumping, and that is true for taking a boat on the open water but is also true for any smaller pursuits too. For some people, the biggest decision in their life is to change their job, car, or move from their home.

It's easy to think only about the negative consequences when making any of these types of changes. It's our nature, and it would be irresponsible not to. But also try to think about the positive consequences that come from jumping: the experience gained, the fulfillment enjoyed.

It's not all been fun and easy by any means. I've made it near the top and dropped back down to the very bottom, started and restarted back at zero more than a few times. But I grew up with many dreams, and I will continue to make jumps so that I can chase them all. It's been a winding journey, but no good sail stays in a straight line.

JUAN ROMERO, the former curator of the National Marine Aquarium and a field producer for the BBC's *Blue Planet* and *Planet Earth*, is an open-sea sailing explorer and consultant to international aquariums.

ETHAN EYLER

Video Game Marketer to Inventor of the Lyft Carstache

TO ME, PUTTING a mustache on a car just made sense. In fact, it was a no-brainer.

I grew up in the suburbs along the Northern California coast with ideas of doing artsy things. In college, I got into creative writing and film and became fascinated with sociology and pop culture. Leaving school, I went into Media Buying for Sony Music, then for a couple of different online entertainment start-ups. In my late twenties, I headed to San Francisco to work for Tencent, one of the biggest Internet companies in China, helping them make video games for the US market.

All this sounds great: when you tell somebody that you design games, it sounds like one of the most creative things you could do. But the reality is that creativity in this part of the business was about toggling the color of the digital cow between green and blue, and then A/B testing the cow colors across audiences to see which age groups spend more money if the cow is blue versus green.

We call these games "social," but they are actually pretty soul sucking: their intention is to trick people into spending money on virtual flowers, virtual coins. Yet when you tell people you work in gaming, the response is, "Wow. How lucky: you get to go play games every day and make up games."

The company was exploding. I was twenty-eight and getting paid well, accruing stock in the company, which would be valuable if I just stuck around. But I couldn't. I needed to escape. My job felt more and more cyclical, repetitive, and almost manipulative. I wandered into a bookstore and picked up a book called *Escape from Cubicle Nation*. The author talked about how if you're truly unhappy for six months or a year in whatever it is you're doing, then you need to just try something else. I believed it then, and to this day I tell others, "If you're that unhappy, try something else." Seems simple, but at the time, it was a scary idea.

I comforted myself by saying that if I jumped and things didn't work out, I could find a way back to what I was doing before. The book's author, Pamela Slim, describes her "van down by the river moment," where her worst fear would be ending up taking a chance and failing, and then ending up living in a van down by the river. That type of scenario is just not going to happen because of a well-planned jump. We have a way of trying to scare ourselves out of a jump with exaggerations, and you shouldn't let that happen.

Even though I wasn't happy in my work, it took up a lot of my time. The idea of starting a full-time business on the side wasn't an option at that point. So I used my spare time to test out creative projects and fun brainstorming on the side. And it was during one of these exercises that I thought to put a mustache on a car.

I was creatively starved, sitting in my car one morning commuting down the US-101 freeway for work. Suddenly, it popped in my head: the front of cars kind of look like faces, and it'd be hilarious if these "faces" had mustaches. It was cracking me up: I kept looking at cars and thinking about each one having a mustache.

I figured somebody must have already done this. It seemed like a close relative to the famous Mr. Potato Head: no way this didn't already exist. I searched the Internet but couldn't find car mustaches. I was shocked. I said to myself in the car, "I'm going to cobble one of these things together and put it on my car, and see what happens."

Initially, I thought that I would use fake hair, and I'll never forget walking into a salon in the Mission district of San Francisco and buying twenty packs of extensions off the wall while the storekeeper's looking at me like, "What the hell is this guy doing?" I went home and tried to needlepoint all the fake hair together. It didn't work. So I settled on faux fur and brought it to my sister, an expert sewer. A few hours later, we had the first Carstache. It looked hilarious. I put it on my car, and the reaction was insane: people literally jumping out into traffic in front of my car, flagging me down, giving me a thumbs-up, asking where I got it, taking pictures. It was just nuts, as if I was the instant celebrity of the city. The feeling was electric.

Here I was, burned out in my day job and now onto something bizarre that people clearly liked. I thought, "Okay, I'm not positive I'm going to be able to make it into a huge business, but I'm going to try. I'm going to give it a whirl." So I talked to my wife just to let her know that I was considering leaving my job to make car mustaches.

My wife was supportive and knew I was unhappy in my job. It was a little more nerve-racking to tell my in-laws: I had married their daughter two years earlier, and I was now quitting my good job to become the basement mustache guy. My boss thought I had gone insane. But I had my mind made up. I quit and said to myself, "This is a pursuit that reflects my creativity and my personality, and I'm going to see this through, and see where it leads me." So I jumped.

My wife and I didn't have endless funds. It took me four or five months of making no money just to launch, but when it did, I seemed to luck out: we got a lot of social media attention (one of the Kardashians posted about the Carstache, suddenly my invention was trending on Twitter) and I gave a bunch of interviews. So looking at it from the outside, you would think—like my friends and family did—"Oh, Ethan has made the new pet rock, and he's going to make millions of dollars," but in reality, even though there was a bunch of press, I wasn't selling enough mustaches to make it a full-fledged business on its own. It was a tough scenario to be in—you're getting these congratulations, but at the same time you're not paying the bills.

I was camped out working in the basement. Every day, I'd sit down there with my dog and just try to hustle. I hadn't planned out a distribution strategy and struggled with sales. Lots of people agreed it was a funny photo, but who's the person that actually wants to put a mustache on their car? Should I license it for sports teams? What's the right market?

A year goes by, and I'm not making a ton of money. It was a tough position for my family. My wife had been supporting us, and I was bringing in a little bit of cash but nowhere near my last job. I'd need to invest more money if I were to grow the business, but that wouldn't be so easy.

In my head, there was a constant negotiation: "How much longer do we give this for it to really turn the corner? How much more money can we sink in from savings to keep this going?" I was betting my own money, cycling through tons of sales strategies—it all became emotionally draining. Imagine making a jump, and everything looks insanely good: "Oh my God. I'm going to sell so many of these." Then the dust settles, and I look at the sales figures and say, "Shit." And then, boom! Pessimism rains in: "If I'm getting all this press, and I can't sell a lot of these products now, how could I ever sell a lot of these products, since I can't possibly get any more press than I have now?"

At this point, it was time to move on. I had come to terms that the car mustache was never going to be an "Ethan gets rich" venture. So I came up with a way to keep it alive as a hobby while freeing myself up to get back to a steady paycheck. I streamlined the distribution and supply chain, licensed the brand, and put the whole thing on autopilot for the next few years.

And yet, my original decision to jump was worth it. It gave me what I call my "hustle MBA." I started a business from precisely the first step onward and conquered every facet involved with operating a company, without having to go to business school and pay a hundred grand to do it. Mentally, the jump gave me the confidence to keep jumping. It gave me the conviction in my abilities not only to be creative but to run a business. It reset my priorities for what I wanted to be doing with my life. Even though this first venture didn't go to the moon, I have always viewed my jump into Carstache as the right move.

Having jumped once, I jumped again, starting a new business in the mobile gaming industry. I was running that several years later when one afternoon I got a phone call.

It was from the founder of Lyft, a company that had bought some of my car mustaches years back when it was a carpooling service called Zimride. Now Lyft was launching a new feature, an on-demand ride-sharing app, and they wanted to put pink Carstaches on the front of every car. The first order was twenty-five Carstaches, and soon after, another fifty.

It was wild: dozens and dozens of these pink car mustaches, passing through the streets of San Francisco. You can ask anyone that lived here at the time—people started to say, "What is going on? Why are these mustaches everywhere?" It was surreal for me. I had never seen a lot of the Carstaches on the road, certainly not at this point. Now there was a mustache popping up around every corner, on every SUV, midsize, and compact.

Fifty Carstaches turned into a hundred turned into a thousand. We couldn't make them fast enough. When I came over to drop off more orders of mustaches, the whole office gave me a standing ovation. The Carstache had become tied to their company identity, their growth. Soon it became clear that Lyft needed my mustache—they reached a point where they couldn't launch a new Lyft driver until a Carstache was ready.

We negotiated a deal where I brought over the Carstache concept and joined the company full-time. Currently, I'm running the Ride Experience team for the company and have transitioned the Carstache into the Glowstache—the glowing mustache, and more recently the Amp, the new hardware device you see on all the Lyft cars today.

It's funny, I've talked to a lot of people about how sometimes you make a jump, and it doesn't immediately work out. And then later down the road, things click in some way, and people say, "Man, you got so lucky with that." But I firmly believe that you create your own luck and that you have to put yourself in a position to get lucky. I didn't know the Carstache would lead me to Lyft and a career I finally cared about, but I knew it was the best representation of my creativity, of my personality. For those reasons alone, jumping to pursue it made sense.

Make a jump, put an idea out into the world, and see what happens. Some things are an immediate hit, and some things aren't, but that's not to say that an idea is not going to have its time and is not going to come around in some way later. You just don't know. But if you don't take the jump, and you don't put those things out in the world and put yourself in the position to get lucky, you don't stand a chance.

If you've thought about something long enough, and you believe in it, you should try it for a variety of reasons. Even if it fails, it's not like the world's going to come crashing down around you. You're not going to end up in a van down by the river. You will learn from following through. I had a crazy idea about a mustache on a car, but there are lots of crazy ideas out there. The learning came from the follow-through.

Start small: make one of whatever you're doing. It doesn't have to be like the real thing, just a prototype, a sample, something you can test out. People will tell you to make a business plan. Don't make a business plan. Yes, you need to do a certain amount of diligence to see if people want what you're building. I didn't do enough of that with Carstache, and it came back to bite me a bit. But on the other hand, don't overanalyze. You've got to break off digestible little pieces of a jump, and take on each piece one at a time. You don't need to write the be-all and end-all business plan before you start your jump.

If you're sitting at a boring desk job and reading this, take some part of your jump that you can accomplish and just chip off that little piece. Make that first thing. It's easy to get yourself into paralysis, where you think, "Oh, I have to set up the perfect plan, and everything has to be perfect for me to jump," but I don't think that's realistic.

A mustache on a car made sense to me—something else will make sense to you. Go for it, stay for the ride, and see where it takes you.

ETHAN EYLER, a former video game marketer, is the inventor of the Lyft Carstache and director of Ride Experience for Lyft.

ABIGAIL OGILVY RYAN

Technology Operations Manager to Art Gallery Owner

MY GRANDMOTHER INTRODUCED me to the wonders of art when I was a little girl growing up outside of Washington, DC. She painted still lifes and landscapes, and her work was in every room of the house. My grandmother had nine kids, and I was always impressed that she was able to follow her passion while raising a massive family—and doing it very successfully. At the time, her life didn't inspire me to be an artist; it just showed me that it was possible to find ways to do what you love.

In college, I struggled with picking my major. I started off taking one of every type of class because I had no idea of what I wanted to do. I wasn't someone who came into college and said, "I want to do premed," or "I'm all set to study econ." Ultimately, I kept going back to art history classes because I adored them. But I kept worrying, what kind of career comes out of this major?

Junior year I worked part-time at a gallery while studying abroad in Italy. I was totally hooked, but coming back to the States, I didn't think I could go into the gallery world. I ended up in online retail marketing, not because I loved it—I didn't—but because the whole process was straightforward: go to the career fair and find a company hiring a lot of people for entry-level positions that seem like, and *are*, good jobs. It may not have been a passion, but it was security: I had a job after leaving school, and that was huge.

I started work a few weeks after graduation. I felt ready. I was really proud of myself for getting a job. It was a hard time to get jobs, I needed to support myself, and this would do it.

Pretty early on, I knew something would have to change. I was just so bored. It was a solid job, and I learned a lot. But I wasn't stimulated. I looked at the founders of the company and felt so much excitement for them: they were doing what made them so happy and successful. And here I was learning a lot and managing a team but feeling totally empty. On the way home from work, I'd ask myself, "Why am I doing this?"

So I left for a smaller start-up. I started working really long hours, and I figured that was good. I'm more or less addicted to the uphill battle of making my life as hard as possible. I thought working a lot would help make me happy. It didn't. I was in social media advertising, and, again, the content wasn't for me. The conversations in my head came back. I kept questioning everything: life is so short, and I'm young, and there's an opportunity to do something I care about. I knew what I cared about, and social media advertising wasn't it.

In a weird way, the start-up helped me jump. If I hadn't had the experience working from eight in the morning until two in the morning, I wouldn't have started down the path toward changing my life. It was pushing me way too hard. Losing personal relationships, working too much on something I didn't care about, having a job push me to such an extreme—I think that actually helped me to say, "Okay, I need to reset and figure out what I find meaningful."

That's when I started thinking about what my grandmother had taught me, of what I had found in Italy, what I had studied in school. I began talking to people about how to open an art gallery.

I talked to as many people in the art industry as possible. I cold-called and threw e-mails across alumni directories, yellow pages, art museums— anywhere. After each person I met, I told myself I needed to get to one more person. And I would get coffee with people. I would ask to get drinks. And you'd be surprised—most people are responsive and say sure. I'd listen to their experiences in art. Are they positive? Are they negative? Did they like being an artist? Did they like being a gallerist?

I ended up sitting down with a lot of the gallerists who failed. They were the most helpful. The conversations allowed me to figure out if this jump was right for me. Every day of the week, I found, and still find, a way to take someone in my industry out for coffee.

The biggest help came from two women in particular. Their trick was simple: they would only speak using "when" and not "if" about my jump. Months before I was even going to try for it, they weren't saying, "If it works out," or "Maybe it'll happen." They'd say, "So when you open your gallery, here's what you'll be doing; here's where you'll be located." Whatever it is you want to jump for, use "when," never "if."

Just as all this research started to come together, I reached a point at the technology company where I just couldn't keep going. When you're doing something that takes so much of your time that you don't enjoy, it's really hard to wake up in the morning and be motivated to do it, and do it well. I got to the point where it was hard to do it at all anymore. I was just going through the motions, and that is not a positive way to run your life. I had to change.

So I quit the start-up. As terrifying as it was, I quit that job with no next job lined up. But I had done my homework, set up countless coffee chats. Most importantly, I had started every thought, dream, and conversation by saying, "*When* I open my gallery . . .". I was going to make it work.

I needed a paycheck, so I walked down the street in my neighborhood, where my local hardware store was looking for a cashier. I was behind the counter a few days later when my landlord came in. He runs a few restaurants in the neighborhood and asked for help, so I ended up managing two of his Italian restaurants for the next year, while still taking shifts at the hardware store, all while working on opening my gallery. I would be financing most of the gallery myself, so cashiering and restaurant managing provided me the cash and with a fairly flexible shift schedule to inch closer toward the gallery opening.

Those days were long, and this part of the jump was not glamorous at all. People would see me behind the counter, or in the kitchen, and question my education, doubt my ambitions. But you know what? That's life. You just suck it up and push through it, and you learn that people will say things. Ultimately, it prepares you to be thick-skinned, and you need to have that when you jump. Crazy as it sounds, these jobs got me one step closer to opening the art gallery; the hardware store was my business school, the pizza joints my crash course on how to survive.

When I had saved up enough money, I pounded the pavement for gallery space. No realtor responded until finally, in January, one told me he could meet the following day. The day after that, I signed the first commercial lease available, pinning an opening date for July.

My timing was right for a jump. I wasn't married. I didn't have kids. There was nothing else distracting me, so I could put my whole heart into this. People joke that I should have a cot in the back office, and I probably should. Things are far from pretty: I'm doing this by myself, and at times it is very lonely and hard to shoulder all the responsibility. Sometimes guys will come in and ask about the paintings. I give the full pitch, hand them my card, and right when I think I'm on track for a sale, they call trying to pick me up. I wish they would call about work.

I still have doubts. I still ask myself all the time, am I going to make my rent this month? Most nights of the week, I'll wake up at 4 a.m., thinking about these things. I tell myself that if I can make it one more month, I can make it to the next month, and then I can make it to the next month after that. I know the first three years will be a struggle. But if I can make it through that, then I bet I'll be in the clear.

If I didn't do this now, I'd have to think about it until I did. And if I get married and have kids, many things could go on pause. So, again, this timing made sense. And that's why I think I'm going to be way ahead of the game in another twenty years when others are just starting, and I've been doing it for a couple of decades.

There's no science to this. Before you jump, just talk to people. Find meet-ups, industry events, anything that relates to people who can help your jump—and go to them alone. It's hard to go to something by yourself, but if you do, you're more likely to go up and talk to someone new than if you're there with a friend. I go by myself to art events in Boston and approach people and just say, "Hi." It can be really awkward, but they usually say, "Oh, you're running a gallery. You know what, I know an artist," or "You should talk to this person." Or, "My friend just closed her gallery; maybe you should talk to her about what happened."

Every morning, I walk through our doors and look around. Even on the worst days, I sit at my desk, in my own gallery, and I feel satisfied. My grandmother's name is on our wall—a reminder to continue to chase what I love.

ABIGAIL OGILVY RYAN, a former technology operations manager, restaurant manager, and hardware cashier, is the owner of Abigail Ogilvy Gallery.

OLAKUNLE OLADEHIN

Health Care Researcher to Nonprofit Executive Director

I'M THE YOUNGEST of four kids born to Nigerian parents who found a way to get Stateside years ago. As a kid in Nigeria, my dad couldn't afford to go to school, so he'd sit outside the classroom by the window until the teacher chased him away. He'd show back up the next day, and the next, until the school told my parents to find a way to send my dad to school so he could stop bothering everyone. They did, but they had money for only one school uniform. So he walked naked to class each day, holding the clothes in his hands to keep them clean.

Education, as you might guess, became everything to my family. My parents lived apart for ten years so they could get a footing in the United States, and when they did, each of my siblings seemed chosen to fulfill a certain destiny for our family. I would be the doctor. From middle school, my dad would ask, "What college do you want to go to?" And just to make him happy, I would say, "I want to go to Harvard." He wanted that respect for our family. Truthfully, I didn't know what I wanted, only that I wanted to make him proud and not let him down. When the time came, I applied to Harvard. I was accepted, and I went. I knew my dad wouldn't let me go anywhere else.

It was at my senior-year prom when I realized something rather embarrassing: I had no idea how to dance. In college a few months later, a friend took me to a break dancing competition, hosted by a student dance club. I knew immediately: I had just found myself.

I pestered my friends to teach me, attended open practices for one club, and joined another. And that was that: I was dancing. If I wasn't studying, I was dancing. Night and day, I'd be in the studio. I felt it was so obvious that I was meant to be dancing my whole life, and I only now had begun to tap into that potential. I didn't tell my parents for two years. When I was home, I'd close the door in my room, put music on, and practice alone. When my parents eventually found out, their response was simple: "We didn't send you to Harvard to dance."

That really rocked me. Like other immigrant fathers, my dad's greatest fear is that I would end up poor, that I'd have to live in a situation like the one he grew up in. A job in health care essentially eradicated this fear; a job in dance did not. I knew my parents were never going to accept me as a dancer. They said, "There are cheaper ways to learn to dance. We sent you to Harvard to get a good education. That's why we're paying this much." Knowing how much they had sacrificed for me, I didn't want to let them down. Yet I also knew I had found something that was going to be a part of my life forever, that I would do no matter what they said. I didn't know how to reconcile those two things.

So I did both, danced and finished my premed track, but it wasn't until I was about to put together my medical school applications that I admitted to myself: I can't commit to this path. So I audibled and took a job researching HIV/AIDS for two years at a hospital in Boston. I worked from nine to five, then danced. In ten minutes, I went from the hospital and into the studio, every night. The schedule gave me the chance to peer into the world of dance, to explore it fully.

I think everyone can dance to a certain degree. But like any passion, like any jump you want to make, you need to commit. If I was studying until two in the morning, I'd still take a break and dance for fifteen minutes. Every single day. There was nothing that was going to keep me from developing as a dancer. I road-tripped to Boston and DC, began teaching at a few studios, judging a few competitions, hosting a few events. Xbox came out with a dance game, and I got a call to help choreograph it. From chasing what I cared about, other opportunities presented themselves.

I became completely uninterested in the hospital aspects of the research, but I was passionate about the people side of care: Why were some people of certain backgrounds coming back more often? Why were these people more at risk, and why do these people have worse health outcomes? So I turned toward something closer to what I cared about: a degree in public health in New York City. It wasn't med school, but to my parents, I could make the case that it was still a viable step toward going to med school. And now I enjoyed the schoolwork and the exams because they related to things that were happening within communities. Best of all, it provided me the flexibility to dance and teach, to be in New York City, the epicenter of our dance world. I dove into these worlds and homed in on my priorities: community, care, and dance.

Privately, I knew becoming a doctor was officially out, and telling that to my parents would be the hardest part. I wouldn't be able to fulfill what they wanted me to do. First the research and now the public health work confirmed there was just no way I'd go down the doctor path. This was a tipping point.

I was sitting in my room thinking, "I have to tell them. I have to tell them." They're going to ask me how applications are going, and I can't lie to them anymore. I knew that in one fell swoop, I would open myself up to something I actually wanted to do for the rest of my life while simultaneously letting down the people who had sacrificed the most to get me to this point. I felt a heavy, heavy burden of letting them down.

It was a very long conversation with my dad. He said, "We never wanted you to become a dancer, and we sacrificed so much. Now what are you going to do for a living?" I didn't have any answers. I just knew medicine wouldn't make me happy. I could do it. I'd done all the requirements to enable me to do it, but I'd be miserable. I don't know if my parents understood it then, or even now, but telling them was a massive release.

Now what? I knew I had two clear interests but didn't know how to apply them toward a tangible jump. I started by asking myself a lot of questions: "Why the heck am I dancing?" I knew it spoke to me, but I also knew I didn't want to be a full-time dancer. I knew I didn't want to teach full-time. What is it? Why am I doing this thing? As I cycled through responses, I started to find ways to use my dancing to help out the community. I started posting workshops within the community. I didn't know what would transpire or come out of these events, but I just wanted to bring people together and dance and feel the joy in community, in bringing people together and realizing we're all the same.

For five, six, seven months, I was hosting these workshops, and I thought, "This is closer to the thing I want." One day, I got a call from a friend I'd met five years prior when she started dating the person who, twelve years earlier, first introduced me to dancing at Harvard. She was now the national program director for Everybody Dance Now!, a nonprofit transforming the lives of urban youth through hip-hop dance culture. She talked through ideas on how to collaborate on some upcoming events, and at the end of the call, she dropped a small hint: "By the way, we're also looking for an executive director. I think you'd be a great fit."

I couldn't move because I knew: this is the thing. This is what I've been waiting for, an outlet that combines my interest for community health and the health of local communities with my passion for dance. I hung up the phone and just sat there stunned. I had bumped into the intersection of my two lives. I realized that my gift for dance could be spread in a way that made the impact I wanted to make. I was convinced that the opportunity was now, believing fully that there's a need in this world that I was uniquely groomed to fill. I could make the jump because I could point so clearly to something I was meant to do.

With some real work, knowing when to jump can become a clear decision. It took two cities, two very different programs, and a few years to understand what the right jump would be for me. As of now, I'm essentially a volunteer for my organization, which is really hard. Nothing is guaranteed, not a salary, benefits, stuff like that. Every morning, I say, "Okay, we are going to make this work so I don't have to go back and do what I don't like to do." And then I get to it.

I was always so terrified of failure because from a young age we are told to be perfect. Any immigrant can tell you that a B in school is simply not an option. I had a real fear of making mistakes. But the more I started to read biographies, the more I asked, "What's the worst thing that can happen?" In looking at my situation, this is a time to take risks. I'm married but don't have kids. We do have a dog. But my wife's been working for a while, and we've saved up. When I assess the worst thing that could happen, the only thing that might be impacted is my ego. My pride might be impacted if this doesn't work, but there's no long-term detriment to anyone close to me that I love. There's no better time for me to lead this nonprofit organization than now.

The hardest thing to do is not care what anyone else thinks. I still feel it when I go to my Harvard reunions. The question is always, "So what are you doing?" And most answers are, "Oh, I'm a lawyer," "I'm a banker," or whatever. Yet when it comes to my turn, my fears are unfounded: I speak about what I'm really passionate about, and people feel it. Where I braced for rejection, there's acceptance.

Whatever your jump is, if you head toward it with passion and vigor, no one will stop you. Even now, my parents don't completely understand what I'm doing or why, but they hear how I speak about it, and they know that I'm on the right path—or at least, my path. And that's what I've learned: live for you. When I wake up, I think of my jump, and I think about my purpose: why I am here, why I am doing this. And then I turn up the music.

OLAKUNLE OLADEHIN, a former pulmonary researcher at Columbia University Medical Center, is the executive director of Everybody Dance Now!, a nonprofit urban youth enrichment organization aimed at improving community health through hip-hop dance.

BRIAN KELLY

Human Resources Professional to
Founder of Travel Rewards Media Platform

MY BIGGEST FEAR is being mediocre. And the idea of becoming the umpteenth guy with a travel blog surely evoked that fear. But I had planes to catch and flights to book, posts to write and seats to save—and a few years of hiring and firing in my HR job taught me one thing: if you're going to get a break in making your career, you're going to make that break yourself.

I was born into a huge Irish Catholic, middle-class family anchored in Long Island. Travel came into my life as an aggressor when my dad's company shipped him down near Philadelphia. We were shocked. At eight, I became Dad's travel guy—ten bucks a pop to book his flights through Travelocity. I was fascinated with computers and this new Internet thing. At twelve, I read about the Cayman Islands and decided it was time to go. I pooled together our family credit card rewards, and we did it. We had never left the country—until that point in time, a big trip was to Orlando. The Cayman Islands experience was mind-blowing.

My master plan for my early twenties was to get into NYU and become a lawyer, so naturally when I got rejected by NYU, I was crushed. I ended up in school back in Pennsylvania where my brothers went. "Might as well be a big fish in small pond," Mom said. So I made the most of it, and I was studying in Spain before graduating when I began playing around more with the credit card rewards system. And I started a personal blog on the topic. I adored writing, and I was obsessed with travel. My blog was the first thing to give me experience with both.

I always wanted to live in New York City, so I squeezed into a job that got me there after graduation, as a buyer in the cosmetics office for Lord & Taylor. It was a sight to see: my 6-foot-7-inch frame hunched over spreadsheets in an office full of women, asking them what lipstick sells best and researching which mascara to buy more of. Forty-five grand a year, locked into a cubicle.

It was terrible. I wanted to take a step—not a jump, just a step—where I could travel as part of the work I was doing. So I pivoted into a human resources role, snagging a job for a Wall Street firm running college recruitment events for graduating seniors. I went from no money, no travel, no time, to a little bit more of all three. I joined the firm in August 2007, the same week the markets started to shatter.

I was accruing $100,000 each month on work expenses, then using those credit card points for first-class seats (once, I ended up sitting next to Madonna), flights to the Seychelles—an alternative, ridiculous lifestyle purely on credit card rewards.

It was on one of these trips that my boyfriend turned to me and said, "Why don't you sell your knowledge to other people? You love booking us trips. I see you light up when you get to the computer. Everyone has points, but no one knows how to use them."

So I bought a domain for ten bucks, called it The Points Guy, and sent out a message to all my friends and family. A couple of days later, I got my first e-mail from a friend of a friend, Loretta, who wanted to go to Cabo San Lucas with her American Airlines miles. The airline website couldn't sort that out, but I could.

I remember when I got the PayPal payment of fifty dollars. I was beside myself: "Holy cow, I can do this. I can make money off what I love."

The idea of forming a company scared me. I'm a procrastinator by nature. My first thoughts were, "Oh, God. I don't want to put together paperwork or hire an attorney. I don't have the money. This is going to be way too complicated." Then I looked into the mirror, poured a gigantic cup of coffee, and said, "Screw it. How hard can it be?"

Turns out, not hard at all. In about an hour, I had put up a Facebook post: "Hey, if anyone needs help using their miles, the Points Guy is now in business." The operation was small potatoes at the start. A few weeks later, people at work started coming up to my cubicle for advice.

But what happens next? I was onto my passion, but my current setup was messy and unpredictable: fifty bucks here, fifty bucks there. Worse, I couldn't scale beyond myself; people were calling me up in the middle of the night: "My daughter doesn't like American Airlines," and "Luft-hansa lost my luggage." My dad sat me down and said, "You need to learn how to make money in your sleep." If I was to really go for this, I'd need to go all in.

There were moments at work that reinforced the need to make a big-ger move. My job at that time was to stand outside a room and fire people all day long. One day, I worked with a manager, and we fired half his team. The next day, I fired him. That job was cutthroat and brutal, but it served up a lesson: you've got to look out for yourself. You can't expect any other person to do that. If I were going to jump, I needed to put the pieces in place, and leap as far as I could.

And then came a breaking point. I was promised a promotion, got the promotion, but didn't get the promised compensation. Instead, my boss says, "You're twenty-seven. Wait your time. I didn't start making money till my thirties." Then she gave me a bottle of Absolut vodka. The sentiment was demeaning and enraging, and that was the day I said to myself, "You know what? I'm going to go full force toward my jump, unapologetically, and just focus on making this work. I'm going to make things happen, 'cause no one else is going to take care of me but me."

I reached out to everyone about my jump. A former coworker and close friend called to invite me for dinner in Staten Island. Her husband was an expert in something called search engine optimization; they knew about my hustle and the jump I was trying to make, and they wanted to help. That dinner changed my life. Over meatballs at the din-ing table, I was given a crash course in monetizing my passions, fusing together writing and travel into something sustainable using advertising.

I made my first blog post on June 7, 2010, and told myself that I would blog every single day afterward, no matter what.

I had a few hundred followers, and it took a few months to get traction, but I loved it. I was thrilled to find a way back to writing, telling stories, and having a point of view that's different from what else is out there. I was homing in on advertising and content when another break hit: a former classmate reached out. He'd been reaching out about meeting up, and I hadn't been able to make the time yet, but he'd persisted and now he shot me an e-mail: "I need help planning a vacation for me and my husband. By the way, you're the stupidest person ever: you're blogging about credit cards, and I work for a credit card marketing company. Did you know you could be making money?"

My writing already focused on endorsing certain credit cards, and now, because of this old college pal's expertise, I began getting a chunk of change if people followed my advice. I was beginning to learn the ropes when a reporter from the *New York Times* reached out—the final piece of luck. I found his e-mail buried in the spam folder: "I hear you're the man on points. I don't believe points are good for frugal travelers. What do you say?" I replied: "Au contraire. Let's meet." We met for four hours. I blew his mind, booked him five free trips to Brazil.

And here's where all these lucky little turns—the advertising, the marketing, the press—swirl together. The same week the *Times* article was to be released, Chase was running an unbeatable British Airways 100,000-mile offer on their latest credit card, and I was getting $100 per referral purchase. This is where all the triangles converged: my readers wanted content on how to get the most out of credit cards. The credit card companies wanted to get in front of my business readers. And the *New York Times* added credibility to it all.

The article was released, and the site exploded, thousands of people going off to buy that Chase card I recommended on my website while I sat there in the shower in my Brooklyn apartment, crunching the numbers from all the referral purchases made, thinking, "Oh, my God. I think I made more than my annual salary today." I walked out of my apartment delirious. Shortly thereafter, I was making six figures a month.

The boom in the Points Guy business was entirely bizarre. I was reporting to my cubicle at the human resources job when I made my first million. It was insane. It was obvious that my desk job was getting in the way of my business, yet when I told my parents my plan to quit, they said I was crazy: Leave just as I was on the cusp of promotion to vice president? My mom said, "The recession's almost over. The firm gives you amazing benefits—how could you leave those?" I just said, "Mom, working at a big company isn't the only way to have benefits. I can just pay for them myself." Obvious as it was, none of us, including me, had ever considered that fact.

I resigned the day the *Times* article came out, stayed on through the next class of new trainees, and then left to begin the life I wanted. I became the Points Guy full-time.

I'm entirely convinced that the Points Guy was made possible by my years as the HR Guy. My clients are the credit card companies that are big finance companies and their compliance departments and multilayers of management. I know how to navigate their processes and how to grow our relationships because I come from that world. I am familiar with legal departments; I have a feel for how to hire. I've cherished my pre-jump experiences because they set the table for today.

Before you jump from what you're doing, remember that you can do two things at once—and you should. I don't recommend taking jumps off cliffs. My move was calculated, and I think that goes for most who jump. Think about what you like doing, how it could help others, how it may fill a need. Let these ideas become your early brainstorms while your paycheck doesn't depend on it. Start playing around with different models when you can afford to guess and check. The concept of my jump changed drastically from the time I started the blog to the time I quit my job.

What most people won't tell you when you start a jump is that you'll need to be a shameless, hustling self-promoter. Do it tactfully. Develop thick skin. I have friends who are musicians who are incredibly talented, but they lack the promotion. I tell them, "You need to go to an open mic night, and just start playing. No matter what field you're in, you need to hustle. You wanna be an intern on Wall Street, you gotta hustle for it. Get out there and meet the people that can get you closer to your jump." I think this hustle factor is often overlooked the most in the jump process.

Above all else, know that to get your break, you will have to jump. No one—not your biggest supporter, not the person you look up to the most—no one is going to make the right decision in telling you when to jump. Everyone's going to have a different opinion. I tried going for consensus so many times: I had 150 smart people sending me in different directions, telling me different things. It's a cliché, but go with your gut. Focus on what you're doing well and what's resonating with people and just drive that home, unapologetically. Then pull the Band-Aid off and jump, because no one else is going to do that for you.

It's been a few years since the meatballs on Staten Island and my first blog post. We're a team of twenty now, partnering with credit card companies on new products, working with global charities and Nobel Peace Prize winners to use our travel to do good. I never imagined this.

There's no greater feeling than the feeling of freedom. I wake up every day eager to look at my e-mail. It's not just financial freedom. It's freedom in the purest of ways: once you have that confidence to jump, you find you have the ability to do whatever you want. Yes, the risks remain real. It could all end one day. The Points Guy could end tomorrow—the Consumer Protection Financial Bureau could come out and say, "You can no longer do credit card marketing on blogs." There's risk in any jump, but that's the whole point: high risk, high reward.

A few weeks ago, I was in West Africa, working with a humanitarian on her philanthropic project. The village named me a tribal chief, dressed me in full tribal garb. Can't make this stuff up: sitting up onstage in a rural village in Ghana with my parents looking on. How did I end up here?! I thought back to the moment when I was in middle school, scared to death of being mediocre. I looked at my parents, and we exchanged smiles. Then it was back on a plane.

BRIAN KELLY, a former human resources professional for a Wall Street financial services firm, is the founder of the travel rewards website and media platform The Points Guy.

BRUCE HUBER

Lawyer to Pastor to Professor

I WAS RAISED in a churchgoing family in Washington State, with plans to get involved in government or the legal world by the time I left home. Through college, everything kept coming back to law and politics on one hand, and my faith on the other. In the end, I'd try one, then the other, before jumping from both.

My first year in the real world was spent interning at a church, an emotionally fulfilling but not so intellectually challenging experience. I wanted something more engaging and thought law school might be just that. Law has the advantage of being a very well-regarded profession in the United States, so my family and friends seemed to think well of me for going to law school. I enjoyed it, got married in the middle of my second year, and realized quickly that my relish for family life would trump any single-minded focus on career.

My wife and I decided to start a family, moved to an affordable neighborhood, and put down roots. It was the height of the dot-com era, and so it wasn't too hard to snag a cushy gig at a corporate law firm in Seattle. I took the bar exam, started working in corporate law, and figured this was it for my career. I was ready to ride off into the sunset.

That was the first of many mistakes of prediction—or failures of imagination. The dot-com bubble popped less than one year in, and my law firm started to suffer as a consequence. More troubling was that I began to realize that none of the work in my job overlapped with what I enjoyed about law or appreciated about law school. The trifecta was that my wife and I realized that the American Dream of moving into the suburbs and buying a home can be a little bit more boring than you think. We weren't miserable, but neither were we feeling particularly fulfilled.

So again I found myself intellectually unstimulated and missing the mark on some very fundamental aspects of my interests. At about that time, a mentor of mine from the church I had attended during college called me up and asked me, "So are you done being a lawyer yet? Wanna come back down here?"

It was a wealthy church, adjacent to a major university. It was a soft landing. They were familiar faces; they provided me with housing; they helped me with my loans. It was not nearly as big a risk as it would appear on paper. The toughest part was knowing that a door would shut, because once you've quit legal practice, it's very difficult to return. But I took that risk.

I remember going around to some of my law firm colleagues at the time to share the news. A few of them quietly expressed the wish that they too could escape the law firm rat race. They'd say, "I'm so envious that you can leave!" or "I want to pull the plug myself, but I wouldn't be able to afford my new mortgage." Or "I just bought a boat." Or "I'm just on the cusp of making partner, and even though I don't really think I want to make partner anymore, I can't just give up now." I left a few days later.

Arriving at the church, I learned pretty quickly that there would be no riding into the sunset here either. If I stayed for the long haul, I'd need a degree from a divinity school and to become ordained within the church, which wasn't what I had in mind. And I had just closed the door on law. I had landed softly knowing well I'd be taking off again soon.

While I didn't know what my jump would be, I put up safety nets in the background. I continued to pay my Washington State Bar license fees even though it was a lot of money, just to keep as an insurance policy. I knew that even if a law firm might not hire me, the state of Washington would at least permit me to go and set up shop and try to do it on my own, if I had to. So I kept that alive.

That gave me a bit of a fig leaf of confidence. The church work was safe and stable, but left me wondering if maybe there was something more. Meanwhile, an old idea continued to creep back into my mind: What about academia? The prospect of getting my PhD and finding a way to reenter academic life kept popping into the back of my head. I stomped it down for a variety of reasons, starting with a few obvious ones: I did not graduate from law school at the top of my class; I was now eight or nine years out of college; I didn't actually think it was possible to head back that way, so late in the game. I told myself, "Put these thoughts to bed. You can either try to go back to being a lawyer, or make do with working in a church for the rest of your life."

The single factor that saved me from this self-limiting talk was conversations with good friends—friends who had known me for a long time and were able to see past some of my rationalizations and excuses. Friends who knew what I had probably wanted all along but was scared to admit. They said, "Look, this is something you've been interested in for a long time. You loved law school. You never seem to be able to get very far away from academic life; even at this church, you're working for the college ministry, and you're doing things on campus. That's just a part of who you are. If this is something to which you are being called, then it's really pretty gutless and faithless of you to resist it."

Early thirties, wife and two kids, another on the way, and I was jumping back to school.

My first moves in this direction were tentative. I broke it down small: first, I'd need to take the standard entrance exam. I decided that's a pretty easy thing to do. I'm not burning any bridges just by taking a test. I did better than I expected, so I decided to take the next step—to talk to some people about where I would apply.

I needed to know the honest truth on this path, and that meant finding people who had gone through it. I dug up old contacts from law school, tracked down folks around the nearby colleges. I reached out to old classmates and professors and sent cold e-mails saying, hey, I know it's been about a decade since I've spoken with you, but would you mind if we meet up and share your thoughts on an idea I have? And since I just wanted advice—not a job or a promise of anything other than advice— most folks were receptive. This was big.

I made a list of the handful of schools that, if I got in, I would make the jump for. Even though the steps had been small to this point, and fairly low cost, they were emotionally preparing me for the possibility that I may actually, at some point, pull the trigger on my jump. And that's a critical exercise to experience, whatever your jump may be.

The applications were reviewed and I kept hearing no, no, no; rejection, rejection, rejection, rejection. Until one day at the end of the process, I heard from my top choice: in. I'd been accepted.

Now the only thing between me and the jump was the money question, and of course the money question is a huge matter for any decision. I was going from career stability to something totally unstable: How am I going to live? How am I going to get by?

Normally when you go to a PhD program, you get an annual stipend, but my program didn't know if they'd be able to offer me anything. This is where my wife and I started having a real serious conversation with my parents and my in-laws. We were well aware that we were a family in need of certain resources simply in order to keep afloat.

And so I found myself making a new set of investigations and explorations: combing through all sorts of California State websites to see what kind of public services were available, and applying for all sorts of scholarships and grants. We qualified for the family student housing and discovered we were eligible for state-sponsored health care and food vouchers.

But most helpful in the preparation was looking back to our own experience when my wife and I were in law school, five years earlier. We had kept a scrupulous record of expenses because we were having the time of our lives and doing so on a shoestring budget. At the time, we thought to ourselves, "Boy, this is really interesting: on paper, we are scraping to get by, and life is perfectly fine. We don't really feel like we lack for anything right now." We kept a record of this for the future so we would know how much it took for us to be happy, as a reminder. We maintained pen and ink spreadsheets that literally tracked every single expenditure we had been making.

Fast-forward, and those spreadsheets made us believe we could do this jump.

My wife and I made a new budget and agreed to take it one year at a time so that if it really didn't work out after one year, we would pull the plug and find more gainful employment. Even though I hadn't practiced law in years, we felt we had something of a backup with my law license in Washington.

I never bothered to see where we compared to the poverty line, but for the next year, the first year of this jump, our family lived off a minimal income. We looked beyond the finances: this was a great adventure. Even though eating out for us meant a taco at a taco bar rather than a nice sit-down meal somewhere, well, we love taco bars. Grabbing a cheap slice of pizza was just as satisfying as eating at a steakhouse. For entertainment, we got creative; I had a free bus pass from the university and would take my kids riding around on public transportation. They were young enough that riding the bus was the most awesome thing in the world.

It ended up being one of the golden eras of my life. Our family of five, enjoying the journey of this jump, together.

I'm a law school professor today, and feel the enormous sense of fulfillment that comes along with doing not only what I want to do and what I set out to do, but in some respects, what I feel I'm called to do. The mix of intellectual challenge and personal relationships that I have with my students is exactly what I am best suited for. In law we talk about the highest and best use of various resources; I feel like this is my highest and best use. I'm doing what I love and what challenges me but also, I think, what helps the community around me in some way.

My work feels neither self-indulgent nor like going through the motions to make a paycheck. I believe I'm getting to pursue my passion as well as to help serve other people and keep my family afloat, all in one fell swoop. But getting to this point required a village. It truly takes a community of people to make a jump. You never jump alone—you're making it with the support of others, with the counsel and wisdom of others, the informed intuitions of other people. You may have confidants around you, or it may take some cold calls. But these people really do exist, and many will want to help—regardless of what your jump may be and when you decide to make it.

A jump doesn't have to happen at once—that's rare. But the little things—the expense spreadsheets, the cold-call conversations, the internal research and brainstorming—that can start now. Stay honest with yourself and when you feel clear about your calling, go for it.

BRUCE HUBER, a former corporate lawyer in the Pacific Northwest and college pastor in Northern California, is a law school professor in the Midwest.

ELEANOR WATSON

Teacher to Ski Instructor

I GREW UP in a village in southern England where everyone followed the rules. In my private school, the boys played football, and the girls sewed. That was that, except for one week each year when we went on our family ski trip. I had learned to ski when I was four, and this week each year was my escape from the way things were. My earliest memories were of being outside in those elements. I think once you've been in the mountains, it changes you. Or at least it did me.

I stayed close to the well-groomed, risk-averse route of academics into my midtwenties. I tested into a good grammar school with intelligent peers, then progressed to university and afterward a master's program before beginning a teaching career. I never stopped skiing—first by joining the ski club as a student and later by leading school trips as a teacher—and all the while I wanted someone to tell me I could ski more, but no one ever did.

Four years into teaching, I became head of the philosophy department, the perfect position in a career that was ideal, living in a nice flat with a lovely boyfriend and our two cats. All of the things I was supposed to want. And then one winter I chaperoned one of our school ski trips, and that's when I said, "Oh shit."

I was taking a long ski lift up with an instructor, hung with him on the run, and distinctly remember feeling happy in a way I hadn't felt in a really long time. By that point, I had felt increasingly stuck in my job; it became clear to me that skiing could give me the sense of purpose and meaning I'd been missing. We started talking. He told me how he'd become a ski instructor, how we were the same age, and how he knew others like me who had done it too. What had been unthinkable was now tangible: there are humans who do this, even other English people just like me. I always thought of the ski instructors as much younger or cooler than me, yet here's a guy bluntly saying, "You can do this, and here's how." He told me the courses to take, the people to talk to.

I came back from the trip and looked at my life. Something within me had changed. I was questioning choices that I had never second-guessed before. As I looked around my social circles, I was clearly out of place. There was a life checklist I was meant to follow. Some of my friends got upset when they weren't progressing quickly enough along that checklist: job, house, pet, boyfriend, marriage. There was no reflection on whether or not that checklist was the right trajectory for everyone. For the first time, I looked on all this and admitted to myself that it wasn't the right progression for me.

I don't know if this is a woman's fear more than a man's fear, but my biggest fear around my jump was not that it involved breaking up with my longtime boyfriend but acknowledging that my new journey could make it difficult to be with any guy. It's not easy to meet someone who's the right person, and if you're traveling on your own to tackle an all-consuming jump, you're only adding more barriers if a match were to happen.

So I had to contend with that one big, scary question: Is this jump worth potentially losing out on a critical aspect of my life that I may not get back again? I knew quite a few older ladies—I didn't know any older men—but I knew quite a few older ladies who were single and never got married. Would that be me? And people around me weren't helpful because they would all say either, "Oh, you're so young. You've got plenty of time." Or, "If it happens, it happens," or other meaningless things that don't actually comfort you since the people saying them have never done what you're considering doing. They never had to choose between a dream jump that meant setting out alone and the other dream of wanting a family.

I decided to jump. I developed a strong conviction that meeting the right person is really just luck. You can't wait around for that stuff. You've got to live your life, not just sit and hope that stuff happens and that you end up happy from it. And what better way to meet someone than doing something that you love, where that person gets to meet the most authentic version of you? For women who may be worried about what I was worried about—of a jump getting in the way of finding the person of your dreams—my advice is to stop it. It will be okay. Go for your dreams, and along the way, you'll meet your mate.

Jumps are worth taking because of the people that come with taking one. Teaching and living in rural England, I was surrounded by people who I didn't feel similar to. In seeking out whatever it is that is your passion, you're going to meet other people who share it: "your vibe, your tribe," as some saying goes. Arriving in Switzerland for new instructor training, I was surrounded by others like me: late twenties and also recently out of a long-term relationship because they didn't have the same dreams as their partners. People who, like me, had been saving up to buy a house and were now using that money on this jump. During instructor training, in such a full, rich way, I was supported.

If you're around people who can't relate to your jump, they can love you and be excited for you, and that helps to an extent. But without going through your jump, they can't actually understand how different you are from them. In my village, my friends were mostly excited about whoever had the newest ring and whatever new baby names were being considered. And I love all that; it's not that I don't love that! But when I tried to say, "I'm really excited about this pair of skis," they'd say, "That's nice." But there was just such a harsh, loneliness-making disconnect.

That was hard. Many people around you may understand life through just one pair of glasses, one type of lens: you do this, then that, then you're happy, and you settle. By jumping, I've taken those glasses off and put on another pair. Now my understanding of my life and what I define as successful is different from the others. Sometimes I still feel they're sizing me up through their lens: "Oh, once you get this out of your system," or

"You should do this whilst you're single," and things like that. What I say is, "No, this is me now. This isn't whilst I'm single. This isn't a phase. I'm nearly twenty-nine. I've done my rebellious twenty-year-old stuff—this isn't the rebellion. This is actually my fulfillment, and this is me doing what I'm supposed to be doing."

And while those statements can be brutally difficult to say out loud, if you're jumping with your gut, you're going to push through. I'm a really indecisive, overanalytical person. When deciding on anything—even something as simple as choosing between two identical biscuits—I find it hard to know which one to pick. Jumping should have been torture. But I don't remember actually making the decision. I went through the process of developing the plan, checking my finances, chatting with my parents. But it never felt like a decision. It just felt right.

That's not to say people won't make it tough on you. They will. I was asked by elders if using money for a future home on ski equipment was rational. The way I looked at it, was it better to spend the money on some-thing worthwhile that would impact my life or to keep saving toward something I was supposed to want? When I tried to post my resignation letter to the school head teacher, she told me, "We think you're doing really well here. We don't want you to leave. I'm not going to accept this for another four days." That was really rare. It doesn't happen. She said, "I want you to be certain that you're not just reacting to all the life changes and that you're definitely doing this." I remember appreciating her sup-port and concern whilst thinking, "I don't need that time. I am definitely doing this."

Ultimately, I jumped because I wanted to be me. I knew I wouldn't meet someone if I wasn't being the most honest version of myself, and I wouldn't want to be with someone who didn't see that side of me, or attract someone who doesn't truly know me. Whatever it may be that calls you, pursue it. You need to be authentic to yourself.

A jump won't always deliver thrilling highs. Even if you hit your plan, you're still going to have days when you want to curl up, shut off the world, and watch Netflix. It's never all smooth. I was quite prepared to jump because I had given myself time to think and plan, but even then, new hurdles and obstacles appeared that I didn't expect, and they take a greater toll on your psyche than you can predict. As we speak, I'm nearly thirty and spending part of the year living with my parents right now, and that's harder than I pictured it would be. Challenges will come your way, even when you make the right call to jump. Change is hard, regardless of whether it is good change or bad change.

It took me a couple of decades to realize I didn't just have to sit around and sew, play with my cats, and save for a house I didn't really want. I wish I'd known that sooner. It's okay to find passion and excitement in areas different from those around you. Follow these feelings to the people who also share them. Mine led me into the mountains—where will yours take you?

ELEANOR WATSON, a former philosophy head of a secondary school, is a ski instructor on mountains in Switzerland and Japan.

UNITED STATES SENATOR ANGUS KING

Lawyer to Journalist to Energy Entrepreneur to Politician

EVERY TIME I make a career move, I try to think ahead five or ten years and ask myself, "How will I feel about this decision looking back on it?" And then I make my best guess at the right move. I asked myself this before going into law, before getting out of law to work in clean energy, before working as a TV anchor, before running for public office. And when I make my guess about what to do next, it really is a guess. We can't underestimate the role that luck and coincidence play in our lives. We just can't. I'm on my ninth career right now as a United States senator. How I got here is just a combination of educated guesses, strange happenstance, and events outside of my control.

For example, the reason I went to Dartmouth was that my sister married a guy who had recently graduated from Dartmouth right before my senior year in high school. I liked the guys at the wedding. So I thought, that's the place for me. Never even visited the place before I went. If my sister had married a guy from the University of Virginia or North Carolina or even Harvard, my life would be entirely different.

I went on to study law at the University of Virginia. Public service appealed to me. I was the UVA chair of the Robert Kennedy presidential campaign in 1968, and I remember well the night he was killed. It galvanized me. I entered a national legal services program and was assigned to Maine. Had never been there before, didn't know a soul. I assumed I'd be sent to Portland. Nope. I joined Pine Tree Legal Assistance in a little town called Skowhegan. This was in the fall of 1969. Skowhegan, it turned out, was a pretty big town. Five or six thousand people. I spent two and a half years there, serving clients. It was a low-income area. Every couple weeks, I would go on the road to the neighboring small towns and meet clients in fire stations and town offices and courthouse waiting rooms. They were looking for advice about various problems. Not just legal problems. Education problems, health issues, housing issues. I could only help them with their legal problems.

Politics was a way to help with every problem. So I went to work for this guy who was running for the US Senate in Maine. He was running against Margaret Chase Smith, who was a really iconic senator for Maine in the mid-twentieth century. Nobody gave him a chance to win. But he did, and I moved to Washington and worked for him for two and a half years. People call the mid-'70s the Last Great Senate, with guys like Ed Muskie and Jacob Javits and Walter Mondale. It was a great place to be.

But I always wanted to get back to Maine. I knew if I stayed longer than two and a half years, the magnetic pull of Washington could keep me there forever. The pension, laying down roots, the whole deal. So I left and went back to Maine to hang out a shingle. I was married and had three kids when we went back. I needed to earn a living, so I started a private practice in Brunswick, Maine. It's a town of twenty thousand people. I was doing okay.

Then a friend of mine, this guy who I worked on the Senate campaign with, approached me. He was the host of a public broadcasting show in Maine, but he was going on a two-week honeymoon. He asked if I'd fill in for him. I'd never done anything like that, never considered anything like that. But he said they'd pay me twenty-five dollars a week. In my first month of being a lawyer, I'd grossed maybe one hundred dollars. So his offer was real money for me. I said yes, did it for two weeks, and was done. Back to law.

Then this anchor friend ran for Congress, so his producer called me up and said, "Hey, you did pretty well for those two weeks, wanna keep doing it?" So I did. It was a part-time thing, with my practice still going, but I broadcast for seventeen years. I was the Jim Lehrer of Maine, if that makes sense. Interviews, debates, documentaries, that sort of thing.

A few years later, maybe six or seven years into my legal practice, one of my clients asked me to become their in-house counsel. I was working for them pretty much full-time anyway. They were doing alternative energy stuff in New England, so I could stay in Maine. I said yes.

So just to keep track of fortuity so far: my sister's husband went to Dartmouth. Robert F. Kennedy was shot. The Senate candidate I worked for won. My broadcast anchor friend went on his honeymoon. Then he ran for Congress. My client needed an in-house lawyer. All of these things happened outside of my control, and each changed my life profoundly.

When I got to the energy company, I was doing a mix of legal and business work. They did hydro projects and this big biomass project. I learned a lot.

I'm sitting at a board meeting for the company in 1988. We talk and realize that the company is slowly going out of business, since our margins are steadily going down and the investment to retrofit hydro sites doesn't make financial sense. At that time, I remembered reading an article by a scientist named Amory Lovins. He wrote in *Foreign Affairs* about how it's cheaper to invest in saving electricity than it is to invest in generating electricity. Basic idea but novel at the time. I could have read any other article in *Foreign Affairs*, but I happened to read that one.

Since we were going out of business anyway and I had nothing to lose, I piped up and said, "According to this article, it's a lot cheaper to do conservation than it is generation. Why don't we go into the conservation business and sell our conserved energy the same way we sell power?"

The Norwegians who ran the company thought it was a pretty crazy idea. But they gave me the time to write up a proposal, so I did my research and wrote it. Then one of our major utilities put in an RFP (request for proposal) that specifically asked for conservation ideas. Done.

Then we all got laid off at the Christmas party in '88. That was one of the weirdest days of my life. My contract went for another year, so when they called me in the room, they asked, "What do you want? Let's negotiate a settlement on your contract." So I said, "Give me half the sal-

ary you owed me and the rights to the conservation idea." They thought
it was a silly idea anyway, so they were happy to say yes.

In January '89 I started a company called Northeast Energy Management, then signed a contract with a utility to start saving them energy by
replacing light fixtures, changing pumps, that sort of thing. This was one
of the first such projects anywhere. And it was very successful. We developed maybe $12 million of conservation projects over the next four years.
Then, an out-of-state utility was interested in getting into conservation, so
it bought the company and I ended up a millionaire. It was more money
than anybody in my family ever had for a thousand years.

So I found myself suddenly with some money and free time. I was still
doing that TV show through all of this, but I was getting frustrated with
Maine politics. The Republican governor and Democratic house were
bickering to the point that there was a government shutdown. One day I
was moderating a panel discussion involving the head of the chamber of
commerce and the head of an environmental group, and at lunch, they
said, "Why don't you run for governor?" If they hadn't said that, I
wouldn't have. But these two diametrically opposed guys both thought it
was a good idea, so I took the idea seriously—and ultimately decided to
go for it.

I got elected as an independent and served for two terms. I think it
was a successful eight years. But when I was done, I was done. My wife
and I bought an RV and took the kids on a five-and-a-half-month tour of
the country. Homeschooled the kids, the whole deal. It was amazing.

I wasn't retired. I was just done with politics. I did some teaching at
Bowdoin and Bates colleges and did some more energy work.

Then, in 2012, Olympia Snowe, one of Maine's senators, unexpectedly announced her retirement. She was just tired of partisanship in
Washington. As an Independent governor, I was able to bridge the
partisan divide sometimes, so I thought maybe I could do the same in
Washington. My main line of thinking was five or ten years into the
future, when I looked back, would I rather have spent my time trying to
help my country in Washington or touring the country in an RV? Once
I put it in those terms, the answer was obvious.

I was fortunate to be elected again, and that brings us up to the present.

If there's anything to be learned from my story, it's that you just don't know what's coming next. The best you can do is prepare yourself well for whatever happens. When David Ortiz, the former Red Sox slugger, stepped up to the plate, he knew he was going to make an out two out of every three times. That's a lot of failure, a lot of uncertainty. When he swung, he didn't know if he was going to connect. But he kept swinging.

And so do I.

ANGUS KING, a former lawyer, journalist, and energy entrepreneur, is Maine's first Independent senator in the United States Congress, a position he has held since 2013. He also served as the seventy-second governor of Maine from 1995 to 2003.

GREG KLASSEN

Garbage Collector to Luxury Furniture Designer/Maker

I GREW UP in Central California on a peach farm. It was my dad's farm, and years earlier, he had left the post office to start it. My dad fought through a disability to be a farmer. One day, he said, "It's time to follow my heart and start farming." He built a very successful farm.

My dad hoped my brother and I would take over the farm after high school, but I wanted to get out of town. I set out for college in Canada, to earn a degree in biblical studies.

Near college graduation, in my early twenties, newly married, and in need of a job, I stumbled into a job recycling wood for a door-making company, driving a forklift around tossing out the garbage. We were trying to pay our last tuition bills and couldn't afford furniture at home, so I'd come back from work with wood scraps and try to make my own.

It was really poor-quality furniture—likely in a landfill somewhere. But a spark was kindled, and I discovered that I loved making things and working with wood. There's something about the material: its natural beauty, how it can be shaped into things, made into something from just a pile of parts or pieces. I spent any waking moment with wood, whenever I wasn't on the forklift.

I kept at it but didn't think woodworking could be practical as a profession: first, I wasn't very good at it, and second, I didn't know how you made a career by making things out of wood. So I kept it as a hobby, and when I finished school, I worked a desk job for that same door company, thinking that's what a college grad needs to do.

I sat at a computer and looked at spreadsheets and numbers and watched my joy slowly wither away. I think there are life-giving jobs and there are life-taking jobs. This was the latter. I continued my woodworking on the side until one day I admitted to myself, "I found something I love. I've got to do it."

There happened to be carpenters from a local cabinet shop in our office installing new cabinets, and I quietly went up to the guy installing the cabinets and said, "Hey, do you guys have any jobs?" He said, "Yeah, sure. We actually need a guy." Within a few days, I left the desk and was working in his cabinet shop.

It wasn't the best job, but I stuck it out, worked there for a year, learned more skills, and began selling pieces at the farmer's market until I hit another point: "If I'm ever going to get good at this, I need more skills." I applied to a prestigious woodworking school in California, but didn't get in. I improved my work and tried again the next year and was admitted.

Two years later, I left school with the confidence that I was a good craftsman. I could create anything that I could imagine. But now came reality: my wife and I had a ton of student debt and a newborn baby, and my salary would be our primary means of income. Was I going to find a safe job, stay practical—do it the "right" way that everyone recommended—or was I going to jump entirely into the deep end?

I went for the deep end. I jumped right in after school—with all that debt, just a few hand tools, a newborn baby, a wife who wasn't working, no savings. We had a few hundred dollars in the bank when I started my business. This was at the beginning of the recession in 2008.

It sounds crazy, but I knew I had to be all-in. I had learned what I was going to learn at woodworking school. If I was to master my craft, if I was going to thrive, I needed to bet on myself entirely. I spent the first six years of business creating my own furniture designs and trying every possible way to market my work, but nothing was working until I finally built up a collection of furniture pieces I was excited about and gained some experience selling my work.

The hardest part was that we were so incredibly poor. We didn't have any level of safety net. When the gas went to empty, I'd fill up just a quarter tank at a time; I would buy just enough wood to make one piece of furniture, and then I would need to sell that piece before I could buy material for the next piece. Starting this jump truly meant starting at zero. I was betting that the immediate struggle would be offset, in the long term, by whatever and whoever I would cross paths with that could inch me along toward my passion in some way, shape, or form.

To be candid, that uncertainty brought with it a lot of emotional risk. I could really feel it. There were a lot of sleepless nights, and there were many moments of self-doubt for those first six years. Am I any good? Am I going to make it? Should I have listened to everyone else who said this wasn't a practical career choice? Should I go get that part-time job to supplement my income? Should I go get a real job? Truthfully, I applied for jobs, ridiculous jobs—one at a timber-framing company, another at a florist delivering flowers. Fortunately, no one would hire me. I even started delivering phone books door to door, but that didn't really work out.

Nevertheless, I benefited from not being distracted. I had set the stage for my jump, and I needed to go for it unapologetically. Preparation is one thing, but staying half-in, half-out leads to mediocrity. You want to plan, but it's easy to stall out in that gray area on the way from planning to jumping. Confirm your convictions, become as skilled as you can be, then go. This approach may not always seem practical, but dreams aren't always practical. They require a risk and a belief in yourself to just jump in and give it a try.

After a few years, the results of my jump were modest, and that was okay: I was able to support my family, and we were able to get by. Six years in, I was in the habit of introducing myself to magazines and websites. One day I sent an e-mail introduction to a design blogger and he responded warmly and offered to feature my work in a blog post. The article quickly went viral and was soon picked up by countless other media outlets, newspapers, and magazines around the world. Overnight I was a viral Internet sensation with my work introduced to tens of millions of people. Immediately, I went from making a lot of cool furniture that few ever saw or purchased to becoming a renowned craftsman with a backlog of orders.

• • •

I feel really fortunate to be where I am. I've worked hard for and earned what's come my way, but I also feel like it's all a tremendous blessing. I lost my dad a couple of years ago, and every day feels like a gift since then. I'm blessed I get to work on what I love every day. Every milestone I have conquered—even during the lean years when a job would pay the bills only for that month—felt like a blessing, even though we were barely keeping our heads above water. I felt blessed to be able to scratch together a living, and I feel blessed now that I can make a real living. It's never been just a matter of "luck."

When I jumped, I never considered failure an option. I was just going to go until it worked. I think I inherited that mentality from my dad. When he started his farm, he never considered failure an option. I've felt the same for my jump. In the times when I needed to come up with cash, I'd find ways to do it, but I never had even a thought about giving up on making furniture as a living because I knew that's what I loved and that was what I was passionate about. It was that simple.

Today, I live and work on a couple of rural acres situated in a field in the Pacific Northwest. I live with my wife and our three kids in a 105-year-old farmhouse that we've been restoring. We're surrounded by raspberry fields on three sides, with soft rolling hills gliding into forest and mountains off in the distance.

I designed and built my own studio: a modern version of a barn with cedar siding and tons of windows and skylights. The walls are lined with big stacks of raw wood slabs that I spend my days transforming into pieces of functional art. My wife homeschools our kids, and I work across the yard, just a ten-second commute from home. My kids often ride their bikes in the shop, and I'll come to the house to eat lunch with them. Sometimes I'll take a break in the afternoon to ride bikes or play with them.

Life has changed a lot since my early days of struggle, but I'm working no differently than before: I'm still doing the work that I love and supporting my wife and kids with it, but now I have removed the stress of figuring out how to make a living at it. That frees me up to put more energy into my work.

It's important to remember why you've jumped, when you are faced with new opportunities like I am now. I'm facing enough demand now to warrant bringing in employees and producing my work in higher volumes, but that's not what I made this jump for. I'm not in this for the money. I jumped to have lunch with my family, play with my kids in the afternoon, and to make a living creating beautiful art. Don't lose sight of what it is you jump for.

With each day life passes by. When you jump for something you care about, you're going to surprise yourself, and you're going to stumble into the next thing that you'd otherwise never see. Whether your passion is for detailing cars or poring over spreadsheets or baking cookies—follow your passion. Start with anything that gets you on the path—for me it was experimenting with making furniture on my back porch—and then follow it.

Know, though, that jumping is going to cost you something. My jump cost years of stress and years of living without. That's just the price you have to pay. It's human nature to prefer a jump to be easy. It's not just about the desire to jump; it's having to accept that it's tough or may not work out the way you thought.

I doubt many people who jump would say, "Yeah, it was a breeze. I didn't have to sacrifice anything." I don't think you hear that too much. It's the opposite: people who are doing what they love have struggled through this, or they had to battle through that. And I think that's the beauty of it: doing work you love is a reward for being willing to take that sacrifice. So leap into that hard choice. From there, you may just find your "luck."

GREG KLASSEN, a former garbageman and forklift operator, is a luxury furniture designer and maker.

Let Yourself Be Lucky

Section Takeaways

Get a calendar, set a date

- "The biggest help came from two women in particular. Their trick was simple: they would only speak using 'when' and not 'if' about my jump." (Abigail Ogilvy Ryan)
- "Nothing about this was spontaneous. We spent almost a year planning, and then we gave ourselves a place and date." (Juan Romero)
- "Knowing when to jump can become a clear decision." (Olakunle Oladehin)

Try even just one thing

- "Put an idea out into the world, and see what happens. Some things are an immediate hit, and some things aren't, but that's not to say that an idea is not going to have its time and is not going to come around in some way later. You just don't know. But if you don't take the jump, and you don't put those things out in the world . . . you don't stand a chance. " (Ethan Eyler)
- "So I bought a domain for ten bucks, called it The Points Guy, and sent out a message to all my friends and family." (Brian Kelly)

- "There happened to be a local cabinet shop in our office installing new cabinets, and I quietly went up to the guy installing the cabinets and said, 'Hey, do you guys have any jobs?' He said, 'Yeah, sure. We actually need a guy.'" (Greg Klassen)

- "I started posting workshops within the community. I didn't know what would transpire or come out of these events, but I just wanted to bring people together and dance." (Olakunle Oladehin)

- "Suddenly, it popped in my head: the front of cars kind of look like faces, and it'd be hilarious if these 'faces' had mustaches. It was cracking me up. . . . I searched the Internet but couldn't find car mustaches. I was shocked. I said to myself in the car, 'I'm going to cobble one of these things together and put it on my car, and see what happens.'" (Ethan Eyler)

Prepare to get lucky

- "I don't think people have good luck or bad luck. The luck is there. You just have to jump to experience it." (Juan Romero)

- "When you jump for something you care about, you're going to surprise yourself, and you're going to stumble into the next thing that you'd otherwise never see." (Greg Klassen)

- "Once you know what you want, once you've started to plan, you're just steps away from running into some luck. You might not collect on that luck until you actually jump; but . . . favorable coincidences begin to appear." (Mike Lewis)

- "All you have to do is keep yourself in a frame of mind to be open to what's dealt to you." (Michael Lewis)

- "Sometimes you make a jump, and it doesn't immediately work out. And then later down the road, things click in some way, and people say, 'Man, you got so lucky with that.' But I firmly believe that you create your own luck and that you have to put yourself in a position to get lucky." (Ethan Eyler)

Then jump already

- "If we kept trying to plan a bit more and a bit more, we'd still be stuck in the harbor with everyone else." (Juan Romero)

- "You don't need to write the be-all and end-all business plan before you start your jump." (Ethan Eyler)

- "The act of preparing to change your life can turn into one of the world's most seductive procrastination tools. Talking about travel and adventure makes for great cocktail conversation, and, dangerously, can go on forever." (Mike Lewis)

- "Above all else, know that to get your break, you will have to jump. No one—not your biggest supporter, not the person you look up to the most—no one is going to make the right decision in telling you when to jump. . . . Pull the Band-Aid off and jump, because no one else is going to do that for you." (Brian Kelly)

- "I casually floated the idea to my mom that maybe, just maybe, it could work out nicely to jump *after* the summer season. . . . She said, 'Mike . . . If you're going to go, go!' " (Mike Lewis)

- "You want to plan, but it's easy to stall out in that gray area on the way from planning to jumping. Confirm your convictions, become as skilled as can be, then go." (Greg Klassen)

You do you

- "The hardest thing to do is not care what anyone else thinks." (Olakunle Oladehin)

- "People would see me behind the counter, or in the kitchen, and question my education, doubt my ambitions. But you know what? That's life. You just suck it up and push through it, and you learn that people will say things. Ultimately, it prepares you to be thick-skinned, and you need to have that when you jump." (Abigail Ogilvy Ryan)

- "When I told my colleagues that I was quitting, they thought I was nuts. They were very sweet about it. They were concerned. They took me into a room and said, 'You're sure you wanna do this? This is a mistake.' I . . . just thought to myself, 'None of these people are qualified to tell me what to do with my life.'" (Michael Lewis)

- "Ultimately, I jumped because I wanted to be me." (Eleanor Watson)

- "People ask, 'How can you do it?' Everyone can do it. Truly." (Juan Romero)

- "Whatever your jump is, if you head toward it with passion and vigor, no one will stop you." (Olakunle Oladehin)

That wasn't so risky, was it?

- "Looking back, it seems like a giant risk to quit a job that paid me all kinds of money . . . for a fairly unknown future as a writer. But I knew I really wanted to do it. There wasn't a shred of doubt, and I was getting so sick of going to work there every morning. So it was not a terribly hard decision, and it didn't *feel* like that much of a risk." (Michael Lewis)

- "I was always so terrified of failure because from a young age we are told to be perfect. Any immigrant can tell you that a B in school is simply not an option. I had a real fear of making mistakes. But the more I started to read biographies, the more I asked, 'What's the worst thing that can happen?'" (Olakunle Oladehin)

- "It's easy to think only about the negative consequences when making any of these types of changes. . . . But also try to think about the positive consequences that come from jumping: the experience gained, the fulfillment enjoyed." (Juan Romero)

- "We have a way of trying to scare ourselves out of a jump with exaggerations, and you shouldn't let that happen." (Ethan Eyler)

PHASE 4

DON'T LOOK BACK

"You come out stronger."

—Matt Pottinger

"AS A REMINDER, Mike, your building access card will deactivate on May 24, as will your e-mail address. Messages will bounce. You'll be out of our system."

Yikes. Well that's one way to say so long. I nodded quietly as a colleague from the human resources department explained the details of my departure from the firm. I had in hand a ticket to New Zealand, a loose plan, and a million unanswered questions. But the human resources department had no questions about my jump: from the company's point of view, in the near future, I'd be gone.

For a split second, I was tempted to reply, "JUST KIDDING!," return to my desk, and pretend I had never thought of leaving. I wanted an open door, a "May Come Back" notice on my desk. A few days later, I even asked a human resources representative if, just *if*, I were to leave and end up coming back, would it be logistically possible to get my e-mail to turn back on? What about my building access card? She smiled and replied, "It's just like turning the lights back on." Never had the possibility of getting to my desk and checking my e-mail seemed so appealing. I wasn't really hoping to turn the lights back on, but I felt some comfort in believing it was possible. My job had formed a big part of my identity: I was known to the world as an associate at Bain Capital. Who would I be when I left?

· · ·

What we think people think of us matters. Some part of us cares and will always care how our friends, coworkers, and family view us. That's normal. And just as we might secretly hope for certain schools, jobs, and neighborhoods to provide us with labels—smart, successful, wealthy— we might equally easily aspire to jumps that do the same, giving us new labels—courageous, crazy, cool. This is part of being human, wanting to fit into a community and to be respected, even admired, within it. But even though all this is understandable and normal, try not to let image be too big a part of your reason for not jumping—or for jumping. Try to make sure your jump is for you and only you.

Shortly before my last day at Bain, an older colleague pulled me into his office. The colleague was a successful manager—the same manager who had warned me early on about the risk of quitting my day job to try to play squash. I expected a stern talking-to, but as his door slid softly closed behind us, this manager told me his own story: of turning down a one-year fellowship position at a global nonprofit organization to attend business school because he didn't want to "get behind" in his pro- gram or career and felt pressure to keep straight ahead. "I enjoy where I'm at now, but what I learned is that in the end, had I jumped, nothing would have changed; I could have made my way back to all this, just a year later." Gazing out the window, he said, "Not jumping has been my single biggest career regret. Rather, my single biggest regret. Period."

It was lunchtime at the office when I made my final round of good-byes. I had daydreamed that this moment would be like in the movies: a sen- timental, sappy send-off. Tears and slaps on the back. Perhaps even some applause as I rode off into the sunset.

But that wasn't what happened. My coworkers were busy with their own lives, and while they absolutely wished me well, they had their own questions to figure out that day. "How great! Good luck! Stay in touch!" they said at lunchtime. Then they went back to work. Life moved on. While others cared, this jump and whatever was to come from it was critical to me and me only. Every morsel of good, every atom of bad, every new challenge and fear, every conquest and milestone I would face from here on was building toward my own learning and experiences, toward my own life journey.

Riding down the elevator, my Bain career compressed into the cardboard storage box I was hugging to my chest, I promised myself I would jump and not look back or wonder whether I was winning or losing, ahead or behind. My college professor Charlie Wheelan liked to remind his students that there are no final rankings in life. He'd often say that obituaries don't conclude with, "John finished in 3,123rd place." And another professor in the theater department would remind me regularly of the advice he gives any student preparing to take the stage, be it in a theater or elsewhere: "You do you."

I wish I could say I left the elevator that day focused on doing me, unfazed by social expectations, immune to self-conscious fears and distractions. That wasn't the case, and it still isn't the case. But before I walked out of the building, I made a pact: to skip the second-guessing. This jump was worth doing. I was all-in.

If you're like me, you may be reading this thinking, "Well, duh. It's easy to say, 'It doesn't matter what people think,' and 'Don't look back,' when your jump happened to go well." I thought the same thing. And yet in those final stages of takeoff, my most encouraging supporters—my loudest cheerleaders, my biggest advocates—were those who had chased a passion and, on a surface level, failed miserably. It was precisely these people, with their "failed" jumps, who were the most unwavering and adamant believers in the value of taking one. As my old boss told me, a jump may be uncertain, but planned right, it doesn't have a massive downside. The people you meet, the story you'll have, the lessons you will have learned, make it an experience worth pursuing, regardless of what happens. So don't waste time looking back.

If you're still not convinced, here's a good test: think up the WORST possible outcome of jumping, and see how bad that looks. For me, it looked like this: quit my job and wake up in New Zealand, lose every match, run out of money, maybe sprain my ankle in the process, and hobble home to live with my parents. After I'd licked my wounds, I'd still be employable to someone, and I would always have a funny story about when I tried to chase something I cared a lot about.

That worst-case scenario didn't seem nearly as scary as the alternative: waking up every morning for the next fifty years wondering what might have been. My close friend Merle (who shared her jump in the "Listen to the Little Voice" section in this book) volunteers at a hospice, visiting regularly with seniors who are, quite literally, on their death beds. The one common sentiment expressed by each patient? The regret of not trying. If you really want to try for something, and you think about it every day, and it's what's in your mind when you go to sleep at night and wake up in the morning, the eventual pain of not trying for it is always going to be greater than the pain of trying and failing. Always.

A few days after leaving the Bain office, it was time for me to leave the States. Before the flight out, my friend Molly took me out for a farewell lunch. Molly was one of my early jump role models, having threaded jumps relating to her passion for outdoor adventures into a successful career in business operations. In between bites of spaghetti, Molly dished her final advice: "When you jump from your job and your life here and unpack all the other distractions, take note of what makes you happy— truly happy—and remember what that is when the distractions come back and life returns to being busy." Before we asked for the bill, I hunched over our empty plates and asked Molly if she had any idea what was going to happen next, because I did not. With her pointer finger, she traced a line diagonally upward, drawing a staircase in the air. "These are the ways we all tend to think of careers." I looked at the invisible staircase and watched myself flying away from it that night, somewhere into the abyss. Then Molly took her hand and traced a second line, this one messy and squiggled, zigs and zags creating ups and downs, like the shape of a W. "These are the types of career paths, and journeys in life, that serve us best."

So that was that. My jump was happening, and the result mattered to me, but what mattered even more was just getting on the plane. I boarded the plane, and I didn't look back.

DAN KENARY

Commercial Banker to Brewery Owner

I WAS A curious kid from central Massachusetts who loved drinking beer. A train ride through Ireland after college left me with an idea that I just couldn't shake: you can spend way, way, way too much of your life at work not doing something you absolutely love and care about. I wasn't going to let that happen.

I grew up in Worcester, Massachusetts, the youngest of four kids born within four years, living in a great house on a street full of big families. We were expected to support ourselves from an early age; there was no such thing as an allowance. So I kept busy. My first memories with beer came in high school: I'd go out camping with buddies, sitting around the campfire drinking cans of whatever was around. I didn't know anything about the beer itself, but I adored the experience—sharing a drink and a laugh with great company.

I was coming up on college graduation in the spring of 1982 and, like most kids my age, had no idea what I wanted to do. I applied all over and ended up being offered a job with the First National Bank of Chicago. My dad had been in business, and I grew up around it, so I said why not and accepted the offer. That summer after graduating, I had a few months free before I started work and I spent them backpacking around Europe with some buddies from school. On the third day of our trip, we found ourselves at a brewery in Ireland, talking about beer.

We knew nothing about beer, other than that we loved drinking it. At that time in the States, the beer world was pretty basic. I remember an exciting beer for us was Molson Golden. We just didn't know anything beyond the light yellow lagers sold everywhere in America. Now here we are at this Irish brewery, and I was a kid in a candy store. We tried the local beer and loved it, and the bartender there told us it was brewed in the town of Kilkenny, which just so happened to be on our train route to Dublin. We had to see it.

We had a tight schedule, but four of us stopped in Kilkenny at the brewery. They gave us the whole history of things and led us down to their tavern. In the tavern were old cellars and a bar, and they gave us sample after sample. We stayed there all day. They ended up driving us to the train station. I would remember that day well. It stood out in my memory as what a brewery could be.

I came back from the trip and moved to Chicago, worked at the bank for a few years in a bunch of areas, doing good stuff with really nice people, making good money but bored to tears. I started thinking, "Is this really what I'm gonna do the rest of my life?" I began looking around at people who were in their forties and fifties, which was ancient to me at that point. They were good people, but I didn't want their careers. Nothing wrong with what they were doing, but I knew if I had to stay in this field for my entire career, I would just go crazy. It was not what I wanted to do.

So in the late fall, early winter of 1985, I said, "You know what? I've gotta shit or get off the pot here. I've gotta do something else." I went and talked to my father about it.

My dad had had one job from when he graduated from college in 1950, having worked thirty-five years as a financial advisor. He had been valuable my whole life as my source for all kinds of advice, but at this point in the game, he just couldn't give me any help. He never switched jobs, and to him and my mother, both children of the Depression, the idea that I would consider leaving a great job at a terrific financial institution was just bizarre. But he tried to understand.

Since I didn't know what I wanted to do, I decided I was going to pursue three different areas of interest. Number one was my love for history, so I pursued the idea of going back to school and getting my PhD in American history. To that end I took the GREs, applied to schools, and was accepted at places. I was offered scholarship money at Stanford. Since I had a finance background, and my dad had known a lot of business managers, I also applied for jobs in other areas of finance. My third area of interest was starting my own company. I didn't know anything about that because nobody in my family had ever tried it. It was a real stretch. But it just so happened a great old pal of mine from college, Rich Doyle, was at Harvard Business School in his second year. Rich was starting a research report on what was, at that time, called the microbrewing industry. That movement was just getting started in the Pacific Northwest, around Portland and Seattle.

I had first met Rich in a freshman dorm in Harvard Yard in the fall of 1978. Rich is a New Yorker through and through, and the most obnoxious Yankee fan I've ever met. So we had a brutal fall of '78 when his Yankees and my Red Sox were battling it out. We bonded over many late nights of drinking beer.

Over time, we kept that relationship going. Like me, Rich had also traveled to Europe, and we compared notes on that. We met up every so often when we were both in Boston, and it was one of those nights when I told him what I was considering. And he said, "Listen, I'm thinking of taking my research forward, converting it to a business plan, and trying to open a brewery in Boston. What do you think?"

Beer became my third option. I had a decision to make: Stanford for the PhD. Another finance gig. Or a start-up brewery idea called Harpoon.

I was flying blind and didn't know what to do. So I decided to learn as much about each decision as I possibly could: what the life would really be like, who I would be working with, what each job truly entailed. If you can reflect on those things, you're going to be able to make a much more informed decision. When I learned about the PhD process and becoming an academic, I decided I really didn't want to do that. The money management business started to look pretty similar to what I had just left, so that didn't seem to make sense. And then there was the last thing, the opportunity with the brewery.

I took a step back. I was twenty-five years old, I was single, and I had a little bit of money in the bank. If not now, when? Now would be a great time to try that. I believed fundamentally that the American beer market was ripe for change. There was an opening. When I traveled in Europe, I tried some incredible beers. But more than that, I saw how the little things—the stories, the history, the marketing behind the beer—were all completely different. They had made drinking beer an amazing consumer experience, one that didn't exist in the States, where beer was viewed as a commodity. There was no experience to it. The lack of a great beer experience in the States felt ridiculous to me. You'd hear young people all the time say, "Oh yeah, I was over in Germany, Ireland, wherever, and the beer was awesome. I came back here and it just sucks."

Coffee Connection was doing it for coffee in Boston. Coffee used to be only at gas stations, diners, premade—you had very little choice. Then all of a sudden you had this place to go for coffee: you walk in and smell the aroma and are swept up in it all. You pay a little bit more, but the experience is worth it. And then you had Ben & Jerry's doing the same thing for ice cream. I felt like beer should be next.

So I said yes to Rich, and we had one other partner, George Ligeti, who also said yes. I left my job in June of '86, and Rich and George graduated around then too. We began turning the original research into a business plan. We raised $430,000 from investors to start a brewery in Boston.

For me, it was a major leap into the unknown: quitting the job while still having rent to pay and, all of a sudden, raising this money. We fell in love with a location on the city waterfront—European beer gardens are located in the middle of the towns, so we wanted the same for ours. We tried moving in immediately but were stalled for months by city bureaucracy and red tape. It was a painful process that almost took out our business before it started, but we stuck it out. A few decades later, the venue has become a tremendous asset: four hundred thousand visitors came through our doors in just the last year.

We moved in around March of '87. We hired for the skills we lacked—a consultant who had installed breweries, a brewmaster who had never been east of Reno, Nevada. He lived on my couch for a while at the start.

Rich and I worked on the walls, built a tour room, laid carpet, painted. We sold our first kegs of beer by early June—an incredibly fast turn-around. It was an exciting time, and when I look back I laugh. It's actually beneficial to take risks like this when you're young because you don't know what you don't know.

Once you get a bit older, you've got other responsibilities, and you want to pick apart each decision. But back then, we were shooting from the hip. We just felt we could overcome anything, and that's the attitude we had to have, and then some. I laugh when I say this, but it's kinda true: waking up and facing the challenges of a start-up is like waking up and taking a punch in the face every day.

It's not easy to know when to jump. I say to my kids, "Listen, no matter what you do, and no matter how long you do it, just do it really well so that when you leave, people think, 'You're a great guy, great gal, leaving a great job. I'm sorry to see you go.'" That way you develop your own great brand, and you take that with you to whatever's next. You build a career that way. It's hard to know where it's going to go, and that's actually kind of an exciting thing, right?

At some point or another, each of my kids has said, "I don't like what I'm doing, I don't like the track I am on. But it's incredibly daunting to try something else, and I don't know what I want to do." I respond by telling them what I learned in their shoes thirty years ago. Brainstorm what you like to do. Research what life looks like doing those things. Then make a choice, and go for it. And if you don't like what you're doing, well, then do it for a year or two. Use it as a building block to whatever comes next. You never know what that next place may be or who you'll meet or where you'll go. That's what makes it fun.

And whatever you go do, don't look back. I never look back. Never, even in the darkest days at Harpoon did I look back fondly and say, "Gosh, I really miss being a commercial loan officer," never once. That place was scratched off once my decision to jump was made. At the time, I had no idea if it was the right decision to start Harpoon. But I did know that I had made the right decision to leave the bank.

Of course, serendipity plays a big role in all of this, but it starts with a personal choice. Take a chance; follow a passion. See where it leads.

And if it leads you through Boston, come find me at Harpoon. We'll have a beer.

DAN KENARY, a former commercial bank loan officer, is cofounder and CEO of Harpoon Brewery.

KYLE BATTLE

IT Consultant to Digital Director at Special Olympics

GROWING UP, I wanted a career. My childhood wasn't one with a lot of comforts; we lived below the poverty line, numbers-wise. It was a struggle. My mother was a drug addict, in and out of rehab, so I ended up with my grandparents for a while. When my mom got clean, I was able to move back in with her, but she had trouble keeping a career going. She'd move from job to job.

For me, a good job was the ultimate dream. I didn't make much right out of college, but it was more than my mother had made for all four years I was in college, combined. Both my grandparents had retired from Procter & Gamble, but my grandfather never made more than $36,000 in a year. And he worked there for something like thirty years. It wasn't much, but we got by. We come from small-town Ohio. That's just how people live.

I grew up with my mom and older brother, Cameron, who has Down syndrome. By the time I was five or six, my mom and I would watch Cameron compete in Special Olympics events. Cameron and I eventually shared the same trophy case; some of his medals, some of mine. The Special Olympics motto is "Let me win, but if I cannot win, let me be brave in the attempt." We both believe in that.

A few years out of college I moved to California looking for steady work, but it wasn't so easy to find. I had been an athlete my whole life but couldn't land anything in sports. At the time, I was living with my former girlfriend, and we were really struggling, living off ramen noodles and even selling her car to make rent. At times, I was ashamed to call home because I knew my family didn't necessarily agree with my decision to move out to LA. And it looked like they had been right.

After about a year in LA, I got to a safe place: a job with a salary, benefits, the whole shebang. The start of a career where I could say, "Okay, now I'll start to build something substantial." I could finally call home. There was a weight off my shoulders, relief for my mom in Ohio: her son had figured it out. For the first time, I felt secure that I wouldn't have to be that guy: that guy who got out, got a degree, went to California, couldn't cut it, and had to move back in with his mom in Ohio. I really didn't want to be that guy.

Right as I was settling in, I came across a notice: a position with the Special Olympics, helping them prepare for their upcoming World Games. My first thought was, "Is this a joke?" Because the job description was so similar to my résumé, a perfect match to my interests. They were not going to find someone who was a better fit than I was. The catch was that once the World Games were over, albeit twenty months away, I would be jobless yet again. The excitement quickly turned to uncertainty: Was the prospect of doing something more fulfilling enough to abandon the security I had struggled the last two years for?

But I had to apply. It was an opportunity I couldn't pass up. The Special Olympics was going to be the biggest event in Los Angeles since the 1984 Olympics. That type of occasion doesn't come around very often. Plus, that was why I moved to LA; to chase my dreams, work on cool projects, and make my future what I want it to be.

The role was a blend of what I knew: my skills in IT, my interests in sports and marketing, my passions for philanthropy and for the Special Olympics. The person who interviewed me for the job was a black Ivy League graduate, like me, and we hit it off. It felt like the decision was made for me. Maybe I should have felt more guilt or should have felt more worried, but honestly, it felt like a choice I didn't have control over anymore. I had fears about my career path and real concerns about cash flow, but a louder, internal voice outweighed everything else: "This is what you're supposed to be doing, so go do it."

The reality was that this jump would toss my professional plans back up in the air. The job I was leaving would be filled as soon as I left, and days after the Special Olympics ended, this new and perfect role would also dissolve.

I jumped anyway. The position wouldn't just be my passion; it would be my springboard. If I helped pull this off—an international sporting event covering 177 countries and thirty thousand volunteers—I would be able to convince that organization, or one like it, that I had what it takes to be a part of their team. Plus, I'd be working alongside big corporations and smart people. I felt that inevitably I would do one thing that blended into something else, bump into someone who would introduce me to someone else. I believed it would work out, even if I didn't yet know how. I took pride in that conviction and put a lot of faith into it. I trusted my instincts.

The job with Special Olympics hit on all cylinders and taught me an immeasurable amount but didn't facilitate the relationships and networking that I was hoping for. Following the World Games, I spent several months unable to find long-term work, with leads often drying up at the last step. I snagged a full-time role at a start-up, but they switched course and stripped my role to a part-time temp position before laying me off. So I started consulting on my own, and my first big contract ended nine months in.

When the next year kicked off, I didn't have a job, I didn't have any projects, and I either had to suck it up or go home. I really didn't want to be that guy. I sent out e-mails left and right, prying at Special Olympics International to see if they would hire me. After being either rejected or ignored, I finally got an e-mail from the guy who had sat in the office next to me at the World Games and had worked full-time at Special Olympics New Jersey. They were looking for a guy like me.

Fast-forward a few months. Special Olympics wanted me on board, to help to build the technical infrastructure that could be rolled out across every state nationally. Exactly the work I wanted, but starting at the state level. I was in the door.

Sometimes you have to take a gamble without knowing what's next, but that's okay when you have a strong conviction for what you're jumping toward and where it will place you. Outcomes aside, you'll be closer to the things that interest you and the people who motivate you. For me, working on a cause that I passionately cared about is what has made the risks worth taking along the way. It has taught me so much about myself, valuable things I couldn't have learned otherwise. The future is still full of possibilities and I know I'm now better prepared to take on those possibilities after having jumped.

Know your worth. Trust and double down on what you can do. My jump was the first time I really bet on myself.

It's a cliché, but it's true: you don't really appreciate success until you fail. That's just natural. I'm not in the clear yet—not even close—but I know what I want, and I'm not going to stop until I have it. I've seen the refrigerator with literally nothing in it. I've survived the humid Midwestern summers without air-conditioning. I've avoided going out for not knowing how to balance having fun with others in social settings and being too broke to participate. I've lived those realities already and, while I appreciate those struggles, I also vow that the next generation of Battles won't ever be able to comprehend it.

KYLE BATTLE, a former IT professional and digital director of the 2015 Los Angeles Special Olympics World Games, is an IT consultant, writer, and filmmaker.

JAMES BOURQUE

Corporate Hospitality Services Professional to
Restaurant Owner

I STARTED THE day mopping. I'll end the night mopping. I'll be back mopping before brunch service starts tomorrow. You always hear this fact about the restaurant business—how most don't make it, how seven out of ten will shut down. I have no idea if that's right, and truth is, I don't care. This business isn't pretty, isn't easy, and isn't for everyone. But starting my own place is what I've always wanted to do, and in 2016 I finally left my nine-to-five to give it a shot.

I grew up the oldest of four in a house full of women: my three younger sisters and my mom. My mother is from Peru, and we Peruvians love to entertain. As a kid, food was synonymous with family: forty or fifty relatives over for Christmas, Easter, Thanksgiving; my mom renting a hardwood floor and having everyone for New Year's. In our family, cooking, eating, and hosting served a higher purpose.

I'm fascinated with the nuances of each dish and drink. A Spanish ham, and the way that the Spanish treat their pigs. A great tequila, and the amount of love and diligence that goes into distilling it. In high school, I'd get home late, and dinner was up to me: reheated leftovers or cook something. At first it was horrible. Then little by little, you get better, and you start cooking for the family, and you start cooking for friends. Next thing you know, you're working in hospitality.

I started out in the imports and exports business after college. They were lofty dreams: travel the world as an international food and beverage businessman. I was trying to export tequila through Florida to Europe, and I did that for eight months or so, but when student loans kicked in, I had to get real. I didn't have the resources or the wherewithal to chase that down any further, so I interviewed for a corporate dining job. It was an assistant manager position at an employee cafeteria in a big company.

I figured someday I would retire and open a restaurant, and I also knew that I needed to learn how to run a business. This was a good opportunity to do both. I approached every task as a learning experience. A big reason I stayed in corporate dining was that I needed to learn, and I couldn't really learn this stuff anywhere else. Whatever your jump is going to be, learn as much as you can before you make it.

I blink, and six, seven years go by. Aside from furthering my educational interests, the job was helping chip away at the financial hurdles: I wanted to open my own place, but I'd need cash. With a single mom (at the time) and three younger sisters all still going through school, God knows we took on enough student loans just for me to go to college. I needed the cash, along with the know-how.

But here's the dirty truth: sure you need the smarts, and sure you need the dough, but those things can become your excuse to never jump—and I watched as it happened to me. As the years rolled, I knew well that corporate life was not for me, but every time I would have that conversation with myself, I'd say, "But it's a paycheck. And I'm still learning. And I have a dog, I have a car payment, and I have rent. I have my student loans. I have to worry about my family. I need to be concerned about not creating an additional burden on my mother." There was always a reason to not jump.

Then one day you wake up, and it smacks you in the face: this is my life. Student loans are my life. My family is my life. My car payments, my insurance, my dog, that's all my life. All that's never going to go away. I will always be paying rent or paying a mortgage. I'm always going to have insurance and grocery bills. Yes, I need a paycheck to cover those things. I wasn't fulfilled with how I earned that paycheck, but that was the one thing I could change.

I'm damn near thirty. God forbid I find myself thirty-five, forty, forty-five—whatever cutoff I've set for myself—and look back, and I'm still doing this nine-to-five hustle.

I had aspirations, and I was not on a path toward achieving them. On the path I was on, I was never going to have time for my friends. I was never going to have time to travel. I wouldn't be making enough to see the world or see my friends in other countries. These were my aspirations; for some people, it's to have a house, have a kid, have a decent car and a dog, and have your weekends to go play T-ball. Bottom line, whatever your dreams are, at some point you gotta be on a path to achieve them. I wasn't.

So I jumped. I quit with maybe two months' worth of savings in the bank, enough to make rent and buy food. I did some consulting for corporate dining groups to give me flexibility and cash for the short term. I put in whatever hours I could, and every other ounce of energy was spent laying down a long-term strategy.

I don't think I fully realized what I was getting myself into when I jumped. The training wheels flew off. I was jumping to start a small, family restaurant business. Shame on people who think that they can "just" open up a restaurant, that you're "just" serving people food, and that's the end of it. This is a family business, and the most stressful part is waking up in the morning knowing I need to show up today, and I need to do a good job simply because if this jump fails, a handful of other people who I love go down with it.

On the safe path, you have responsibility, and there are people who are dependent on you, but you can call in sick. And someone above you can step in and do your job for a week. You can take a vacation. Someone else can cover for you. But if I take two days off now? The whole thing could fall apart.

Running your own thing isn't always pretty, and it's not for everybody. It's really not. Sometimes I don't think it's for me, and I'm all-in. There are mornings when I wake up and think, "God, I just want two days off—or enough time to take a nap, maybe catch up on *House of Cards*." That goes through my head for about an hour or so, and then I start anew. I close my eyes and remember why I jumped. I look around at the chairs, the tables, the bar. That always triumphs.

If you jump, be ready for bumps in the road. We were finalizing our opening plans when our first lease turned out worthless; we were two weeks in the test kitchen when our executive chef quit. Back to zero, facing a deadline to open that was weeks away. For a lot of people, this would have been it. Within a week, I looked at around twenty locations, talked to a bunch of landlords, made a bunch of negotiations, sat down and got one that worked. We got the keys on November 18, and we had the doors open by December 17. Be ready for the bumps.

I'm a firm believer that I am the sum of all of my life experiences, so even those dark times have helped me get to where I am today. Never look behind you. I hired a new bartender, and I was talking to him about his jump—he wants to start an events company. I told him that you always need a contingency plan. You have to have plan B, plan C, plan D. For me now, it's not so much, "Do I go back to corporate?" as it is "How do I maneuver and take what I have here to the next step?"

This restaurant could very well fail. Knock on wood, I don't want it to, but I don't think failure is the question in making a jump. The question is, what can you do from here? How do you make this part of that bigger plan that creates stability for a future that you own, that you create? What will you do when things go wrong? You can see it as the world crumbling, or you can say, "Well, I have all of these pieces: let me catch what I can and see what I can do with them."

I keep coming back to the idea of agency: the difference between life happening to you versus you making life happen. People say, "Well, I wasn't given the opportunity. I wasn't set up for success." You have more control over your life than most people give you credit for, and it's not always easy, and it's not always fun. But when you jump, you are going to make a mark. Outcome aside, that's a really good feeling: knowing that you took an idea, you applied yourself to it, and then, at the end of the day, you tried. My restaurant has an identity, it's growing up, and it's on its own now. For that alone, my jump was worth it.

Remember that no jump is life or death. Sometimes at the restaurant, when things get really tense, people get pissed off. If a dish goes out wrong, people take it emotionally, and there are two things I always remind people. One: it's just food, it's not neurosurgery; no one is dying. And, more importantly, there's always dinner tomorrow. As shitty as things get today, there's always tomorrow, and if we messed up today, we still have the opportunity to do it better tomorrow, to fix it tomorrow.

Win or lose, success or fail, I'm moving straight ahead.

Because there's always dinner tomorrow.

JAMES BOURQUE, a former corporate hospitality professional, is a food and beverage entrepreneur.

ELIZABETH HAGUE

Secretary to Photographer

I COME FROM a family of creative types who inspired me to do something interesting. I fell in love with art, took up photography, and dreamed up a world where I worked for myself, taking photos when and where I wanted. So I went for it, and it all worked out.

Well, not quite.

Our generation grew up being told we could do whatever we wanted and however we wanted. So I fully believed that after we left college there would be perfect jobs waiting for us.

Not quite.

I graduated in 2007, right before the economy dropped off completely. My degree was in film photography—not digital, but film: old school, antiquated film. The day I picked up my diploma was the same day I heard they were planning to tear down the film labs at my school.

As the economy got worse, the jobs that I felt were promised to me simply evaporated. In its place was a cold reality: holy shit, I have a ton of debt, there are no jobs, and I have a degree that's not going to help me get anywhere. Yet I cling to these grandiose dreams of being the next Annie Leibowitz. What happens now?

I grab the first job that will take me, a ten-dollar-an-hour secretary job at an eminent domain office. My job is to help take people's land.

The worst frigging job in the world. I live in a shitty apartment with a shitty boyfriend in a shitty job.

My only outlet is photography. I am freelancing in my spare time and gradually have a few more projects thrown my way. On the weekends, I go shoot something for six hours as an assistant somewhere, and I make, two, three, four, five hundred bucks sometimes.

Here, my jump emerges. I realize that I can start my own gig as a photographer and escape this life of just awfulness. Doing that would mean moving back in with my parents. It would mean learning on the go: I studied art, not business. It would mean a high chance of failure, especially in the economic landscape of that moment.

I look at the risks and think: I have an apartment full of thrift store furniture and a crappy boyfriend who doesn't know what he wants to do either. What am I really losing here?

So I jump.

What happened next was the same thing that has happened to every failed business. Not enough lead generation, not enough money coming in. Somewhere, things went wrong: I didn't shake enough hands, or people didn't know enough about me; there was some magic thing that was missing that I could never track down. I wasn't able to produce the amount of work I needed to produce to sustain myself in any feasible way.

The cruel reality was that what worked for me as a side gig on the weekend didn't work for me as a real job. Jumping from hobby to livelihood required finances to cover health insurance, operating costs, and equipment. I couldn't keep up and racked up debt upon debt, with no escaping.

It's incredibly embarrassing in our society to fail. Many people don't accept the notion of failure, and they don't encourage you to experiment. So when you actually do fail, there's a sense of worthlessness: Why didn't I do better? How could I have not made this work? I labeled my company failure as a personal one, which made it all the more embarrassing and devastating. I didn't want to share what happened with anyone. Yet just a couple years later, this experience turned out to be critical, essential. And I want to share with you why.

Picking up the pieces meant going back to square one, looking for a job again. But this time, things were different. I decided I was not going back to my old crappy life and that I'd think much broader in my search. It's embarrassing to admit that until that point, I had considered only a narrow life vision—the type you dream up or see on TV—and had never pushed beyond that scope. I wasn't going to make that mistake again.

I learned two big things. First, I needed to find jobs that might not be perfect but would build the groundwork for future jumps. And second, I had to believe in whatever I did next. Even though I felt helpless, failed and unemployed in my parents' basement, I assumed control over the situation. I could do whatever I want.

I researched different industries besides just photography. I didn't settle to be another secretary at some blah blah law firm. I took time to find things that somehow related to what I liked doing. Eventually, I got a temp job on the set of photo shoots. It wasn't anything fancy. I wasn't the photographer. I was in the back, holding up props for them to shoot. But I approached it with positivity. I was involved in something tangential to my interests, and that was a good start. I told myself, this is a great step that I'm making on the journey toward finding what I want to do. I'm going to be the best prop holder they've ever had.

Luckily, a while later some folks took note of my prop-holding skills, and they offered me a permanent position. It wasn't my big life goal, but there were pieces of it that made me happy. I told myself, "Say yes, then figure the rest out." It honestly was the best frigging decision I have ever made, in my entire life.

When you jump, prioritize what you need most, and solve those items first. At the top of my list were paying my bills and being happy; further down was being my own boss. When I started my new job, I solved for the top and put the bottom on hold. And that's okay: checking off priority number eight wasn't going to matter if I couldn't figure out number one.

That was really hard—not to try and solve for everything all at once. But sacrifice is abso-freakin-lutely the key to getting what you want. A jump isn't done in a day. But that doesn't mean you won't do it in a couple of years, or even six months from now. You don't know. You just don't know.

Being at that company with people ten times smarter than I am, who had twenty years more experience than I had, taught me the things about my new industry I didn't know, things I never would've learned on my own. I became so valuable because of what I learned about digital branding that I actually got head-hunted by another company. I transitioned to working for a dot-com, and from there I built up the funding I needed to make my own jump once again—to a digital media company. This time, I was way smarter. This time, I was ready.

None of this would have happened if I hadn't first jumped and failed. If you look around your life today and if your alternative to jumping is staying in a miserable job or with a miserable boyfriend or in an awful apartment—or some combination of all three—and never moving forward, then it doesn't make sense to *not* jump. Results aside, you'll be making moves toward happiness—and even if you don't get all the way to happy, at least you'll have gotten a toe off the ground.

You'll be less miserable. And the potential gains are just so much better than the potential embarrassment of a failure. Truly. When you're lying on your deathbed, are you going to be excited that you stayed in your shitty job? Are you going to be upset that you didn't take that opportunity when you had the chance? Are you going to be happy, saying, I tried everything I possibly could to make a life I'm proud of?

There's no guarantee that what I'm doing now will be 100 percent successful. There's no guarantee in anything. What matters is that I'm living a life I want to live. The journey that comes with taking a jump will always be worthwhile to you, period.

Failed jumps will expose you to new skills and experiences, and you'll become more and more valuable on the job market. Yes, failure can be embarrassing; just deal with it. And once you get used to failing—when you become an expert at failing—it's not nearly as scary.

Be less afraid to be happy. My parents are now retirement age, and they have become a bit more reflective. They talk about how they wish they had taken a jump when they were younger. Don't have these regrets.

When I look back, I think the lofty promise made to our generation might actually be true: there are dream jobs and fulfilling careers available to us. We just have to jump—and sometimes fail and jump again—to reach them.

ELIZABETH HAGUE, a former secretary, photographer, and photo shoot prop holder, is the cofounder and owner of Wildcat Echo, a boutique full-service digital and branding studio.

JACK MANNING (PSEUDONYM)

Private Wealth Manager to Sober-Home Operator

I'm a worrier. Anxious, neurotic, type A. Been that way my whole life. People like me don't usually belong in a book on risk-taking. But all that stress finally caught up with me and worked out for the better in a way I would never have imagined.

Today, I have a story to tell. About the time I stopped worrying and started jumping.

I had a normal childhood in southeast New Hampshire, with a loving older sister and two caring parents. My father is a great guy, and I am superfortunate to have him. But he is also an extremely dominant personality and was the driving force behind a gold standard I set for myself as a kid. At the earliest age, my goal was to follow in his footsteps, and that meant getting the best grades, becoming the best athlete, attending the best school, winning awards: appearing really successful.

Along the way, I missed the memo that said that in order to attain the good grades and awards, it requires really hard work on a day-to-day basis. So I had these lofty goals of what I should be, without having developed the tools or the work ethic to achieve it. That amounted to a lot of worry and anxiety—fear to step outside of my lane in life, fear of trying for anything other than what my dad wanted for me. I grew up very scared of wanting anything other than his version of success, and I scrambled to obtain and then maintain those standards.

When I was around fourteen years old, I started getting in trouble every couple of months because of drugs and alcohol. It was apparent right from the start that I wasn't predisposed to trouble with drinking and doing drugs; it was an escape from my fear and worrying. When I'd get in trouble, I assumed that getting good grades or winning awards would fix the problem: that it'd bring me happiness if I could just get back on the beam, dust myself off, clean up my appearance, correct people's perceptions of me. And so began a pretty vicious cycle of getting hurt chasing what I thought would make the hurt go away. Things got worse. I desperately tried holding on to this gold-standard pursuit while things fell apart.

In my junior year of college, I went to the hospital for a big surgery. Afterward, I never kicked the pain medicine they gave me for it, and my abuse of the pills skyrocketed. My sister intervened, and when she did, I threw my hands up. I was scared, alone, powerless. I needed help.

The plan was twenty-eight days of inpatient rehab. I agreed to that, and then I told myself I'd head back to college and to my sports team and prove to everyone that I was okay. After those twenty-eight days, I agreed to a one-month outpatient sober house. One month turned into three; I became active in the sober community and took a job working in the stockroom in the local Pottery Barn. For the first time in my life, I was happy.

Three months turned into eleven months in the sober home. I had found a new version of myself, and it was radically different from the one I had imagined. I left clean and content and went back and graduated college. But as I started my career, I still couldn't shake my dad's expectations for me, and I got a job in his line of work, private wealth management. He's been in it for forty years and has this big book of business, and we always assumed that I'd take it over some day. It was my destiny.

I was really naive about what the job actually was. I didn't think much about what it entailed; I went into it because it was what my dad did. I saw the things that it afforded him. I looked up to him and believed that I could eventually take over the family business.

For the first two years, I had blinders on. I was in the zone. It was a total sensory overload, being in a new city, having a new profession. I wasn't thinking about what I was doing. Once I settled into a more comfortable position, I stepped back. It was the first time I stepped outside the box and looked at the job, and me in the job, from a thirty-thousand-foot view. My job was about getting wealthy clients and managing their money. There were few parts that felt right. I thought, "Okay, what am I doing here? This is what I'm doing for the next thirty-five years of my life. Is this how I want to spend my time as a human being on Earth?"

I looked at all the clients I was servicing. They were incredibly creative entrepreneurial types that found the courage to follow their passions. I heard their stories about how they started in one type of job and then broke off to try something they cared about, about how they realized when their first or second job wasn't what they were destined to do. I wondered what that must feel like, to follow a passion—or to even have one.

Around that time, I was introduced to a guy who runs a big health company. We met up and started schmoozing (I was hoping to get him as a new client). As we got to talking, I told him that I was sober. He told me about this gap in the health care industry around sober rehab homes, about how many fraudulent people there were in the business, and how there was such a need for good, honest help. I could relate exactly to his point: many people leave inpatient rehab and go straight home, transitioning from total support to zero support. He said there needs to be an intermediate level of care for people at an affordable price, and how someone like me would be perfect for it.

Instantly, I saw that this was something I could help with. And with this entrepreneur telling me his story, I could step back and see a jump: chasing something I cared about, starting an organization, and, most importantly, waking up every day in a life that actually fit me. I went back to my desk for about six months with the idea rattling around in my head. As I looked at it from a professional angle, the operational model seemed feasible. As I looked at it from a personal perspective, it seemed like my calling.

In thinking about what I was currently doing, my gut feeling about it was always a little bit off. I would get this pang in my stomach because I knew: "I'm doing something that I don't want to do, that I'm not passion-ate about, that I'm not good at, to which I don't know how to add value." When I started to think about going into sober homes, it was the exact opposite: "I can talk about this. I want to talk about it. I want to help these people. I can make my own organization." Working with sober homes felt like destiny, in a way that made sense, in a way that the gold-standard chase never did.

It wasn't easy to jump. In my job, I was performing well in a corporate training program where less than 10 percent of the people successfully make it through, and I had made it into the first quintile nationally. I had done the hard part: I had found good clients and built a good book of business. Rarely, if ever, does someone in our business doing this well step away from it all. I dreaded the reactions: "What the hell are you doing? You're on a path to be super successful at this. Why are you doing this?"

But I was no longer thinking only in terms of social expectations and social norms. I was now thinking in existential terms. I really was. I real-ized that I was doing this job because I was scared of doing anything else. If I continued to do it, it would be out of fear. But to finally have found a calling, a vocation, which serendipitously came to me, felt like a no-brainer.

The bigger hitch in my jump was explaining my destination. I real-ized that in one fell swoop, every single person in my life was going to find out my story of battling drugs and alcohol. You don't start a sober home without a story yourself. But if there's one thing I learned from my own journey, it's to be comfortable with who I am. Getting sober is now the experience that I'm most grateful for in my life. And so, ultimately, I didn't give two thoughts to what people would think about it.

I began my jump before I left my job, taking on the process of acquiring the property, raising money, nailing down the details, all while working my original nine-to-five. For a six-month period, I knew that I was going to jump, but I wasn't telling anyone at work, and I wasn't tell-ing any of my clients. That cognitive dissonance was tough to deal with on a day-to-day basis. But when the time came to go all-in, my path was clear. And there haven't been many decisions in my life that are clear. Like I said, I'm pretty neurotic. To have such conviction and confidence about jumping—to have such clarity and lack of fear—was a sign. It felt right.

After I jumped, I took a road tour of all the treatment centers in the country, presenting to medical directors, visiting the centers any way I possibly could. I was totally new in the industry, and all of a sudden, I was coming across experts who had been in the industry for thirty years. Everyone knew each other. I was the new kid on the block: How was I going to make a sober house center that could make a difference?

Miraculously, we filled our sober house within one month of opening our doors. By the end of that month, I was responsible for sixteen men, all in the very early stages of sobriety. The hard truth about sobriety is that the relapse rate is extraordinarily high. But in that first year, of the forty-five or fifty guys who visited our center, only one relapsed.

The best part of the jump was the men I met, the people that came through our doors. These were guys that were homeless, on the street. They had good families but had taken their drug use too far. After they left, one became an electrical engineer, one started a demolition company, and another began work at an insurance company. And these were people who had not spoken to their families for years, now going over to their families' houses for dinner on a regular basis and mending broken relationships. It was a really incredible experience to see the transformation of the guys from when they stepped foot in our house to when they left.

Over time, it turned out things weren't all gravy. I was very involved on a day-to-day basis with each one of the guys. I got superintimate and wrapped up with each one of them. I didn't do a great job creating boundaries. They all became very close friends of mine. However, as I learned firsthand, the operating model for a sober house creates a perverse incentive structure: it rewards relapses. Patients who relapse come back, and that's where the money is in the rehab world. I should have seen this coming, but it made me sick.

The rehab world preaches about being of service, but depending on relapses in order to exist as an organization directly opposed this. I struggled with the decision for months before settling on the reality in my gut: I would have to jump again.

Just a year after making my jump into starting the sober home, I'm turning a new page, moving on and starting over. I don't know exactly what will come next, but I certainly know that jumping one year ago will never be something I regret. That jump distilled basic elements of a job that I now know I need: I found that the idea of a nine-to-five is actually something I appreciate, and that I highly value the normalcy of a work routine. I also discovered that I need to leave the big city: on a day-to-day basis, I can handle it, but over a long period of time, it has a negative impact on my psyche; I stress out and burn out. I want to be closer to my family, and a big part of wherever I jump next will be to get closer to them.

I'm not living in fear anymore. The other day, I read a short story about a man on his deathbed. And someone asked him what his greatest regret was, and he said that he worried too much in life. I can really understand that. In starting a sober home, I learned that I can live my life either holding faith in things turning out okay, or I can spend the time between now and that deathbed just worrying.

I'm going to jump again. And I'm no longer worried about what happens next.

JACK MANNING (pseudonym), a former investment professional and sober-home owner and operator, is currently starting over in a small city in New England.

MATT POTTINGER

Journalist to United States Marine

IN JOURNALISM WE talk about story arcs, although I'm not sure my own journey clearly fits into one. It took a war and a tsunami, and one big jump, for me to learn that that's okay.

My parents divorced when I was a little kid. I grew up with my mother and stepfather, moving around a fair bit for his work. I was lucky to go to a high school that offered Chinese, and through learning about China, I became interested in journalism. I studied the language a little bit in high school, and then, in my junior year of college, did an exchange year in Beijing, at Beijing Normal University.

On long weekends I would jump on a train and go to some part of China just to see what was happening. It was the early '90s, and here I was, a twenty-year-old student crisscrossing the country, listening to anyone I could find. It was an incredible time in history: the country was emerging out of the devastation left by Mao and attempting to reform its economy and open its markets, all while dealing with fallout from the Tiananmen massacre a few years earlier. I was writing, keeping a journal, and sending letters home. I decided that after college I'd find a way back as a journalist and chronicle the rise of this future power.

And that's what I did. After graduation I moved to Beijing and covered China for Reuters for a couple years, and then the next five for the

Wall Street Journal. I relished the job. I loved having a front-row seat into the rise of China, covering wild stories. I was quite happily established as a reporter, doing a lot of investigative news pieces and writing for the front page of the paper. If I had stayed on at the *Journal*, my next job might have been bureau chief somewhere in the world. And from there, I probably would've become an editor later on in my career or a columnist—the end goal in my type of work.

In the early autumn of 2001, I returned to New York to meet with the managing editor of the *Wall Street Journal*, as well as our foreign editor, to discuss story ideas.

The *Journal* headquarters in those days were right across the street from the World Trade Center, so my father had suggested meeting for breakfast at Windows on the World, in the World Trade Center, before my meeting next door. At the last minute, we canceled that plan so that I could sleep in and spend a little bit of extra time writing up the story ideas that I wanted to discuss with the editors. A couple of hours later, as my father and I drove into the city together, we got word that an airplane had hit one of the twin towers.

Less than two years later, the United States invaded Iraq; a year in, the war was going terribly wrong. I was stunned at how badly we—as a government, but also as a nation—had misjudged the nature of the war we had launched. I was disturbed by what this would mean for the United States and for our future.

I kept reporting until the events of 9/11 and the turmoil of the Iraq war eventually led to a crossroad: I can stay doing what I'm doing—writing and watching and witnessing what's happening in the world—or I could try to dive into the center of events as a direct participant—even if in a very small role. More to the point, I started to feel like if I didn't get involved, I would one day regret not having done so.

That haunted me: there are important historical events unfolding right now that are going to reshape the future—possibly not for the better—for my country; do I want to be on the sidelines or on the playing field?

In the fall of 2004 I was back in New York at a Council on Foreign Relations lunch event, and I happened to be seated next to a guy who was wearing a regular suit but in fact was an active-duty marine colonel.

I spent the entire event asking every question I had. I was incredibly impressed by him: how he held himself and how he described the marines that he led, their sense of perspective as well as their ability to maintain high morale, even in very challenging times.

As we wrapped up, I made a tiny, flippant remark. I was thirty-one years old at the time, and I said, "It's too bad that I'm too old to be a marine because it's something that I never considered as a kid or as a younger man." I went to a liberal prep school outside of Boston. Military service as a path forward just wasn't on the menu.

The marine colonel asked, "How old are you?" I said thirty-one. And he said, "We still gotcha."

He said if I could pass the physical fitness test and get good recommendation letters, I might be able to get a waiver for my age—the cutoff was normally twenty-eight. If that worked, I'd get a ticket to Officer Candidates School and a chance to pass a ten-week boot camp down in Quantico.

I was just stunned by that. From the event, we went straight back to his office, and he called up a recruiting officer and made an appointment for me. The next day, I was sitting in this marine captain's office, and we were staring at each other across the desk, both of us in disbelief that I was there. He gave me a thick packet of application paperwork. I'd have to try to dig up my college transcripts; it had been ten years since graduation.

I took all that stuff back to work with me in China while at the *Wall Street Journal*, and now had this strange sense of possibility that there was this alternate future. Now that it was possible, was it something that I wanted to follow through with, or not?

It was another catastrophe—the Indian Ocean tsunami of 2004—that gave me the resolve to follow through with this impulse to become a marine. The tsunami struck just after Christmas, killing hundreds of thousands in South and Southeast Asia. I scrambled to Thailand to cover the event, and did some of my reporting on the US military response to the tragedy. I was extremely impressed with the marines and sailors I met who were running humanitarian operations across the region. Many were barely older than kids, but they were professional and extremely committed.

When I got back to Beijing a few weeks later, I began doing a lot of reading about the Marine Corps, while confiding in only one person, a young marine captain I happened to meet who was studying in Beijing. This guy, who didn't really know me at all, immediately agreed to start training me: in the darkness of mornings a few days a week, we'd do long runs, short sprints, reps of pull-ups. On weekends, we'd hike the Great Wall. As I became more physically fit, I became more confident that this was something that I would be able to do. From there, I began confronting a bigger question: Is this something that I should do?

My greatest moment of doubt came on a training day, while finishing a twelve-mile climb on the Great Wall, on this unbelievably hot and humid day in July. The marine came down with heat exhaustion and was throwing up—though that didn't stop him from completing the hike. I thought I was in pretty good shape until my fingers swelled like sausages. I had developed hyponatremia—when you sweat out all the necessary salts in your body—and I ended up tied to an IV drip in a hospital emergency room for the next twelve hours.

After that episode, I knew I needed to share my jump plans with my family. It was mid-2005, when the news was just filled with stories of servicemen getting cut to pieces in Iraq. I dreaded telling my mother. She was absolutely distraught. She made no effort to hide it and tried to marshal every argument she could to deter me. All of her points were quite rational arguments: that this was going to be a terrible detour into the abyss, that I could end up with all my limbs blown off, or be burned alive.

Even if I made it through, she said I would have sacrificed my career, which was going well. I would be behind. I would be unable to catch up. I would've lost that income. I would've lost the momentum and status. I may end up with posttraumatic stress. All these were things that I'd thought of, and they were things that I was scared of. I didn't argue with her on any of it. I let her tell me her thoughts and fears. And then I took a weekend alone to think it all through.

What it came back to was this sense that if I didn't try, I would live with regret—and the kind of regret that you carry around from inaction felt much worse than the regret that you might feel from having taken an action. True, I might end up dead or disfigured, or with my mind injured.

All these things were possibilities, but if I didn't follow my instinct and my desire to jump, I would carry around the regret of having failed to even try. And somehow, that felt viscerally worse to me than thinking about the risks. At the end of that weekend, I emerged and told my family, and very shortly after that I told the *Wall Street Journal* that I was leaving to join the marines.

My colleagues were speechless. They didn't know what to make of it. Some of them thought that this must be political: this must be a part of a long-term plan to run for Congress. I told them the truth, that I am doing something that I feel in my bones is right.

I got a call from the managing editor, the top dog of the paper. He said he's known many good journalists who previously served in the military, but he'd never known one to go in the opposite direction. His brother had served in the army. He told me he was supportive and proud of the decision and that if I got injured in pre-deployment training, there'd still be a place for me back at the *Journal*. I'll never forget his support. Ultimately, all of my colleagues were there for me. They were speechless, but they were there for me.

It was definitely a leap of faith then, but now I can say with confidence that some of the reasons we give ourselves for not making a jump—rationalizations we make, excuses we come up with—are fears that, in hindsight, should never hold people back. Especially fears about money, and particularly if you don't have kids already. I was single at the time and didn't have kids. I took a huge pay cut—so what? I never think, "Oh shoot, I wish I had stayed on longer so that I could have had two or three times the salary that I made as a marine." It just never comes up. Even if I'd had kids at that point, I don't think it would've necessarily stopped my jump. Concerns about paychecks or income levels in your twenties or thirties are ridiculous. In hindsight, a steady paycheck is a flimsy rationale for not pursuing your gut.

In the long run, your jump is a positive for whatever comes next. It doesn't have to be forever. I thought at the time of my jump that maybe I'd come back to journalism—and someday I might. You emerge from any jump humbled by the new learning, educated with new skills, closer to a completely different group of people than you ever would've been associated with otherwise. You come out stronger and probably in a better position to do whatever it was you were doing before you made the jump.

I was thirty-two by the time I got commissioned as a second lieutenant in the Marine Corps. I was almost a decade older than my classmates at officer candidates school, and those guys I served with are some of the closest friends I'll have for the rest of my life. The ride has been amazing. I just can't imagine my life today without having jumped.

In the moments after your jump, embrace what jazz musicians call "shed time": the time in a shed where you are locked away, trying to learn your instrument, understand your craft, master your skills. No matter what jump you take, there's going to be a certain amount of shed time involved.

Embrace this time. You may have to start new at something; your career arc may reset. So what? That's part of the fun of it. That's the journey.

MATT POTTINGER, a former journalist for the *Wall Street Journal* in its Beijing bureau and a former United States Marine, is currently serving on the National Security Council.

SARAH DVORAK

Retail Operations Analyst to Cheese Shop Owner

I GREW UP in Wisconsin in a boisterous Italian family that loved coming around the table for meals together. That's something my mom instilled early on—we always ate dinner together, mostly home-cooked. So I've always been fond of the eating experience, and not just because it tastes good but because it brings people together and creates genuine, memorable experiences.

I left the Midwest after college, with hopes to head west. I bowed to the pressure to have a job lined up right when I graduated, and I found one as a business analyst for a corporate retail chain in California. I was always driven to work and to make my own money, so I was thrilled to graduate in a timely manner and start working. It felt good to do that. But after a year and a half, I found myself looking for what was next, and what I was passionate about, which ultimately led me to food. I was having these mini aha moments: eating the perfect tomato, tasting the best taco. Many of these seasonal, amazing food experiences drew me closer to the food world, and ultimately I went to an info session at a culinary institute up in Napa and came home feeling the need to pursue a life in food. I decided on my jump: culinary school and then become a chef.

Preparing for culinary school required a real understanding of a kitchen, so I took a day off work and ran around to different kitchens in town: "I need to get some experience—I'll work for you for free. What do you think?" I found a chef who, after assuring me that I would hate myself for doing this, took me on board and allowed me to come and work for free on Saturdays and Sundays while still maintaining my corporate retail job.

Four months in, they offered me a paid position. Excited at the opportunity to make $10.50 an hour, I quit my job to become a full-time back-of-house employee at Jardinière, a lovely restaurant in Northern California.

Up until this point, I was giving up all of my free time, all of my weekends, to work in this kitchen—and this pushed me to jump. That's something I always tell people: "Get out there. If you're thinking about something, go do it, and see if you actually like doing it." I did my research, I enjoyed what I saw, and I went forward. My mom was literally crying herself to sleep: here goes her daughter, quitting a solid post-college job to scrape by in a kitchen so she could later go to culinary school and make no money. But I felt an inner pull toward this world, or to at least explore this world. Making things easier, I had no real responsibilities as an adult; I didn't have a mortgage—I was living in a house with six roommates. It was my time to explore this.

In jumping, I didn't totally think through that I'd be making $10.50 an hour with no benefits, no nothing. I didn't consider the money part as well as I should have. My job called for twelve hours of work per day but only paid for eight. And while there is certainly the privilege of being in a well-respected kitchen, which is awesome, and I think it is worth the sacrifice to a certain degree, it's ultimately not enough money to actually live on.

Making things tougher was that I had no real savings at this point. I was a year and a half out of college, so I didn't have the time to put cash away. And then there was the timing: I was in the kitchen from noon until midnight every day, so I didn't see my friends. I was missing birthday parties. I had no social life because my entire social network was outside of that world, and when you're at work for twelve hours a day, there's not a lot of time to see anybody.

This sounds bad, and most of it was. But there also came a lot of good in my jump. I learned the right questions to ask myself: What kind of lifestyle do you want? More basic, how do you want to be spoken to on a daily basis? Do you want to be yelled at? Or do you want to have seemingly adult conversations? Do you want to work late nights or early mornings?

I learned that I did truly enjoy food; I just needed to find a way in which it worked for me and for my long-term happiness. I learned how to pair a passion with economic stability—no one had told me how to line up your finances behind what you jump for. It made me think ahead: I knew that eventually I want my own family, and eventually I might not want to live with six roommates, things like that. The right jump would have to solve for these things.

Most important from this jump is that I fell in love.

With cheese.

Our restaurant had an amazing cheese program; it was my happy place. In my darkest moments, where I was getting yelled at for taking too long to shuck a dozen oysters, I would take a second and walk toward the cheese. I'd think, "Oh, this is so amazing. I love it."

I grew up a pretty standard cheddar girl in Wisconsin—my mom would buy Asiago every now and again at the Italian market, but mostly it was just one type of cheese around our house. In the kitchen, I was enamored by just how many different types of cheese there could be, and it all starts from the same single ingredient. The idea of fermentation really lit a fire in me in terms of chemistry and science and microbiology that I just never had before. I never thought I liked science. It really intrigued me, and I found myself determined to learn more about that process and what caused milk to turn into this amazingly diverse food. That, and the people.

The people in the cheese world are truly salt of the earth. I knew I wanted to be surrounded by these people. It was hard for me to relate to others in a job where core incentives were more financially driven. My female coworkers would come in with these giant diamond engagement rings, as if to tell everyone else: "mission accomplished." That didn't get me excited in the slightest. I wanted to be around my people. And my people, I feel, are people who care about the environment and who care about other people. A collaborative, lovely group of down-home people.

The people were the most compelling part of beginning to work with cheese, even beyond cheese itself.

I left the kitchen and returned to a desk. On paper I did a reverse of sorts, going back from food and into a retail job at the Gap. It didn't feel like a failure. It felt more like a victory in that I had just tried to make it in a kitchen, and now I could check that off my list of potential paths and move forward and try something else. My mom was super-stoked that I was going back to a nine-to-five job; my friends were really supportive.

I made myself cozy in my cubicle and breathed a sigh of relief. I was now getting paid again and had bought some time to figure out my next jump. And that time was invaluable: I spent the first half of my five years in inventory management and the second half in merchandising. I had a mentor who was an Excel guru, and he taught me how to run a business and how to be organized in doing it. I got smart on merchandising—buying things, anticipating trends, making something that people would like. I don't know how I could be running a successful business without those experiences.

And outside of work, I continued to retest my passion for cheese. On business trips to New York, I'd explore the food scene while I immersed myself in it from all sides. I helped out at a farmers' market nonprofit, joined the California Artisan Cheese Guild, volunteered wherever and whenever I could. I needed to know if my fling for cheese could be satisfied as a hobby, or if it was something more.

It was something more.

Five years into the Gap, I was fully immersed within the organizations and people driving the cheese industry forward. I needed to know the community that would receive my jump, and this community was welcoming, kind, and collaborative. Each experience brought me to the point where I finally said, "That's it. This is what I want to do. I want to start a business that supports these people and gets me into this community. Because these are my people."

My last step was attending the American Cheese Society's annual meeting: networking, cheese shows, competitions, social hours—a dream for us cheese people. From there, I spent two weeks in Europe to visit historical cheese landmarks. I told myself that when I came back from that trip, if I was still very passionate about this jump, then I was going to quit the Gap.

Two weeks later, that's what I did.

The hardest part, again, was dealing with my parents. They are from a generation that went to work, and that's what they did. They didn't necessarily have to be passionate about it. Work was work. They wanted a better life for their kids than they had—their parents had struggled through the Depression. My mom couldn't get it: "Work is work. So whatever you do, it's going to be work." And I said, "I just disagree."

Ultimately, my parents became my largest supporters, but they were still tremendously worried. Fortunately, I had my local community. In Wisconsin, I would tell people my idea, and they'd say, "Oh, interesting." But around my neighborhood in California, I'd tell people my idea, and they'd say, "Yes. You gotta do it. Go for it."

One friend was blunt: "You don't like your job. You're not getting any younger. You don't have anyone relying on you. What sort of book are you writing for yourself? Do you want to look back and say, 'I worked another twenty years at this job that was never particularly meaningful for me. That was fun.' Or do you want that story to be different?"

I knew I wanted my story to be different.

Deep down, I know I don't do my best when in a very comfortable situation. If I'm being challenged, it's a struggle and it's superhard and it's stressful, but I ultimately feel like that's where I thrive. To be at my best, I needed to jump.

Money came into play again, but this time I had some savings. I could configure the roommate situation to save a few bucks—it was really scrappy, but it was possible.

I quit the Gap, and the next thing I did was drive around the country for two and a half months visiting cheese makers. I met a lot of folks who struggled to get their products to market. From making the cheese then marketing it and fulfilling sales—making cheese is just not a realistic job for anyone. But they were committed to doing it because they loved it so much. I felt these people needed a mouthpiece. Slinging around the country by car, I knew I was passionate about the product. I was passionate about the people making it. And I was invigorated about the fact that someone needed to share the stories and get them out there.

I opened Mission Cheese in April 2011. There was a huge learning curve because I had a bunch of new employees whom I adored but who knew nothing about cheese. I started off working around the clock, and that's just not sustainable. You can't work fifteen-hour days for any extended period of time. Around six months in, I was getting pretty burned out. There were really dark times where my friends would send me pictures from the park and be like, "We wish you were here," and I would just start crying immediately. I was underfed and sleep-deprived.

It was really hard, but I slowly started to step back and trust others with my jump and its success. Two and a half years in, I felt, "Okay, I think we can probably start a family now." I ended up having a baby, and the process was an amazing milestone for me in that I had to step away completely. I forced myself to believe that I could jump, while also being a mother.

I think a lot of people hold a romantic view of running a café or a shop or your own business. You just hang out there, and it's awesome, and the customers are your friends, and it's your home away from home. It's not actually so romantic—no jump is pretty—but for me, it has been the right choice. You have to define what you want from your jump; for me, it was impact. From our 650-square-foot cheese shop, we're supporting people, serving as the mouthpiece to those who need it. And while this original goal feels complete, I know there's going to be a new one coming, and that next jump will be different from the one before it, and the one before that. And that's okay.

Before you jump, do your research. I had a friend who thought she wanted to open a Korean small plates café. I told her to work in a business like that to see if she'd enjoy the work that she'd be doing. So she went to Korea and came back and ultimately didn't do it. You have to get out there and get your hands dirty. It's the only way to figure out if you actually like it, and it's not something that's been romanticized in your brain, and to see if the day-to-day work is something that you'll enjoy.

The lovely thing about making a jump is that a lot of people who have jumped prior are willing to pay it forward. If someone tells me they want to open a cheese shop, I say come on down and hang out here and see if you like it. I really think that's the main thing before you jump: taste it, play forward the reality, and draw a business plan, straight up. What does it look like? I think that forces you to think through all the things that are scary.

And while jumping may look scary, the alternative is much worse. The longer you stay in a role that you don't like, the more trapped you feel. We only have one life, and for me, even now, I'm thirty-five. I may be working for another thirty-five years, and that's as long as I've been alive. I want to enjoy that time, and I want to feel like I'm doing something that I care about, and I want my son to see me doing something that I care about.

Not jumping is a disservice to yourself. Ultimately, if you don't try new things, you're never going to learn what you like or don't like. And I think that's the beauty of Mission Cheese. Even if I closed tomorrow, I have learned so much about what I like to do with my day and what I don't like to do, and what drives me, what motivates me, that I would know well how to spend my next days afterward. And I don't think you learn that without challenging yourself in uncomfortable ways.

SARAH DVORAK, a former retail inventory planner, back-of-house kitchen attendant, and retail merchandising associate, is founder and owner of Mission Cheese, an American artisan cheese bar.

DANNI POMPLUN

Bartender to Yoga Instructor

IF NOT NOW, when? And if not me, who?

Bartending always came easily to me. Downward dog, not so much. I should be the guy pouring you a beer, not telling you how to exhale. I jumped a few years ago, and to this day I still wake up scared. But the above questions kept reappearing in my head. Eventually, I had to answer them.

I was born in East LA, the youngest of three. Mom was an alcoholic and a drug user, in and out of prison. Dad was absent for mostly everything. I think his way of coping with things was just not being there. By the time I was around seven years old, we kids had to take care of ourselves. Mom would go on late-night trips and not be back for a long time.

I was pulled in and out of school while my mom was running from the law. By the time I was in middle school, Mom was locked up for the long haul, and I was living with my dad, with a rough stepmom. We kids had to fend for ourselves. I didn't have much in the way of educational skills. I didn't know how to read or write very well, so I relied on social skills. I found friendships and connections with other human beings as ways to cope.

I left home for good at sixteen. I had just come out to my dad, and he didn't take it so well, so I moved on. I got a fake ID and started working two jobs in LA, eventually taking shifts in a skate/surf shop. After a while, they asked me to manage the store, and I thought, "Well, why not, I've got nothing else going for me." And so I did. I lived with a fight-or-flight mentality the entire time. I wasn't doing something I loved, but that had never been an option: "All right, well I got to survive, so I'm going to do what I got to do right now."

I moved down to San Diego at eighteen and lived with a girl I met on Craigslist. Social worker, supergrounded—a really down-to-earth chick. A few months in, she says, "Hey, do you want to come with me to this yoga class?" I said, "What's yoga? Yogurt? Sure, I love yogurt."

She corrected me, and when I told her I wasn't interested, she wouldn't stop.

I was dragged into class and got hooked. It immediately became my escape, my time-out.

I let it all slip when I turned twenty-one a few years later and started partying hard. I covered up my insecurities with drugs and booze, and addiction kicked in. I ditched yoga. And then I lost a partner, my first run-in with death. Things got worse.

My roommate, the social worker, gave me an ultimatum: "I can't keep living with you if you're going to continue to live your life this way." A yoga studio had opened up a couple blocks away from the house. To keep my roommate in my life, I took a class. I totally got my ass kicked.

And that's when I stopped pretending. I threw myself into yoga—an outlet that, for the first time in my life, became my rock, my true pillar of stability. I was exposed to this foreign, fluid language where people talked about things like compassion and growth and self-worth and self-acceptance, words and ideas I'd never heard before. Until then, I had been fighting to breathe. Doing yoga gave me the chance to stop and think.

I was going to yoga nonstop until nearly a year later, when I left one of my two bartending jobs and couldn't afford to go anymore. I told one of the teachers. She said, "If you want to keep doing this, you can scrub toilets."

So I started scrubbing toilets, and after a while, I was promoted to mopping floors. And then to scheduling and desk duty. My teachers slipped me into teacher training, and when that was about done, one of my instructors asked me to teach a class. I said, "I'm not actually going to teach yoga." He said, "Great, be there at noon." Suddenly I was impacting people, and people were appreciative, and we were forming these authentic connections. In these one-off teaching moments, I saw something else for me, something so different from the world I had been living in. I wanted to ditch my day job and teach yoga full-time.

But I was too scared. I stuck to what I knew: my job managing a popular bar, making great money, being everyone's go-to guy. I couldn't visit a store or restaurant without somebody knowing me. I created a veil that I was popular, and I wrapped myself in that. I'd had no self-worth before; now my self-worth was based on money and being everyone's guy. I'd gotten sucked into that. I knew the jump I should make, but I craved the attention of being a bartender. I wanted to do yoga, but I really wanted to keep being seen as the cool kid.

A few years later, I turned thirty and moved to Northern California. I was keeping this terrible secret, this hope and dream, bottled as it kept bubbling up inside of me. It came to a head when I sat down one afternoon with one of my teachers. I said, "What do I do? I really love this yoga thing, but I've got this bartending gig that's making me a ton of money, and it's the only thing that I've known how to do really well for the last ten years."

His response: teach.

It was so obvious, but it still hit me like a ton of bricks. It was like, oh yeah, maybe I should just start doing the thing that I like to do. The bar was fun and easy work, and people loved me there. But if I was totally honest with myself, it felt empty. I just didn't want to be there.

Knowing this didn't change the fact I was terrified to jump. I remember riding on my scooter and my head being completely filled with this decision: Should I do this or should I not do this? Who am I to try and do this, and am I going to be good enough? It was a struggle to understand the concept of transitioning my identity toward something that I love, as opposed to something I was dependent on.

I was afraid of my own success. What if I was good at teaching? Sometimes, I think we're more afraid of success than we are of failure. That's a really scary thing—to have something really good happen, especially when you've had a bunch of not really good things happen. My fear also had to do with self-worth: Who am I to teach these people? My whole life, I had been a giant fuckup. Am I supposed to be teaching anyone?

I'm wrestling hard with this decision when one of my students takes me out for a cup of coffee. She asks me straight up, "Why don't you teach full-time? And I said, "Oh, I don't want to be a full-time teacher." She looks at me dead in the eye: "Stop bullshitting me; why don't you want to be a full-time teacher?" I could only look back at her. She saw through all my excuses.

I felt safe at the bar. I was working twenty hours and getting paid for forty, making great money, traveling each month on my own. Why would anyone give that up?

My student said, "You need to do this. I can see that it's in you and that you've got a gift." I remember going back home and not sleeping. I stared at food and tried to eat, but I was so perplexed. One day soon after, I was preparing for one of my classes with this incredible heaviness in my head. I was just so consumed: "What do I do? I really want to jump."

I was shaky and queasy in my belly. I thought, "I have to tell my students. I've got to share this, because if not, I'm not going to be able to teach this class." I sat down and looked at everyone and unloaded: "Dear yogis, I think I want to quit my job and do this full-time."

Immediately, the entire class of thirty-five students started clapping and cheering and hollering, "Yeah, do it!" I told them how I was living in fear. But what is fear? It's really just false expectations appearing real. I had all these made-up scenarios in my head, scenarios in which I wasn't going to be good enough, and I wasn't going to make it, and I wasn't going to be able to sustain my life. All that stuff was supposedly going to happen.

But after I had told not only a couple of friends but also a full classroom of students, I had no choice but to do it.

I sketched out a nine-month plan but unloaded my jump on my boss two months in, right before my shift at the bar.

I said, "I think I'm done here." He said, "Oh, you're sick, not feeling good?" "No, I think I'm done here." "Well, what do you mean you're done here?" "I don't think I can work here anymore." "Why? Do we need to pay you more?" No: my gut, my heart, everything that's been a part of my being and my sustainability is pulling me in this other direction.

My boss looked at me. He said, "Man, I can't get mad at you for that. You've got this thing that's firing you up. Go do it." It was like everything that had escalated inside of me for years suddenly spilled out in one conversation.

Now that I had said my jump out loud to the people who needed to know, it was liberating; it was freeing. And I had created space for other things to come my way. As soon as I made it known I was set on teaching full-time, things started happening. The rightness of my jump only became more clear: of course this is the thing I'm supposed to be doing.

My jump brought me into the now, into today—where I'm personally thriving, where I'm happy. I work more, but it doesn't feel like work. I never walk into a yoga class thinking, "Ugh, I really don't want to be here." I always leave thinking, "That was fucking awesome." And that's the best feeling ever. I left on fine terms with my boss, and I'm sure I could go back to the bar, but I jumped and I've got to see this out. I've got to try to live for me.

Success is unique to each of us. Every night when I go to bed, I feel satisfied with what I have going on, and I don't long for the things I used to need. Now, let's be real: there's still not a day that goes by where I don't think, "Oh my god, what am I doing?" There's still not a day that goes by when I don't think, "What the fuck did I leave? What am I doing? I live in one of the most expensive cities in the nation." I still freak out and say, "Oh my god, I've got bills to pay, rent to make."

But these fears are always going to be there. I think that no matter what, for me, they will be there. I have a choice to either live in that fear or not live in that fear. So when fear swirls around and comes on by, I choose not to get involved. I say, "Hey, thanks for playing but not today." I push it off to the side. It's about knowing fear is there but recognizing that I have a choice to either play into it or not.

Know that you are never alone in your jump. I was worried about whether people would accept my decision, yet the response from friends, even from strangers, was overwhelming. "You're excited about this; you're ramped up about it? Come talk to us. We'll help you out." The more you share your jump and the more you put it into words and share them out loud, the more others will want to support you. People want to see people succeed, and the people that love and care about you want to see you win. Let them help you win.

No one else is going to live your life again. No one wants to look back and say, "I didn't try it out." Jump, and when you get stuck, because no doubt you will, think back to the questions I still ask today:

"If not you, then who? If not now, when?"

DANNI POMPLUN, a former bartender, leads yoga classes, retreats, and teacher trainings throughout the United States and overseas.

MANISHA SNOYER

Actress to Education Entrepreneur

GROWING UP IN a low-income household with a single mom, I knew that if I was going to achieve anything in this world, I'd have to create it myself. From the beginning, I've thought of myself as an agent for change. I knew that change wasn't going to be handed to me. I'd have to make it happen.

I was a child actress, and I loved the theater. I found a way to a performing arts school and then to France to study acting, before landing in New York City for more acting. Coming from a family of teachers, I started tutoring to make some extra cash. I taught everywhere: from the most elite private schools in New York City to at-risk after-school programs as a substitute teacher.

The acting was moving along, but at a certain point, I realized that path was not for me anymore. That realization was excruciating because I attached my identity so strongly to being an actress. But I wanted something more. As humans we heal where we're wounded, so perhaps in some ways my upbringing, which lacked guidance and direction, was what pushed me toward desiring a leadership role in the education world. When you think of taking a jump, you think of going away from some boring office job to being an artist or an actor. For me, it was the other way around.

I brainstormed ideas while renting out spare rooms on Airbnb to make ends meet. I had grand, change-the-world ideas but saw that it would be easier to aim for something more concrete and pragmatic. So I organized a summer camp program teaching a group of students about social entrepreneurship. The camp was comfortable. In terms of paying the bills, this was it. All I needed was sixteen students to make things profitable. But nothing about the camp would make the magnitude of social impact I was interested in.

So I press reset, buy a flight to California to attend a conference that I hope will help generate more ideas about what I should do. On the plane, the man next to me launches into how he wants to move out of New York because he's worried about his daughter's education—private school is so expensive, and public schools are too standardized and over-crowded. I say, "Well, I've been around teaching for years. There are other options for learning. New York has plenty of teachers, plenty of spaces to teach. All you need is a place to bring them all together."

He said, "Make that place."

It was so clear: my marketplace would empower parents and teachers to start their own schools, classes, and workshops to fit the unique needs of their families and communities. A jump toward this marketplace would fit the type of leadership role I wanted to take in the world, in an area I cared about. I hadn't even stepped off the plane, and the idea had arrived.

I freaked out. I had been banking on a foolproof idea like the sum-mer camp, and somewhere in the sky I became destined to build a Web-enabled teaching marketplace. To make this jump didn't feel like my decision; the idea just took hold and plowed me forward. I felt I had no choice.

I'm an easygoing person, but for those first weeks after the idea came to me, I was overcome with this terror—a terror so intense that I'd wake up in a sweat every night. I felt more anxiety than I had ever experienced in my life. This was after years of meditation and psychotherapy. I tried to think logically: "What's going on? Is this jump worth it?" While running through these thoughts in San Francisco, I spotted a fortune cookie message in the street. It read, "Fear is the necessity of invention." I took that as a sign to keep going.

Renting out my extra rooms is what made my jump possible. Financially, it placed me in a situation where I was slightly uncomfortable, which forced me to push my business forward, and at the same time, renting the rooms provided enough cash so that I didn't have to go out and get another job, because it would have been impossible to do this jump with any other side gig. I'm going overtime, full-time, all the time. I just don't have the extra time or attention required for any part-time desk job.

It's been hard. I think that a lot of people look down on first-time founders. And that can feel discouraging. And then I look at our largest competitor, who has raised $133 million in capital, and here I am, a nobody. The other challenge is being a female entrepreneur. There are a lot of people who will treat you like a child and think your idea is sweet, or try to give you a lot of advice that is not helpful. So starting a company requires a really strong inner anchor.

And if, at some point, things change, and this business fails? I believe that there is no failure. I've learned more about myself this year than I have at any other time in my entire life. The jump has provided my own education at an accelerated scale. I've learned what I want my business to look like and, more important, what I want my life to look like.

Don't let prejudices out in the world deter you. When you jump, you'll find it funny how things can tip your way. Once, I had to revamp the website but couldn't find the funds to do so, and my room guest, a talented graphic designer, came to the rescue—at no cost. Later, as I was struggling to hire a computer scientist as a cofounder, my guest at the time was a computer engineer: every morning, I would complain to him for half an hour, and then we'd sit down and have breakfast and figure out how I would push forward. I'm financing this business solely off my room-hosting income—no banks or investors—so these little pieces of luck go a long way.

I feel strongly that this idea chose me and bit me, and there's really no turning back. I can't imagine doing anything else right now. With every card I played, there would be another one waiting for me to turn over. The idea began to live inside me. I simply became its driver. And I stay grounded: I have my long-term strategy, my short-term strategy, and my day-to-day strategy, so that I never let anybody tell me this is not what I should be doing or that I don't have the skills to do it.

Before you jump, get really clear on your values. Don't let your thinking become too lofty on one hand or too grimly rooted in reality on the other. You have to have both. Focus on what your day-to-day life, post-jump, looks like. Someone who loves pies may decide she's going to go out and make a pie shop, and then as she jumps for it, she realizes that making pies every day is grueling. Yes, it can actually be a horrible process, making pies.

Be honest with yourself: What are your reasons for wanting to jump? Is it because you don't like working for a boss? If so, you have to be careful that you don't become the mean boss to yourself. Do one thing at a time, and then celebrate each success—especially the little ones. But don't forget to keep your feet on the ground.

I started my marketplace in January 2015 and launched in November of the same year. Since then, we have grown by 400 percent. We have a community of over five thousand teachers. We're profitable but, more importantly, we are making a real difference in education. It's been an amazing ride.

MANISHA SNOYER, a former actress and summer camp operator, is the CEO and founder of Cottage Class, a community marketplace for preK–12 grade education that empowers teachers and parents to start schools, classes, homeschool programs, and camps to fill unmet educational needs in their communities.

JACOB LICHT

Corporate Lawyer to Government Lawyer

I GREW UP a Danish immigrant in Los Angeles, finding joy in art and argument. During school years, I became torn between the two. In college, I got lost in studio art while studying prelaw. I considered art school, but I had witnessed the career of my dad, an artist and photographer, and I had seen how hard it was for him to make that work. While I admired his dedication and happiness in the pursuit, the more practical side of me took over: I could develop a stable career as a lawyer.

I went to law school—can't say I loved it—and tried to veer away afterward. I got another degree in urban planning and found myself in real estate, thirty years old and newly married. When that market tanked in 2009, I gave up any lofty ideals and interests and quickly retreated to a traditional corporate law gig, protecting the environmental interests of energy companies.

I think having a sense of general purpose in what you do each day is not too crazy to hope for. Each day, it became clearer that a corporate law position was not going to sustain my sense of purpose for the next thirty years. It was hard to believe I was put on this planet to minimize hydraulic fracking companies' risks.

I wasn't looking for a total life makeover: there were pieces of law that I really liked, and so I began to dig more into those pieces. And that was when I found a posting for a litigator at the US Department of Justice (DOJ). I knew I enjoyed trial law, and this would give me a chance at that. More importantly, the job description was to help take out the bad guys. This was the type of impact I had dreamed of making through law. I would stay in my industry but make this pivot.

The only catch? Unpaid. Internship. With no full-time option afterward.

I was thirty-four. I had two young children. My wife was employed, so fortunately we had her paycheck (which obviously made it possible for me to consider an unpaid position), but there was something crazy about jumping this way: I have two graduate degrees. I'm getting paid well. I'm on this path where I could become a partner at a big, respectable firm. To ditch all that and work for free just sounded nuts. When I brought it up to peers, they said, "It's an internship. Unpaid. What are you doing?"

The DOJ was very up-front with me that there was absolutely no guarantee whatsoever of the position turning into something paid. The federal government was in a budget crisis, and the result was a hiring freeze for all full-time positions. That raised a lot of eyebrows from friends. My family tried to stay supportive. But there's always going to be an underlying pressure: you know you should be out there making money. How could you not want to make money?

I was lost. Do I apply for this "job"? Can it be called a job? What is a job? I told my wife, "Hey, this sounds far out, and it also sounds like a great experience. But I know we can't really make this work." And this was where she gets all the credit. With a million reasons to say no, her first response was, "I think you should apply."

That says a lot about my wife. She had seen me be really unhappy for a number of years at that firm. She felt that this would reset my thinking around what was the right pursuit because it was so clear that this corporate law job wasn't it.

Her support was great to have, but I also needed some tactical strategy. First, I tracked down the person who would be my boss for that year, to make sure I would get what I was signing up for. Sure enough, even though I wouldn't get paid, I would get real, tangible value in the form of experience as a trial lawyer for the US government.

I'd had enough jobs to know the key questions to ask before jumping.

In a way, it was a big plus that I was jumping at age thirty-four and not, say, twenty-four. If I were twenty-four, I wouldn't have known to ask certain things: What exactly will be my duties? How am I going to be managed, and how much freedom will I have? What can I take from this experience? I took those questions to a few other attorneys who had taken similar positions—some whose jobs had worked out, others whose jobs hadn't—and tracked down a guy who had made my jump exactly. He told me about little things, and that sealed my conviction. Apparently, I'd be given the title of special assistant US attorney, where "special" is used as a synonym for "unpaid."

My wife and I developed a spreadsheet of what our home finances would look like with just her income. What would our cash flow look like? Where would we cut back? I was making more than half of our household income—how do you reduce your household income by 60 percent and make that work? We'd have to make sacrifices, change our day-to-day. These were the final checks we made before I jumped.

The chances of the internship turning into a job were really low, but I decided to roll the dice—that Congress would pass a budget, that the Department of Justice would use the additional funds to hire new assistant US attorneys, and that when both of those things happened, being in this unpaid position would somehow help my chances beyond the normal 1-in-200 odds for the gig.

If my sole objective in jumping had been to land a full-time job, this pile of slim hypotheticals would have convinced every reasonable cell in my brain not to try.

But for my jump, I defined success differently: if this year of experience would get me closer to what I should be doing professionally, then I was going to call that a win, whether or not I had a job at the end of the internship. For years at my law firm, I'd think, "Shit, I don't know if I should be a lawyer. This is not fun. This doesn't have meaning. I don't know what I want to be when I grow up."

Getting closer to that answer—of figuring out what you want to do, how you want to spend your days—is reason enough to jump. My jump was going to point me in a more informed direction professionally—and gaining that clarity alone made the jump worth the risk. The immediate outcome was less important. And that sounds soft and lofty to say, but looking back years later, I came out of my one-year "special" assignment with more conviction around my career ambitions than from all my other years of law practice combined.

The act of jumping itself will put your life back in your hands. Whether it works out or not is irrelevant—the fact that you made the choice will change you. Above all else, my jump gave me a newfound sense of control over my destiny, even if I didn't know what was about to happen. I was in an unhappy situation, and I was able to say, "You know what? I can change this. I don't know where it's all going, but I know that where I'm at right now is not where I need to be." That sense of control was really important.

Jump to learn. When I was in a corporate law job with clients, my learning curve had slowed to a near stop. Particularly when you're earlier in your career, learning needs to be the number one priority in what you do, much more so than a paycheck, maybe even more than stability. Those skills you learn early on are going to catapult you further in your career and faster than other folks who are stuck doing the same old same old. Prioritize learning.

To the chagrin of some family and friends, I jumped to become the thirtysomething unpaid intern for the US government. Ultimately, the budget unfroze, and I was hired as a full-time (and paid) assistant US attorney (no longer "special"—ha!).

I look back at my dad's career with a better understanding of why he pushed forward in his passion, even with its uncertainties and risk. There's not a price you can put on doing a job that actually makes you happy. And that, itself, is worth jumping for.

JACOB LICHT, a former corporate lawyer, is now a prosecutor for the United States Department of Justice.

ANOOPREET REHNCY

Investment Banker to Fashion Entrepreneur

I WAS BORN in London; I'm Indian and one of three daughters. Both my parents were born in East Africa, to parents who moved there from India to start businesses—true entrepreneurs. Politics turned dark and both families became refugees overnight, fleeing on a day's notice and landing in the UK, with no assets or plans, but with a steadfast determination to succeed—there was no other option.

My mom's family started over from scratch, in a countryside town outside London. I grew up obsessed with painting, fashion, dance, and all things artistic. My grandma is a tailor and I used to watch her closely. She made all of our family outfits for special Indian occasions. She made my mom's wedding outfit.

My dad founded a sports retail business with a garment-printing arm. I loved seeing new designs from Nike and Adidas even when I was seven or eight years old, but I would always feel the need to doodle and re-design what I saw. In my early teenage years, during school lunch breaks, I started peddling all sorts of things—from apparel to kit bags to neon shoelaces—to my friends, and later I custom-printed clothing to wear on school trips and holidays. It made me realize that I could apply my creativity together with the art of selling, and create something that people could buy.

There's always been a certain kind of hidden pressure, well—not a pressure, just something ingrained in my family, that, when you have something good, you have to hang on to it. You never know when it could disappear. Hearing of their struggles to achieve success motivates me to achieve and to give back to my parents, because, after all, they've worked so hard to give us the best upbringing and education.

This desire to achieve pushed me toward a financial career early on. I worked very hard to gain admission to the London School of Economics, and from there worked even harder to pick up all sorts of internships. When I landed a gig at Goldman Sachs, and then JP Morgan, it felt like, wow, things can happen, I can do this.

Investment banking fit well with what I was supposed to be. In the Indian community, the recommended career choices are accountant, doctor, lawyer, or banker. That's about it. And at weddings when people ask, "What's your job?" if you say, "I'm an investment banker," it's the perfect, 10 out of 10 answer. It's almost as if you're credible, you're worthy, you'd be a great match for a partner. There's always been that attitude among the Indian kids that I know: they have to get to the top.

I was a couple of years into the quest to the top when my partner, Bipan, came back from a tough trading day. He also worked at an investment bank. We sat down, and he said, frustrated, "Why can't people be black and white?" There's office politics in banking just as there probably is in every large corporate environment, and Bipan and I didn't feel cut out for that environment. We questioned, why can't things be more straightforward? Why can't people be transparent? It was from that idea that Bipan and I thought, "There's no one really out there representing the concept of being black and white, transparent and honest."

We're both straight-up people. And we both were fatigued with the chase for what we thought we were supposed to be doing. We thought, "Let's champion this message of transparency and not be afraid to say it how it is." How would we do this? That's when my gut spoke up: a clothing brand. What better way to champion a message than to wear it?

It wasn't that hard to leave what I had thought I wanted for so long. I had worked so, so, so hard from the age of fifteen to become a successful investment banker, perhaps partner of a firm—that was my ambition—and to work in a fancy, big office in the heart of London. Here I was seven years toward that goal, yet seeing that desire snap. That dream was all done, and I had to accept that. To my parents and others, I was giving up a great career, a fantastic salary. They asked, "Are you really going to be able to do it and survive?" Yes, I had complete faith that I would survive.

Aside from my own belief, my banking job had equipped me with relevant industry research. Working as a consumer specialist on equities, I was surrounded by information about brands—P&G, L'Oréal, Coca-Cola—and my work meant accessing all the information to understand what was making these companies successful. I'd use the information to consider: What's missing in the market? What are the hot areas? Where are the areas for growth?

For months, I had written my own memos on the consumer world, sending them out to coworkers and clients. I now wanted to use my viewpoints and that unexploited creativity to add more value to the world.

The day we received our bonus, I jumped. Leaving the bank felt like a massive relief. Even though we didn't have anything set up officially, just a few designs flying around on sketchpads, I was excited to finally get working full-time on something that came naturally to me and that I was passionate about. I was finally free to prove to the world that I didn't have to stay in one scripted role as a young Indian woman in finance. The decision was easier to make with Bipan quitting at the same time, so I wasn't on my own.

My friends weren't surprised by my decision to jump. Even while I was committed to banking, people would say, "You should sell paintings and design clothes on the side. You can display your art in galleries. You can do XYZ." They always believed that my creative gene was being wasted sitting in the office.

I leaned on family and friends who were supportive of Bipan and me and our black-and-white concept and did everything within their power to help us. We tracked down the best production factories across the world, created our own fabrics from scratch, built the website, taught ourselves how to use design programs, got our heads around import and export regulations, directed photo shoots with models we spotted on the street, and so much more.

There have been so many ups and downs from the day I decided to jump, right until this very day. So many screams of joy, so much anger, so many sleepless nights, so much frustration, so many educated guesses, so many emotions. One of the hardest things right at the beginning was people saying to me, "You don't have a clue about fashion. You're not a fashion designer. You don't have a degree in fashion. You'll need to hire a designer; you can't do it." I took all the criticism on board but never let the negativity make me doubt my abilities.

Persistence is the most important skill in starting your own business. You can't just try once—you try again and again and again. Early on, we set ourselves the seemingly impossible goal of reaching the biggest celebrity possible, a woman who embodied our message, a role model. We tried every method possible to reach her with a sweatshirt design that was inspired by her.

After a few tries, we received a response from her team: a dancing emoji.

We were floored. A response! Obviously, they've responded for a reason—but what does a dancing emoji mean? How do we reply? Is it good? Is it bad? Do they want the product? All these things are running through your head, and your mind is running at a hundred miles an hour. You've got to act really rationally but you're so excited. I'm a massive fan of this woman. But you can't let the fan girl inside take hold of your business mind!

So we told her team our story, about the sacrifices that we'd made to pursue what we believed in, and what we're trying to create for the world. We sent them our products, and a few weeks went by.

We were really having a tough day the moment it happened, one of those soul-searching days that come with any jump. I felt we needed to do something different, to get more visibility. But what the hell should we do? Bip and I were rethinking every part of our plan when the window on my laptop screen appeared.

One of my friends in the United States congratulated us in a post on Facebook. And there it was, the money shot: Beyoncé, Queen Bee, modeling our sweatshirt, emblazoned with our very own slogan design "Queen Bee *noun*. I call the shots."

The biggest celebrity in the world, the most iconic person in fashion, music, and pop culture, supporting our brand, our concept. Wearing something I designed.

I was in shock. I couldn't say anything whilst Bip was yelling, screaming, jumping. Our website crashed, and we sold out our entire inventory. Beyoncé had uploaded multiple images to her Instagram, website, Facebook, and Tumblr and the world went wild.

The elation turned to chaos: glued to our seats and hunched over screens, we immediately started replying to every single tweet, message, and comment and reached out to all the media outlets that were wondering which brand Beyoncé was sporting. Without thinking of a strategy of how to respond to millions of people just between the two of us, we just went for it all night long, and I don't think we slept for about seventy-two hours.

We were hit from all sides. We should have been soaking in the victory, but all was chaos. Those couple of days, that month, was physically draining and straining. Not what you'd consider going through after hitting a lifetime achievement like this.

I wish it were true that if Beyoncé wears your product, you're going to be a million-dollar, billion-dollar brand the very next day. Sadly, it's not that easy. You can't rely on one person, event, or milestone to make your jump work out. You have to continue pushing harder, and that's exactly what we did. As a result of not sitting back to enjoy the moment, our brand is now present in over thirty countries and in dozens of carefully selected stores. But we're only on our third collection and we've still got a hell of a lot to show to the world. We want everyone to believe in the concept that we have created and to know that we're the brand standing for it. We're not even close to what I think we can achieve.

Jump for what makes you get up in the morning. Confirm this is part of your proposed jump before you make it. I found out pretty quickly that my "dream" of becoming a banker wasn't what made me happy. Chasing money wasn't what made me happy. I didn't want to have that lifestyle.

You have to be mentally prepared that it's not going to be a smooth ride. People are going to knock your jump. People are going to say that you can't do it. You don't have the skills; you're never going to make it. But you've got to form the toughest skin and not let anyone kill your jump.

You're not going to lose anything by jumping. You'll gain skills, meet fascinating people, and have so many things to add to your CV. The fact that you jumped shows a lot about your personality, in that you're a risk-taker, and most importantly someone who is not afraid to stand up for something you believe in—your passion.

ANOOPREET REHNCY, a former investment banking professional, is the creative director of A Black And White Story (ablackandwhitestory.com), a fashion brand she cofounded in 2014 with Bipan Ahuja. Both made the Forbes 30 Under 30 list in 2017.

BRENDA BERKMAN

Lawyer to Firefighter

SOME JUMPS DON'T end well. Don't mistake that for a reason not to try. I was on a quest to serve when I was stopped by one of the more powerful organizations in the world, head-on. A decision to jump would change my life, but it would come with a real price.

I grew up in the 1950s as a sports-playing tomboy from a lower-middle-class household outside Minneapolis. Nobody had gone to college in my parents' generation, and if you were a girl, you were to become a secretary. Or maybe a nurse or a teacher. Didn't matter though because once you got pregnant, you were done working. Back to the house.

That didn't sit well with me. As a child, I was determined to someday serve my community, pinning my hopes on becoming a firefighter before being shut out, before being told that wasn't in the realm of possibility for women. I discovered law one summer after college. If I couldn't serve people as a firefighter, I figured law was the next best way to serve.

That summer I met the lawyer for the fire officers' union in New York. Through him, I met firefighters. I could tell how much they loved their job. That stuck with me as I went back to finish law school. And then, just a few months before my graduation, New York City announced that it would allow women to take the test to become firefighters.

I decided to take the test, even with the law gig lined up after graduation. And then something crappy happened: they changed the test so that none of the women applying could pass. When the city rejected our appeal to reconsider the test, my lawyer-to-be reaction was swift: "Well, this has the potential for a lawsuit."

I thought I'd be good at firefighting. And I really wanted that opportunity to provide for my community: What job sacrifices more than this one? Entering burning buildings and rushing to car accidents—you help people. You are counted on. I wanted to be counted on.

And then there was this other thing. I was tired of being told you can't do something because you're a girl. That had always seemed stupid to me. If it was your passion to play baseball, why couldn't you join Little League if you were a girl? My mother tried to sign me up for Little League, and they wouldn't let me in because I was a girl. Not because I was a bad ballplayer—I was a good ballplayer—but because I was a girl. This had to change.

I moved forward on the lawsuit as I started my job as a lawyer, juggling both at first. Five years later, the lawsuit forced a decision: I had to testify in court that if I won the case, I would leave law and take the job. The city was claiming that I was pulling a publicity stunt as a bra-burning feminist and that I didn't really want to be a firefighter. So I had to take the stand and testify under oath that I would become a firefighter if we won. Why would a lawyer leave her job for firefighting? Most people did not see the logic in that. They absolutely didn't see the logic in that.

New York's fire department is considered the roughest, toughest, most macho group around. And the idea that this little pipsqueak young woman might be challenging their all-male club of ten thousand firefighters drew a lot of attention, and it wasn't attention that I wanted. I wanted to be a firefighter; I didn't want to be a movie subject.

I jumped.

I testified under oath that I would do it, that I would leave law if given entry into FDNY. I jumped because I felt like this was an opportunity to really change our country for the better, even if just slightly. It's one thing to have a personal passion for something and say, I want to jump because this is my passion. And that's great; you only have one life to live, so people should do what they enjoy doing and what they feel is right for them to do. But if you have others that you can help by jumping, then that's more than reason enough to go.

The hardest part was knowing that in this jump, it would just be me, on my own, for at least a while. Maybe forever. No other woman had come forward. That was the hardest obstacle, being so alone. Next was dealing with family. My lawyer father-in-law was not thrilled: he had represented these fire officers for years, and the idea of his daughter-in-law going from lawyer to firefighter seemed ridiculous. Even my mom thought I was nutty: here I had a bachelor's degree, a master's degree, and a law degree, and I wanted to take a job that's dangerous, entails a 50 percent pay cut, and requires only a high school diploma. But I knew I had to try.

I won my lawsuit, a few other women came out of the woodwork, and in 1982 we retested and were admitted as the first female firefighters in FDNY. Many of us, including me, were fired directly afterward; we had to bring more lawsuits to get our jobs back.

Winning the lawsuit was only the beginning of the torture, not the end. Harassment, discrimination, death threats, draining of air tanks, physical abuse—you name it. The self-doubt and internal questioning only increased because there was so much opposition to the women coming on the job. Also, my family believed that winning the lawsuit created problems between the firefighters' union and my father-in-law, even though they were his big client for nearly three decades, and even though he didn't support my lawsuit. The impact of a jump has a far-reaching ripple effect on your nearest and dearest. And it's not always a positive one.

Nothing is guaranteed in life—you have only what is in front of you right now. And who's to say that this single narrow little road is the one you're going to stay on in life? Unlikely. There are going to be plenty of unexpected twists and turns where you will have a choice to jump, and that's the beauty of it really—it's your choice. Never feel someone or some group of people is making the choice for you. You can take advice. You can research and investigate and take small steps toward your goals and your passions, but eventually, it's your choice what to do. And that should be thrilling rather than feared. Otherwise, why be alive?

It wasn't a sweet ending after the first lawsuit. It didn't even end after the second lawsuit and getting my job back. The hurdles went on for my whole career, and that was twenty-five years. There were always some people who thought that it was okay to harass me and discriminate against me because I was a woman—the woman who ruined the fire department. There was a considerable personal price to pay as a result of my jump.

But I wouldn't change a thing. Because this was a jump worth fighting for.

BRENDA BERKMAN sued the New York City Fire Department to eliminate job discrimination against women. When she won in 1982, she quit her law practice and became one of the first women firefighters in the FDNY. After twenty-five years and promotion to captain, Berkman retired in 2006 and became an artist.

BRANDON STANTON

Bond Trader to Photographer

I LOVE, LOVE, love taking photos. But photography wasn't some life-long passion or inevitable calling. And when I jumped, it wasn't clean or pretty, and certainly not based on a clear-cut view of the next twenty years. Instead, my jump was a decision: to trust myself and work hard, to leave a planned life for something seemingly impractical.

I started photographing around six and a half years ago. It wasn't a hobby I had as a kid or in high school or even in college. I picked it up while working in Chicago as a way to relieve stress as a bond trader. I was twenty-six and wanted a creative and artistic escape on the week-ends because I was spending every other waking moment thinking about the financial markets. My job was completely consuming my life, and because of that, my entire identity was wrapped up in how well I was doing in the markets. Say it was Friday. If the day went well, I'd feel great the whole weekend. If Friday went horribly, I'd spend all weekend miserable.

I needed something that would create some pocket of air in my life, something that I could value other than trading. I bought a camera as a way to create that breathing room, and I started going through down-town Chicago and photographing all kinds of things. It wasn't people at first.

I enjoyed trading. It was fascinating to me. It was invigorating. It was intellectually interesting. I enjoyed the people I worked with. It was exciting, an unhealthy kind of excitement—in the way that drugs or gambling are an unhealthy kind of excitement. I enjoyed trading, but the end goal was always money. The input was my time and my thoughts and my energy. And no matter how much I enjoyed the game, the output was money. Because I was doing a specific form of trading, I couldn't talk with my friends about it. I was doing relative-value trading and fixed-income securities trading—very particular stuff, complete with its own vocabulary.

This job and this life made me very isolated from society. The work placed me in a parallel world where I was doing something that nobody else understood and that had no output other than money. For those reasons, there was something unfulfilling about the work even though I enjoyed it in a lot of ways, even though I did look forward to going to the office. About four or five months after picking up photography, I lost my job. The trading firm was about to go under. At that point, I had a decision: Stay in the game and climb aboard another trading firm. Or take photos.

I knew if I didn't jump from this industry, and if I stayed any longer in the practical world of trading bonds, it would be very hard to leave, because the work was prestigious. Just a few years earlier, I was spending Thanksgiving and Christmas admitting to my family and friends that I'd flunked out of school and was working at Applebee's. It was very embarrassing. Three years of hard work later, I got to come home and tell everybody that I was trading bonds at the Chicago Board of Trade, which was exciting. It felt great. Maria Popova, founder of Brain Pickings, talks about the danger of prestige and the feeling it gives us: how good it feels to be doing something that makes us feel important. It locks us into places. Money wasn't the most tempting reason for me to stay—it was the feeling that I was doing something that very few people had the chance to do, and feeling like it would be stupid to give that up. I think that's why it was so hard to leave. I didn't want to give up that feeling of coming home for Thanksgiving and Christmas and seeing my family and knowing that I'm doing something that made them proud.

And yet at that time and place, I simply loved photography. I just enjoyed doing it. I mean, I sucked at it in a lot of ways. Sometimes I'd get lucky and take some good photos, but those were just luck. Regardless, I loved it. It was like a treasure hunt. I really enjoyed doing it. All I wanted to do was photograph.

And that desire led me to jump. I made what was a very selfish decision: to restructure my life around doing something that I enjoy. Up until that point, I had spent all of my time trying to make as much money as possible. In my jump, I wanted to, for the foreseeable part of my life, attempt to make just enough money so that I could control my time.

I focused exclusively on how I would spend my days. I would switch priorities and put time above money as the most valuable resource. Instead of structuring my life to have as much money as possible, I was going to structure my life to have as much time as possible. I thought if I did that, I could answer a simple, important question: What is it that I should be doing?

It's easy to label a jump as a black-and-white narrative: "Oh, I was chasing money and doing something where I was sacrificing my true enjoyment for money. Then I left, and I started embracing what I really wanted to do." That wasn't the case for me. And my jump wasn't exactly from the world of finance but from the world of practical decisions. I chased a thing that had no previous example of anyone ever making money doing it—documenting random people in a very serious way, daily. I wouldn't be using my degree, wouldn't be applying for any sort of other trading job, wouldn't be going into sales. It was a jump from the practical to something that on the surface seemed completely impractical.

I set a modest goal: take some time off and photograph. I didn't have a lot of money saved, and so my ambitions were basic; my only goal was to make just enough money to control my time. I believed I had a unique enough eye that I could maybe do some sort of street photography that was good enough so that I could sell prints and pay my rent and photograph all day long.

As I set out, I wasn't afraid of failing, because I had already failed so miserably in college. In college, I thought I was too smart and too good for school. I resented people telling me I had to go to college and it was the only way to success. I signed up for five classes in one semester, didn't go to any of them, and got five zeros at the University of Georgia—

zeros—and flunked out of school. Soon, my friends began graduating and going on to start jobs. It felt awful, like everyone was talking about me, looking down on me, wondering what happened to me, calling me a fuckup. At that time, I was living in my grandparents' basement. I was working at Applebee's.

That's where I learned what the worst possible failure feels like. And from that, I became immunized. Slowly, I rebounded. I returned to school, passed my classes, and pushed my way into the job in Chicago trading bonds. I started reading a hundred pages a day, and I did that every day for the better part of the next decade. It created discipline. I had put my life back together after hitting rock bottom, and bouncing back from that bottom proved to me something—that I could fail by society's standards and I could come back.

I was telling everybody I knew that I was going to be a photographer. I aimed to take random pictures of people on the street and post them on Facebook for free. Somehow I was going to figure out a way to support myself: "I'm gonna figure it out," I thought again and again. Of course there were the detractors—the people talking about me and laughing behind my back, saying that I was doing something impractical and ridiculous. That I was lazy, would never make money, didn't want to work. "Yeah, I wish I could just be taking pictures all day too. Get a job." Those kinds of things.

But having failed before, I was familiar with this position. I knew the pressure. I could withstand other people thinking I was failing in order to do something that I really wanted to do. And so, I jumped. I left Chicago and decided to move to New York and try this photo project, which everyone thought was crazy because, remember, I had no experience.

The decision to jump was originally short-term, which made it easier. It was all incremental. It started with "For the next foreseeable time of my life, I'm going to do only what I want to do. I'm gonna do it all day long." And that sounds simple, but here's the main thing: very few people actually put in the work to follow their dream. Look around New York City. Listen to all the people who tell you they're musicians, who tell you they're photographers, who tell you they're artists, who tell you they're painters. And then you ask them, "Oh, really? Tell me about your average day. What are you doing on a weekly basis to do these things?"

And you learn, eight times out of ten, that the person is doing just enough work to own that identity, to be able to call themselves that. Many people use "follow your dreams" as an excuse not to work: "Oh, I don't have a job because I'm chasing my dream of this." In reality, you're going to bars, and you're saying you're chasing your dream to hang out with your friends, to play video games, to practice a couple times a week just enough to say that you're chasing your dreams. But chasing your dreams becomes an excuse to not work hard.

When done correctly, and very few people are doing it this way, jumping is nothing but hard work. That's all I did. I didn't go out. I didn't go to concerts. I didn't know anybody in New York. I didn't hang out with friends. All I did was photograph. I treated it like a job. I didn't treat it like any job. I treated it like a job that I did all day, every day. During those early days, I would go out and I'd take forty portraits a day. I wasn't even telling stories at that point. I was just doing photography. The Humans of New York that later became successful looks nothing like the Humans of New York that unraveled as I landed in New York with two suitcases, not knowing anybody. I saw New York for the first time two months before I moved here. I'd photographed for the first time eight months before I moved here. And now I was in New York working full-time on a photo project.

Photography is all I did. It's all I did. That's the thing. You can tell people, "Take the leap." It doesn't matter. It doesn't matter unless you're the kind of person with the discipline and the work ethic to work all day long at what you want. And this is what gets lost on many people who want to jump. We live in a competitive world where everybody wants to leave their job. Everybody wants to be doing something creative and something that they love. The most competitive market in the world is doing what you love. And like in any market, the person who works hardest is the one that's going to be able to succeed. It takes a massive, massive amount of work to build a life around doing what you love.

That's why, ironically, jumping to follow your passion requires much more discipline than it does passion. Passion wears off after a few months. It's not like it's going to be fun all day. You have fun at moments, for sure. But for me, it got to the point where I was waking up and I had to force myself to go out and photograph. Every time I went out and photographed, I really loved it and I enjoyed it. But it got to be where it was discipline that was sustaining me—discipline that I built up after I flunked out of college, when I told myself I was going to read one hundred pages of a book every day no matter what. I was going to practice piano for an hour every day no matter what. I was going to exercise every single day no matter what. I did all three of those things every single day for years. That built discipline, and that's what got me through my jump and taught me how to do something every single day without fail, no matter how I felt. That's the key to making a jump. It's not passion. It's discipline.

So I kept it simple. I was determined to photograph every single day, no matter how hopeless it felt, no matter how sad I felt, no matter how lonely I felt, all of which I felt very acutely when I first arrived in New York. I was here alone over the holidays. The two people I knew in New York went home, and I was here for two weeks, which were depressing as hell, the toughest two weeks of my life. I went out and photographed every single day. Christmas Eve all day, Christmas all day.

It was just me. And here's the other thing: the lion's share of the effort in taking a jump comes before anybody's paying attention. That's why it's so hard, because everyone wants attention these days. Our currency right now is attention. People tend to think, "Oh, I have this idea. It's going to get me attention." Then they do it for two weeks, and nobody's paying attention. Nobody pays attention to an idea for two weeks. You might get lucky, but it's not going to be sustainable. People pay attention to work, and you have to work a long time before people will give you the gift of their attention.

I was very, very respectful of my audience, and I still try to be, which is why you don't see any ads or promotions. I felt like I owed them, so I would work all day long and post nothing but pictures, post nothing but stories.

I never had a doubt about my jump working out. When I started, I told myself, "I'm going to photograph ten thousand people in New York City." This is the most diverse place in the world, and I knew nobody else was doing it on that sort of scale. I knew that it was a good idea. I knew that the idea had the potential to succeed. If it wasn't succeeding, it was because I wasn't good enough yet. It took a year of working every day before I could fully pay my rent. But I never said to myself, "This is not working because it's not a good idea." I told myself, "This isn't working because I'm not good enough yet. I need to get better. I need to improve." Malcolm Gladwell's *Tipping Point* gave me my new mantra: that there's no way that I can fail because I can always get a little bit better. If I keep getting a little bit better, a little bit better, a little bit better, the work gets a little bit more interesting. It's going to reach a point where suddenly people are going to be checking it out, not because I'm telling them to, but they're going to be checking it out because it's good enough and it's interesting enough.

And it took a while, but it reached that point. It reached that point where I'd done it. I had approached hundreds and then thousands of people. My photography got a lot better. I had started organically interviewing people and talking to the people, and at some point, things tipped. I'd gotten enough experience and I'd put enough pieces together where I earned the attention of other people. I earned it through months and months and months and months of jumping, doing and thinking about nothing else. I finally earned the attention of other people.

Once you truly earn the attention of one person, somebody that believes in your jump not because they're your friend or your cousin or your mom but because you've honed your skills to the point that you've earned their attention, that's when you become successful in your jump. Because the world is such a big place that if you've worked hard enough to earn the attention of a single stranger, then it's just a matter of time before you reach more people just like that person.

Jumps should start small, with a clear purpose in mind. Back when I was nineteen or twenty years old, I wanted to change the world in a bunch of huge ways. That's why I flunked out of college, because I thought I was too important and my mission was too big to concern myself with the small things. That sort of mind-set led me to a place where I was humbled and brought down.

When I jumped into photography, I put all my thought into the small things that I could do every single day and not into the big things like impacting society and impacting the world, creating social change.

Paradoxically, the more I focused on the small things that I can control, the more of an impact I've had in ways that I could have never imagined when I was nineteen.

Last year, Humans of New York raised over $10 million for charities. We have over twenty million followers from around the world. Am I living a very comfortable life now that I'm very grateful for? Yes. Is it extremely fulfilling to me that so many people are paying attention to what I do every single day? Yes. It feels great to be able to impact that many people. It's a wonderful, wonderful, wonderful feeling.

Is that why I jumped to become a photographer? No.

I jumped because I love, love, love taking photos.

BRANDON STANTON, a former bond trader, is a photographer, author, and the creator of the Humans of New York project.

Don't Look Back

You will come out stronger

- "You're not going to lose anything by jumping. You'll gain skills, meet fascinating people, and have so many things to add to your CV. The fact that you jumped shows . . . that you're a risk-taker, and most importantly someone who is not afraid to stand up for something you believe in—your passion." (Anoopreet Rehncy)

- "Sometimes you have to take a gamble without knowing what's next, but that's okay. . . . Outcomes aside, you'll be closer to the things that interest you and the people who motivate you." (Kyle Battle)

- "Getting closer to that answer—of figuring out what you want to do, how you want to spend your days—is reason enough to jump. . . . The immediate outcome is less important." (Jacob Licht)

- "You emerge from any jump humbled by the new learning, educated with new skills, closer to a completely different group of people than you ever would've been associated with otherwise. You come out stronger." (Matt Pottinger)

Prioritize learning

- "Jump to learn. . . . Learning needs to be the number one priority in what you do, much more so than a paycheck, maybe even more than stability. Those skills you learn are going to catapult you further in your career and faster. . . . Prioritize learning." (Jacob Licht)

- "Being at that company with people ten times smarter than I am, who had twenty years more experience than I had, taught me the things about my new industry I didn't know, things I never would've learned on my own." (Elizabeth Hague)

- "I approached every task as a learning experience. . . . I needed to learn, and I couldn't really learn this stuff anywhere else. Whatever your jump is going to be, learn as much as you can." (James Bourque)

Develop some mental discipline

- "Ironically, jumping to follow your passion requires much more discipline than it does passion. Passion wears off after a few months." (Brandon Stanton)

- "Prioritize what you need most, and solve those items first. At the top of my list were paying my bills and being happy; further down was being my own boss. When I started my new job, I solved for the top and put the bottom on hold. . . . That was really hard—not to try and solve for everything all at once. But sacrifice is abso-freakin-lutely the key to getting what you want." (Elizabeth Hague)

- "You can tell people, 'Take the leap.' It doesn't matter. It doesn't matter unless you're the kind of person with the discipline and the work ethic to work all day long at what you want. And this is what gets lost on many people who want to jump." (Brandon Stanton)

- "You have to be mentally prepared that it's not going to be a smooth ride." (Anoopreet Rehncy)

You can avoid regret

- "What it came back to was this sense that if I didn't try, I would live with regret—and the kind of regret that you carry around from inaction felt much worse than the regret that you might feel from having taken an action." (Matt Pottinger)

- "While jumping may look scary, the alternative is much worse. The longer you stay in a role that you don't like, the more trapped you feel. We only have one life. . . . I want to feel like I'm doing something that I care about, and I want my son to see me doing something that I care about." (Sarah Dvorak)

- "One friend was blunt: 'You don't like your job. You're not getting any younger. . . . What sort of book are you writing for yourself? Do you want to look back and say, "I worked another twenty years at this job that was never particularly meaningful for me. That was fun." Or do you want that story to be different?' I knew I wanted my story to be different." (Sarah Dvorak)

- "And whatever you go do, don't look back. I never look back. Never, even in the darkest days . . . never once." (Dan Kenary)

You may wake up scared

- "For those first weeks after the idea came to me, I was overcome with this terror—a terror so intense that I'd wake up in a sweat every night. I felt more anxiety than I had ever experienced in my life. I tried to think logically: 'What's going on? Is this jump worth it?' While running through these thoughts . . . I spotted a fortune cookie message in the street. It read, 'Fear is the necessity of invention.' I took that as a sign to keep going." (Manisha Snoyer)

- "I jumped a few years ago, and to this day, I still wake up scared." (Danni Pomplun)

- "The reasons we give ourselves for not making a jump— rationalizations we make, excuses we come up with—are fears that, in hindsight, should never hold people back." (Matt Pottinger)

- "Fears are always going to be there. . . . So when fear swirls around and comes on by, I choose not to get involved. I say, 'Hey, thanks for playing but not today.' . . . It's about knowing fear is there but recognizing that I have a choice to either play into it or not." (Danni Pomplun)

Put in the shed time

- "In the moments after your jump, embrace what jazz musicians call 'shed time': the time in a shed where you are locked away, trying to learn your instrument, understand your craft, master your skills. No matter what jump you take, there's going to be a certain amount of shed time involved." (Matt Pottinger)

- "Get your hands dirty. It's the only way to really figure out if you actually like it, and it's not something that's been romanticized in your brain, and to see if the day-to-day work is something that you'll enjoy." (Sarah Dvorak)

- "When done correctly . . . jumping is nothing but hard work. . . . Once you truly earn the attention of one person, somebody that believes in your jump not because they're your friend or your cousin or your mom but because you've honed your skills to the point that you've earned their attention, that's when you become successful in your jump." (Brandon Stanton)

- "You can't just try once—you try again and again and again." (Anoopreet Rehncy)

Get good at failing

- "Some jumps don't end well. Don't mistake that for a reason not to try." (Brenda Berkman)

- "Failed jumps will expose you to new skills and experiences, and you'll become more and more valuable on the job market. Yes, failure can be embarrassing; just deal with it. And once you get used to failing—when you become an expert at failing—it's not nearly as scary." (Elizabeth Hague)

- "As I set out, I wasn't afraid of failing, because I had already failed so miserably in college. . . . And from that, I became immunized." (Brandon Stanton)

- "I don't think failure is the question in making a jump. The question is, what can you do from here? . . . You can see it as the world crumbling, or you can say, 'Well, I have all of these pieces: let me catch what I can and see what I can do with them.'" (James Bourque)

- "None of this would have happened if I hadn't first jumped and failed." (Elizabeth Hague)

- "If, at some point, things change, and this business fails? I believe that there is no failure. . . . The jump has provided my own education at an accelerated scale." (Manisha Snoyer)

- "It didn't feel like a failure. It felt more like a victory." (Sarah Dvorak)

Welcome happiness

- "Be less afraid to be happy." (Elizabeth Hague)

- "Jump for what makes you get up in the morning." (Anoopreet Rehncy)

- "There's not a price you can put on doing a job that actually makes you happy. And that, itself, is worth jumping for." (Jacob Licht)

- "That's a really scary thing—to have something really good happen, especially when you've had a bunch of not really good things happen." (Danni Pomplun)

- "If your alternative to jumping is staying in a miserable job or with a miserable boyfriend or in an awful apartment—or some combination of all three—and never moving forward, then it doesn't make sense to *not* jump. . . . You'll be making moves toward happiness—and even if you don't get all the way to happy, at least you'll have gotten a toe off the ground." (Elizabeth Hague)

- "And yet at that time and place, I simply loved photography. I just enjoyed doing it. I mean, I sucked at it in a lot of ways. Sometimes I'd get lucky and take some good photos, but those were just luck. Regardless, I loved it. . . . And that desire led me to jump. I made what was a very selfish decision: to restructure my life around doing something that I enjoy." (Brandon Stanton)

- "For the first time in my life, I was happy." (Jack Manning)

Haters will hate—and your parents may cry

- "My mom was literally crying herself to sleep: here goes her daughter, quitting a solid post-college job to scrape by in a kitchen so she could later go to culinary school and make no money. But I felt an inner pull." (Sarah Dvorak)

- "I dreaded telling my mother. She was absolutely distraught. She made no effort to hide it and tried to marshal every argument she could to deter me. All of her points were quite rational arguments." (Matt Pottinger)

- "My lawyer father-in-law was not thrilled. . . . Even my mom thought I was nutty: here I had a bachelor's degree, a master's degree, and a law degree, and I wanted to take a job that's dangerous, entails a 50 percent pay cut, and requires only a high school diploma. But I knew I had to try." (Brenda Berkman)

- "People are going to knock your jump. People are going to say that you can't do it. You don't have the skills; you're never going to make it. But you've got to form the toughest skin, and not let anyone kill your passion." (Anoopreet Rehncy)

- "Of course there were the detractors—the people talking about me and laughing behind my back, saying that I was doing something impractical and ridiculous. That I was lazy, would never make money, didn't want to work. 'Yeah, I wish I could just be taking pictures all day too. Get a job.' Those kinds of things." (Brandon Stanton)

- "To the chagrin of some family and friends, I jumped." (Jacob Licht)

There will never be a perfect time to jump

- "There was always a reason not to jump. Then one day you wake up, and it smacks you in the face: this is my life. Student loans are my life. My family is my life. My car payments, my insurance, my dog, that's all my life. All that's never going to go away. . . . I wasn't fulfilled with how I earned that paycheck, but that was the one thing I could change." (James Bourque)

- "In hindsight, a steady paycheck is a flimsy rationale for not pursuing your gut." (Matt Pottinger)

- "I had fears about my career path and real concerns about cash flow, but a louder, internal voice outweighed everything else: 'This is what you're supposed to be doing, so go do it.'" (Kyle Battle)

Jump for the life you want

- The act of jumping itself will put your life back in your hands. Whether it works out or not is irrelevant—the fact that you made the choice will change you." (Jacob Licht)

- "There are going to be plenty of unexpected twists and turns where you will have a choice to jump, and that's the beauty of it really—it's your choice." (Brenda Berkman)

- "I keep coming back to the idea of agency: the difference between life happening to you versus you making life happen. People say, 'Well, I wasn't given the opportunity. I wasn't set up for success.' You have more control over your life than most people give you credit for." (James Bourque)

- "Know your worth. Trust and double down on what you can do. My jump was the first time I really bet on myself." (Kyle Battle)

- "Serendipity plays a big role in all of this, but it starts with a personal choice. Take a chance; follow a passion. See where it leads." (Dan Kenary)

- "If not now, when? If not me, who?" (Danni Pomplun)

Conclusion: **Jumping Again**

TWELVE HOURS AFTER boarding the airplane in San Francisco International Airport, I landed in Auckland, New Zealand. I was the world's 290th-best squash player.

My plans set me up to stay one month in one country. After that, I had only a few leads to pursue.

I knew my jump wouldn't last forever, probably not even for years—nor did I design it as a long-term jump. I understood that my commitment to couch surfing out of a suitcase, living with strangers, and traveling every few days would last only for so long. I laid out my goals simply: a few months, maybe six. Crack the top 200 in the world rankings. Make a story that I could be proud of when I was eighty and reflecting back on my life.

But after that first month in New Zealand, something funny happened: I began to get lucky. A fellow train passenger's grandparents in Poland, a training partner's high school friend's sister in Portugal, a coach's former player in Japan, a high school classmate's childhood buddy in South Africa—logistical solutions and squash-playing opportunities began to unfold. Bigger tournaments, better players, a ranking into the top 250, 200, then 150, 120. And a couch surfing odyssey that kept on going, thanks to players and host families, friends of friends, and complete strangers.

· · ·

When my jump ended, sixteen months after it began, I had been ranked the 112th-best squash player in the world and had traveled to nearly fifty countries, on six continents, and across two hundred thousand miles. Almost every night, I was someone's guest: another player, an old classmate, a fellow bus passenger.

I had lived out of my pair of Levi's and a roller bag, said yes when offered a seat at the dinner table or a stool at the bar, and had polished off wedding cake with newlyweds in Chile, parachuted in the South Pacific with the 1990 skydiving world champion, played guest of honor at a school show-and-tell with a ten-year-old who had never met an American until the day before when one woke up on the couch in her family's house in the southern farmlands of New Zealand. I had tagged along to the best dive bar in Zimbabwe with my friend's friend's mom's best friend's sister, crashed Van Morrison's seventieth-birthday jam in Northern Ireland, road-tripped through the Moroccan desert with a pair of best friends I'd met in the airport a few hours earlier.

Why had I ever doubted this jump? I had hit the goals I had set out to reach, and once I had done so, I felt, for the first time since hearing the little voice, a sense of peace. During one of my final flights on the pro tour, on a plane somewhere high over Bulgaria, I felt it in my gut. This jump was over, and I was ready to move on.

As my pro squash jump wrapped, I guess I could have spent the flight home soaking in all the experiences I'd had. Instead, all I could think of was how alarmingly close I had come to not jumping at all. If I were to draw a Venn diagram with two circles, one that included everything I'd feared most before jumping and one that showed everything I most value from the experience of having jumped, they would perfectly overlap under one label: the unknown. The unknown is what nearly convinced me not to jump, and it is what ultimately delivered the people, experiences, and lessons that made my jump experience special to me. The unknown is where I found my luck.

When I caught up with friends and former coworkers after I returned home, they'd refer to my decision to jump as a no-brainer. And I'd smile and think back to the nights alone staring out my office window and into the map of the world pasted next to my desk and at the quote by Jeff Bezos I'd posted above my computer. What will you be most proud of when you're eighty? In retrospect, my jump was a no-brainer, sure. But it was a full-brain pursuit: it took my intense devotion, my all-encompassing investment. And I built the experience around listening, thinking, planning, and, finally, accepting. If it weren't for a network of others who helped me and a voice in my head that wouldn't shut up, my incredible experience of turning full-time squash pro, even if only for a time, wouldn't have happened.

The man and I were sitting side by side in the back of the crammed cabin, two strangers in an airplane high above South America, sometime toward the end of my tour. Tall and middle-aged, wearing a suit and speaking with a cowboy accent, he stuck out. He was the only other native English speaker on the plane.

We'd talked very little during the flight, but as the plane angled toward the ground, he turned to me and asked, "What's next?" Was I going back to my old job? I said I didn't know. "But I am going to try and write a book." He asked what the book was about, and I told him, and he laughed. I sat awkwardly in silence. Then the cowboy in a suit started telling his story:

"I haven't jumped yet, but I'm going to."

Below us, the plane wheels touched down onto the asphalt in São Paulo.

"Son, you know what evil is? Lots of people think murder or cheating. We talk about this a lot in church, this question of what is evil. But to me it ain't murder or cheating." I pretended to follow. "For years," he continued, "I've been playing second fiddle to a business partner back home in the States. He takes most of the profits without doing the work. I'm in my fifties, but I've had enough, been quiet too long." He slowly unfastened his seat belt: "To me, *true* evil is when someone or someplace takes your agency. That's true evil." The last of the passengers in front of us began to stand and shuffle toward the plane doors ahead. I stood to reach for my suitcase and follow the single-file line.

"Tell me when that book of yours comes out," he said.

* * *

The hardest part of jumping, I discovered, wasn't leaving for a new life—it was coming back to where the old life had been. It's one thing to tell yourself you are a sponsored athlete with a purpose, on a world tour with some pocket change and tournaments ahead. It's another thing to look into the mirror at twenty-seven, rounding the corner toward thirty, finances running low, sleeping on your buddy's couch.

I browsed a few job boards and began going through the motions. And then I stopped. I had another jump to make.

So I crashed on my friend Crosby's couch for a month, and then for five more. (Thank you, Crosby.)

I had a story I wanted to tell, about a journey I almost didn't take. Not only that, but I had a collection of stories to share, stories that had piled up over the past few years in my flattened, stained backpack, of jumps made by others that had inspired mine; jump stories that had made my jump possible. So I borrowed a computer, put on my worn pair of Levi's, and ironed my fraying button-down shirt. I sat down at the end of a booth in a coffee shop down the street from Crosby's house. Ever so faintly, I could hear it: a little voice.

Acknowledgments

(or, The Story Behind the Story)

If there is a story behind the story, it's how a collection of friends, family, coworkers, and strangers around the world made my jumps possible. A jump is never made alone, and my two jumps, first to play squash and next to turn my experience into this book and into a platform, would not have been possible if it were not for having many others around me. This section won't do full justice to the people and their generosity who contributed (and continue to contribute) to my dream, but I will try my best.

Before there was a book, there were two twentysomething guys sketching up their dreams in adjoining workspaces in late January 2013.

This book is dedicated to that other guy: my friend and former colleague, the late **Corey Griffin**. Because it was Corey who immediately believed, and expected, this to be a book—and vowed to never let me off the hook until I made both jumps happen. Corey was a legend, with a booming laugh and an unyielding conviction that anything can be done. We were office neighbors for the better part of three years when I barged through his door with an idea that could help us make our jumps. Corey being Corey had me sketch a book cover, told me it'd be a bestseller, and asked about its progress over lunch breaks and beers after work up until I left. This book wouldn't exist if it weren't for Corey. I am grateful to his brother, **Mike**, sister, **Casey**, and the rest of the Griffin family for supporting this project in his honor. For more on Corey and his incredible legacy, please visit www.coreygriffinfoundation.org.

The next night, I sent a scan of the book cover sketch to my friend **Loretta Cremmins** and that weekend shared it with a college professor, **Charlie Wheelan**. First over e-mails with Loretta and then using sticky notes at the Hanover Starbucks with Charlie, the two put wheels on the project. My college roommate, **Tom Mandel**, selflessly put his creative writing genius to work on editing the very first paragraphs of the book. If the Knicks weren't so lousy to watch in 2013–15, Tom probably wouldn't have had this free time on his hands, so a related thank-you to the Knicks executives for the misery that is the Andrea Bargnani trade, among many others.

My parents, **Michael** and **Betsy Lewis**, supported every ounce of my ambition while rightly pointing out the things that mattered most before any type of jump: earning a solid reputation, working hard, not expecting any guarantees. My siblings, **Emma Lewis, Becca Hade, Molly Bevan, Kate Laing**, and **Whitey Reid**, were by my side in the two years of brainstorming that followed.

I shared everything about the little voice in my head with my cousin **Sheryl Sandberg** and her late husband, **Dave Goldberg**, and they are responsible for every part of its journey into reality. From the moment I confided in her the idea to go play squash, to the day I came home to unpack a few years later, to the first stories I shared in the book project, Sheryl remained proud, smiling, and standing in my corner. Sheryl, you and the kids are my rock, and I could not be more grateful. This journey has been, and continues to be, my attempt to answer your question of what I would be doing if I weren't afraid.

As I thought more about this voice, I confided in a handful of role models—my heroes and examples of not simply how to work but how to live: **Frank Britt, John Blasberg, Deb Conrad, Dirk Reynolds**, and **Justin Gmelich**.

My friends took on this mission alongside me. **Emily Broas, Dan Hochman, Fernando Rodriguez-Villa, Rory Grant**, and **Pat Collins** pushed me through the unsexy steps by getting me on track with maps, routes, goals, confidence, and storage space. **Bobby Blatt, Jeff Cole**,

Steve Anastos, Andrew D'Ignazio, Nick O'Neill, and **Greg Arch** checked in early and often, and kept me on my way.

So many other friends put themselves out as a sounding board, again and again: **Noah Carr, Will Hochman, Emily Hochman, Eric Tanner, Peter Nicol** and **Jess Winstanley, Meg Dudley, Chris Hanson, Debbie Sterling, Lizzy Auld, Taylor Halsted,** and **Tessa Lyons-Laing.**

As I tried to become a pro, the Boston squash community at the University Club took me in: **Chris Spahr, Dan Roberts, Fernanda Rocha, Gil Gallotto, Jay** and **Elizabeth Bride, Jeannie Blasberg, Bill Nimmo.** When I went out to sponsors, a handful offered money for, well, not a whole lot in return: **Amrit Kanwal, Digger Donahue, Andy Goldfarb, John Nimick, Sandy Tierney, Alan Lewis, Matt McPherson, Zander Lurie, Jack Sweeney, Evan Goldberg** and his wife, **Cindy,** and **Tim Wyant.**

When it was time to leave Bain Capital Ventures, the team was fully behind me. **Paige Caporelli** gets credit for the pep talks in the copy room, while many other colleagues shared their honest advice, including **Todd MacLean, Jeff Crisan, Shannon Harrington, Janine Strate, Jeff Glass, Jared Kesselheim, Scott Friend, Matt Harris,** and **Mike Krupka.**

A handful of family friends helped push me through the last paces before the plane: **Dave Eun, Scott Tierney, Sarah Leary,** and **Molly Graham.** It was **Scott Mitic** who told me the difference between crazy and stupid on the sidewalk in Palo Alto, and those words helped me define my life.

And when I landed on the other side of the world, I don't know what would have happened if it weren't for my childhood buddy **Adam Fried,** who pulled out a couch for me in Sydney on three different occasions, believed in the Jump Curve framework when I wrote it down on a napkin, and believed in me during many long nights at the kitchen table when I wasn't sure I believed in myself. In what otherwise would have been a lonely pursuit, Adam made this project a team effort. I treasure the adventures we've had and the ones we continue to find ourselves in as roommates in San Francisco.

The book grew legs when key people emerged at my side: **Nicole Rotonda, John Ingram, YS Chi,** the real **Michael Lewis,** and **Cass Sunstein.** If it weren't for **Domas Girtavicius** and **Agne Selemonaite,**

I wouldn't have that story for my future grandkids about that one time I officiated at a Lithuanian wedding.

Crosby Slaught, I owe you a really, really nice couch. And **Charlie Ryan**, same for you. It is because of these two and their fellow roommates **Claire Dougherty** and **Emily Hanna** that I was given a critical six months to pitch this book: while eating their eggs and sleeping in their living room. From that time on North Point Street came a book proposal and a company.

Also from my honorary roommates came the meeting with Emily's sister **Amy Hanna**, who became my friend and teammate in the early stages of building the When to Jump community, and who helped me drive the mission forward. Amy, I know you don't like the spotlight, but thank you for being my friend, and thank you for believing.

Several folks helped get me through the book-writing process, starting with barista **Tristan Ragan** from the Peet's on Chestnut, **Merle Saferstein**, **Buzz** and **Liz Ann Doherty**, **Tara Bratt**, **Meghan Kelleher**, and **Rahul Malik**. I made a few best friends out of this time: **Abby Sordoni**, **Aisling Blake**, and **Mike P. Lewis** went well beyond any normal terms of friendship to troubleshoot ideas, brainstorm new plans, and share in the mini-milestones. Above all, they made themselves available to listen, always.

Every person in the book went to great lengths and effort to relive details, conversations, anecdotes, and memories—solely to expose their most honest, vulnerable self for the reader. Without exception, each interview was a treat, and I cherished and am honored to have had the opportunity to enter each of your lives and share in each of your journeys.

The road to publishing started when my friend **Emily Hirshey** introduced me to her dad, **David Hirshey**, who passed me along to his friend and literary agent extraordinaire, **Alice Martell**. Around the same time, my friend **Hannah Weber** and her dad, the PR whiz **Larry Weber**, helped me form a cohesive vision. **Arianna Huffington** understood my vision immediately and worked with me to expand it, helping bring When to Jump videos across the Web and to audiences around the world. **Alex Cushman** and **Mike Adelman**, and later **Natasha Chu** and **Andy Hoffman**, helped organize and formalize everything.

As my jump to make a book slowly grew to other platforms, many others pitched in with ideas and expertise: **Tim Schwartz, Matt** and **Pete Callahan, Dan Harris, Graham Abbott, Sam Gould, Alissia Miller-Kofman, Alan Meckler, Alex Korchinski, Chris Lehane, Caitlin Choate,** and **Janet Hanson.**

And then there's the book you're holding now. It was a few months into 2016 when **Barbara Jones,** my wonderful editor at Henry Holt, along with her editorial assistant, **Kanyin Ajayi,** took my proposal, imagined it as something much bigger, then made a bet and dug tirelessly, seemingly endlessly, into every word and detail to see that bet through. Along with Barbara and Kanyin, a core group of colleagues on the Henry Holt team was with me from our first meeting, eighteen months out: **Maggie Richards, Pat Eisemann, Jason Liebman, Ruby Lee,** and **Jessica Wiener.** In the UK, **Liz Gough** at Yellow Kite believed our message should be in the hands of audiences overseas, and she helped make this happen.

As we took the book and began to turn it into a platform, so many people stepped up to help and must be thanked, starting with **Summer Dickey, Jon Slavet, Jeff Crowe, Martha Beattie, Kyle Battle, Ned Berger, Nate Chambers, Andrew Scully, Sean Donahue, Brian Doyle, Lisa Horwitz, Diana Friedman, Max Montgomery, Rachel Allen, Delaney FitzPatrick,** and **Jekka Kuhlmann.**

Finally, there were the couches and the people they belong to. This book came from the story, and the story was made possible by the friends of friends, players, host families, train passengers, and other beautiful strangers who went out of their way to help out a squash-playing couch surfer chase down a dream. To the many people who helped make this dream come true, thank you. Truly, thank you. I've got a couch with your name on it in San Francisco.

ANDORRA
CRISTINA MIR BAUCELLS
EDUARD ROSELL CUBI
ALBA CASANOU MALLOL

NORWAY
IZABELA SZELEMEJ
DAN HOCHMAN / JOSEFINE ÄLMEGRAN
TALE HELLAND / KAROLINE TRESVIK
ADRIAN OSTBYE

SERBIA
IVAN DJORDJEVIC
MARKO MATANOVIC

GERMANY
ANNIE MUNGER

IRELAND
PADRAIG JONES
NIAMH O'CALLAGHAN
BRIAN BYRNE
JAN VAN DEN HERREWEGEN
GRAINNE O'TOOLE
Ó MURCHÚ EÁNNA

NEW ZEALAND
JOHN FLETCHER
GLEN WILSON   LANCE BEDDOES
PAUL COLL   MICHAEL PITTAMS   MICHAEL SUNDERLAND
TRACEY KIMBLE   DOMINIQUE LOWRY   BEN GINDROD
MICHAEL SUNDERLAND   JULIE GARDNER   GRANT CRAIG
MARTIN KNIGHT   MEGAN BELL   BRIAN BELL   KEVIN MUIR
ADEN MUIR   TAYLA MUIR   ANDERSON ROMERO   JOSH ROMERO
CHRIS VAN DER SALM   JASON VAN DER WALT   PAUL GROWCOTT
HALEY EVANS   JOELLE KING   KIM TAYLOR   RACHEL CAPIZZI

USA
BECCA HADE / TIMMY HADE / MOLLY BEVAN / TERRY BEVAN / BILL BEVAN
MARTHA BEVAN / KATE LAING / WHITELAW REID / BRI REID / NICK O'NEILL
HELENA LANCASTER / SARAH FELDMANN / MIKE BUSH / JOE COLEMAN
TOM MANDEL / ERIC TANNER / GRAHAM ABBOTT / WILL HOCHMAN
JAMIE BERK / WILL NEWNHAM / MEREDITH GREENBERG / CROSBY SLAUGHT
ALEX ARMSTRONG / JANET HANSON / CHRIS HANSON / MARTIN HEATH
DIANA FRIEDMAN / SHERYL SANDBERG / JOHN BLASBERG
JEANNIE BLASBERG / ANNIE BLASBERG / JACK BLASBERG
CHARLIE BLASBERG / JORDAN ESTEN / KAITLIN SENNATT / JOHN ROBERTS
DAN ROBERTS / ARTHUR GASKIN / ANDRE MAUR / BUSANI XABA
RICHARD ELLIOT / MARK TALBOTT / DEBBIE BROWN / ROBERT GRAHAM
ORLA O'DOHERTY / FERDINAND GEITHNER / MARK WIELAND / BEN GETTINGER
DREW JOSEPH / EMILY HOCHMAN / MICHELLE SULLIVAN / BENNETT SIEGEL

MOLDOVA
IGORI DINGA
LIDIA SCARLAT
SERGIU DURLESHTEAN

POLAND
KAMA KHAN
GRZGORZ KULTYS
MARZENA MARCINKOWSKI

FRANCE
ARTHUR MOINEAU / BEN DESOMBRE
NICOLAS BARBEAU / PIERRE BADY
VINCENT DROESBEKE NADVORNIK
JÉRÔME ELHAÏK / ANTOINE BARON
ALEX LAVAUD / ADAM PECAS / VICTOR CROUIN
JEROME DADOT / DAMIEN VOLLAND
BAPTISTE MASOTTI / GREG ARCH / CHASE LANG
JEAN JACQUES VALLOT / DAVID SCHOUMACHER
FRED DOMAIN / SAMUEL CHALAYE / AMANDA TEDONE
CHARLOTTE URGESE / SARAH HADDADI
VICTOR MONTSERRAT / ALEX LAVAUD

BRAZIL
MANOEL PEREIRA   MARCOS ANDRE
MARIA SYLVIA DIAS   FLAVIO PEREIRA
DANIELA AGGIUNTI YOSHIDA   JANAINA ZEN
LUCAS PINTO   CAROL B AREDE   DIEGO ROCCA
JULIANA PEREIRA   KIKI SILVA   RAFAEL ALARCON
FRANCO OTAVIO TOBIAS MARTINS   GLAUCIO NOVACK
LEONARDO DAHER   JOSE HENRIQUE LOPES
GABRIELA NORONHA   VINICIUS RODRIGUES
DIEGO GOBBI   BETO SCIENCIA
HUGO VARELA

NEW CALEDONIA
DAVID NAVARRE • JEAN-MARIE BALCON
NICOLAS MASSANET • ALEX COLLENOT
FREDERIC BAUD • SEIGNER NATHALIE
LOAN SEIGNER • STEPHANIE MONCLIN
YENDI SEIGNER • LORENA BUR
VINCENT HARDEL

ZIMBABWE
ROS MILLAR   CATHERINE RESSIJAC
RICHARD FOX MORRIS   HENRY MILLAR

SOUTH AFRICA
MEG DUDLEY • JONATHAN JUST
EMMA LEWIS • GAIA BONINI • NEIL OOSTHUIZEN • JASON ELLEY
PHILIPP FASCHING • FIONA WILSON • JOSEPH OU • NICCI EVANS
PAULA MILLAR • ANJA SCHIEGL • JUSTINE SOFFIETTI
OWEN DE JAGER • KATIE LOUISE MILLAR • BEN STOFBERG
LAUREN HODGSON • DESI HODGSON • CHARLES HODGSON
MELISSA MEYER • STEVE ANASTOS • CHRISTINA ANASTOS
ERIC DURELL • STROTHER SCOTT • JANINE LEGER
MARGOT LEGER • JEAN-PIERRE BRITS • CRISTO POTGEITER
TANIA RAWSON • PETE RAWSON

TURKEY
MARIA CLAUDIO
ASHLEY ZANDY
SALLY ANNE ALDOUS
KATE SANER

CZECH REPUBLIC
JAN KOUKAL

GREECE
ANNA-LOUISA CHALIASOU
DIMITRIS SPARTALIS
EFTIHIA SPARTALIS
DIMITRIS NIKOLAOU
HARRY LONDY
ELIZA KARGIOTI
GIORGOS AGGOURIAS
GIORGOS MISSIKOS
HARALAMBOS LOUKARAS
KIKI SPARTALI
NIKOS DIMITRIADIS
DIMITRIS PITSOS
VASILIS BARDIS

PARAGUAY
TOMMY BURT
PETER CREED
TODD HARRITY

GIBRALTAR
ANTHONY GILBRINDLE

I ♥ [soccer player icon]

LITHUANIA
AGNE SELEMONAITE
DOMAS GIRTAVICIUS
EDVINAS DOVYDAITIS
JEKATERINA MAKAROVA
MANTAS KOCIUNAS

CHILE
FRANCISCO CAMPOS
ARTURO TEIXEIRA
CLARO TAMMY

SWEDEN
ELVIRA SVEDMALM   CARL JOHAN TROSDAHL
KARIN BIRGERSON   LOVISA FORSTADIUS
STEFAN ADAMSSON   MAGNUS RYDERSTEDT

ARGENTINA

RODRIGO PEZZOTA
ROBERTINO PEZZOTA
ANDREGOR ROCHA · FERNANDO ROCHA MATURI
ANA LAURA ROCHA · PELO ROCHA · PABLO ROCHA
CECILIA ROCHA · ESTEFANIA ROCHA · RODRIGO OBREGON
FRANCISCO OBREGON · ELIAS SANCHEZ
FERNANDO SARMIENTO · NAHU RAMOS · DANIEL RAMOS
JUAN CARLOS TYMKIW · FELIX FERNANDEZ RIESTRA

JAPAN

YOHAV WAKABAYASHI
KEN OKADA / ALEX HARING
MAYUKA KOWAGUCHI / J MORGAN KEIM
CARLY SILVERMAN / DAN ABBOTT
CHRISTOPHER RYUICHI YAMAMOTO
MARIANA JIMENEZ-HERNANDEZ
SOFIA DURAN STONE / YANA ANDREYCHIKOVA
DANIELLA SANDOVAL / ANTJE VON LOEPER

FINLAND

JAAKKO VAHAMAA · MATIAS TUOMI · TATU KUUTIL

MOROCCO

NAJEH TALIB
ZOFIA STARK

NORTHERN IRELAND

ADRIAN LEESON · REBEKAH LEESON
JEFF HARRISON
THOMAS W P HARRISON · JOEL HINDS

ESTONIA

ALIIS ALLAS
ARDO NÕMM
JANIKA HIRVI
KÜLLIKI KRISTIANSON
JERE ROBERT HIRVI

AUSTRALIA

ROB HELLAUER XAVIER BURTON MATTY HOPKIN
DOMINIC BENACQUISTA PETE AITKEN
DONNA URQUHART MARY CLAIRE O'BANION MANUEL WANNER
DOMINIQUE RATCLIFFE JESSE KEGAN JAKE EBEID
AARON FRANKCOMB DARCY EVANS LAUREN HENDRICKSON
REYNA PACHECO TIM BATTY
MITHRAN SELVARATNAM BETH MADISON DAVID CROMWELL
ADAM FRIED LEWIS DOUGHTY MOANA GRAY SELENA SHAIKH
HARRY ZEITLIN JAMIE MCCROSKERY KIM ARE KILLINGBERG
ALBERT SHOIHE NATTY DIPOLD SAXON HILL PHILIPPA HILL
HANNAH DAWES CAMERON PILLEY ELISABETH CANCIO PHIL ROSS JEFF GAETO
ISAIAH BERG NICK DAWES LIZ MILLER DAWES LIISA RUSSMANN
RAJ RAY JONAS DAHLER SCOTT DAWES
LAUREN CARNEY PETER SAXBY
JOERI HAPERS

PORTUGAL

ANTÓN GALÁN TORREGO
CLÁUDIA ARAGÃO
ALEXANDRA TELES
PATRICIA VARANDA
JOANA SIMÕES
MARIA GALÁN TORREGO
DOROTHEA ESC
VASCO CONDE
NATALIE WIERZBICKA VELAZQUEZ

QATAR

EVER RAMIREZ MENDOZA
GOSIA GOSIA

BULGARIA

STOIL JILEV

LATVIA

RAIVIS LUCIJANOVS
ALEXANDER SAUTIN
MIKS UZANS
IEVA RAUDSEPA
PAULS RAUDSEPS
VALENTIN HAIDUCHENIA
Илья Михальчук

BELGIUM

STEVE BRENNAN
B

ENGLAND

TRISTAN EYSELE
ADAM MURRILS
STOJAN DRAGOMIR NEDELCHEV
ALEX NOAKES
PHIL NIGHTINGALE
JULIAN TOMLINSON
DAVID WARDLE
STEFAN SUSEMIHL
JULIA CARAM
LEONARDO PINTO
EMMA RADFORD
FERNANDO RODRIGUEZ VILLA
JESSE ENGELBRECHT
PAUL RAWDEN
TOM RICHARDS
CHRIS SIMPSON

UNITED ARAB EMIRATES

FRANCIS UY BARBARA LANG-LENTON
CLAU LANGARRI PIERRE HEITZMANN
CHRIS SIMPSON ALEX INGHAM
JAMAL AL-BARWANI
DAVID HALEY AHMED AL KIREMLI
KHAWAJA ADIL MAQBOOL
MELANIE BECK SANDEEP RAMACHANDRAN

UKRAINE

NICK TALBOTT RUSLAN SOROCHINSKKY
OLGA SEVERINOVA JAMES GROSVENOR

HOLLAND

MARC TER SLUIS · REINIER VAN LANSCHOT
THOMAS SCHNEIDERS · STEPHANIE VAN RAPPARD
MARTIJN KOOLEN · MAURITS POT · BOBBY BLATT
EMILY BROAS · MADDIE BROAS · TIM BROAS
JASON MORRIS · BART RAVELLI
PIEDRO SCHWEERTMAN · SEBASTIAN WEENIK
ALEXANDRA DOUWES · EVERT DOUWES
OLIVIA DOUWES

DENMARK

JENS SØNDERGAARD · NENA KUM
HENRIETTE EDERB

MALAYSIA

SANJAY S CHAL
MUHAMMAD HANNAN
ADDEEN IDRAKIE / GURSHAN SINGH BHANDAL
TIMOTHY ARNOLD / MOHAMMAD SYAFIQ KAMAL
MADELINE GILL / JAAFAR SADIQ / LOTTE ERICKSEN
ALEXANDRA FULLER / CHEYNA TUCKER

FRENCH POLYNESIA

PATRICK MORELLE
REBECCA BROCARD
CYNTHIA ROIGNET
GIUSEPPE MANCA
HERVE ROIGNET
NICOLAS BARBEAU
RIDGE CHUNG

GILLES CONAN
MIKA REPRESENT

AUSTRIA

JOEL JOY

SOUTH KOREA

KJ KIM
MATT OH

WALES

JENNY HALEY
DAN BERGIN
ABBY HICKS

SPAIN

BERNAT JAUME
EDMON LOPEZ MOLLER
NICK STAUNTON
ROB STAUNTON

Hi, I'm _____

(your name)

My jump is _____

(your jump)

Fill in the blanks, then head to whentojump.com/lastpage

Made in the USA
Monee, IL
14 April 2024